My Music, My War

Lisa Gilman

MY MUSIC, MY WAR

The Listening Habits

of U.S. Troops

in Iraq and Afghanistan

Wesleyan University Press   Middletown, Connecticut

Wesleyan University Press
Middletown CT 06459
www.wesleyan.edu/wespress
© 2016 Lisa Gilman
All rights reserved
Manufactured in the United States of America
Designed by Mindy Basinger Hill
Typeset in Minion Pro

Library of Congress Cataloging-in-Publication Data

Gilman, Lisa, 1969–
My music, my war: the listening habits of U.S. troops
in Iraq and Afghanistan / Lisa Gilman.
pages   cm.—(Music culture)
Includes bibliographical references and index.
ISBN 978-0-8195-7599-9 (cloth: alk. paper)—ISBN 978-0-8195-7600-2 (pbk.: alk. paper)
1. Iraq War, 2003–2011—Music and the war.
2. Afghan War, 2001—Music and the war.
3. United States—Armed Forces—Iraq—Attitudes.
4. United States—Armed Forces—Afghanistan—Attitudes. I. Title.
ML3916.G53 2016
780.88'355—dc23   2015022965
5   4   3   2   1

To the veterans who so generously participated in this project. THANK YOU.

CONTENTS

PREFACE

I first began to think about doing a project with Americans participating in the wars in Afghanistan and Iraq in 2004. I was concerned that our country was sending troops to two wars that we had initiated, yet there was little information available at the time from media or scholarly sources about the people fighting those wars. The little that I heard through television, radio, or print media was usually cloaked in polarizing rhetoric from one political side or the other to bolster an argument. I heard some portrayals from the right side of the political spectrum about the heroes fighting to protect Americans and to bring freedom to Afghanis and Iraqis. Alternately, I heard stories from the left about soldiers as victims who were severely injured or had lost their lives fighting in the wars, which were presented as unjust. Missing was information about the identities of these men and women or about their perspectives on what it was like to be at war and what impact the experience had on them in the short and long terms.

The first phase of the research began in the summer of 2005, when I spent two weeks in Colorado Springs, Colorado, home to multiple military establishments—Fort Carson Army Base, Peterson Air Force Base, and the United States Air Force Academy—and near to Schriever Air Force Base. As a folklorist also trained in ethnomusicology, my plan was to conduct ethnographic research that would include observing the dance practices of soldiers in between deployments and interviewing them about the corporal dimensions of their work and leisure time activities. Right around the time that I went to Colorado Springs, troops had been discouraged by their command from talking to reporters because of concerns about negative publicity. I was assured by the public information officer at Fort Carson that soldiers off base were protected by free speech laws; however, I quickly found that soldiers whom I did not already know were reluctant to talk to me, linking me, an academic wanting to write about their experiences and perspectives, with journalists who had similar objectives. My research assistant, who accompanied me for this fieldwork, had been an officer in the U.S. Army and was serving in the Army National Guard at the time. One day while hiking near Colorado Springs, he fortuitously encountered someone with whom he had served in Germany and who agreed to participate in an interview. This interviewee, an officer in the U.S. Army and a helicopter pilot, put me in touch with several other officers in his unit. Over the course of these preliminary interviews, I came to realize just how important music was and quickly shifted my focus from dance and corporality to musical listening.

As an ethnographer, my preferred research method is participant observation. Choosing to study musical listening at war posed some obvious challenges, because I could not easily join soldiers on tour to participate in their activities while listening to music with them because of restrictions to access, my own concerns about the risks involved, and my parental and work responsibilities. Soon after shifting my line of inquiry to music listening, I therefore also adapted my methods to primarily conducting interviews in person, by phone, via e-mail, and through social media sites in order to gather empirical data about musical engagement at war. As a result, a significant part of this study relies on narratives about musical listening that happened in the past, so it is ultimately a study about memory and personal experience narratives of war and musical engagement.

After my initial interviews in Colorado Springs I continued by interviewing some combat veterans who were students in my classes at the University of Oregon in Eugene, where I am a professor in the Folklore Program and English Department. Some of them later put me in touch with other veterans living either in Eugene, whom I could interview in person, or elsewhere, whom I interviewed by phone, e-mail, or Skype. As word spread about my project, people I interviewed, colleagues, and friends from around the country put me in touch with veterans who subsequently introduced me to others, some of whom I interviewed using e-mail as well as the other methods listed above.

By the conclusion of the project I had interviewed thirty-five people either in person or via phone, e-mail, or Skype and had had numerous less formal conversations with many more. Of those interviewed, all but one, the spouse of a veteran, were or had been in the military. A majority of those interviewed had deployed one or more times to the Iraq war and some to both the Iraq and Afghanistan wars. Four of the people I interviewed were women; the rest were men. Twenty-seven identified as white; three as African American; one as white, Native American, and Mexican American; one as Italian and Latino; one as Caribbean American; and one as Peruvian American/Latino (see appendix).

When I first began this project I tentatively explained to potential participants that I was interested in interviewing them about music and their experience at war. I anticipated that many would be ambivalent about participating and that they would question why I was asking them to talk about something so trivial, given the intensity of war. But almost everyone I approached was enthusiastic, and many responded quickly by telling me that "music was huge over there," or something echoing a similar sentiment. Many also explained that they had been reticent to participate in interviews about the wars with other scholars or journalists because of the difficulty of discussing some of their experiences and feelings and also because of the political biases of much of the discourse about the conflicts. Talking about music provided the possibility to discuss their experiences in ways that gave them a focus, and also, very important for anyone struggling with the aftermath of war, relative control over the subject matter. I was not asking them to discuss what they had done, witnessed, or experienced; rather, I asked them to reflect on their memories of music listening, and most were acutely aware of how vital music was and continued to be in helping them make it through difficult times.

In spring 2009 I met Benjamin (Benji) Lewis, a white veteran of the U.S. Marines, an antiwar activist involved with Iraq Veterans Against the War (IVAW), an association of activists organizing against war whose membership is restricted to combat veterans of the Iraq and Afghanistan wars. Benji was also a member of Veterans for Peace (VFP), an organization that includes veterans of any war in addition to civilians who share the organization's objectives.[1] Benji gave a talk in Eugene about his experience as a marine, the reasons for his political transformation, and the antiwar activism that had become the focus of his life. I introduced myself to him and interviewed him about music a few days later, on April 29, 2009. He subsequently introduced me to some of his friends, also young combat veterans, who were involved in the antiwar movement, specifically with the nonprofit Coffee Strong, at the time an antiwar coffeehouse and resource center run "by veterans for veterans" located outside Joint Base Lewis-McCord in Lakewood, Washington.[2]

My introduction to the Coffee Strong activists diverted my attention from this book project. For two years, what little time I had for research was devoted to making a documentary, *Grounds for Resistance: Stories of War, Sacrifice, and Good Coffee* (Gilman 2011), about the Coffee Strong activists.[3] Though I largely put writing about music and war on the back burner during this time, researching for and making the film afforded me the opportunity to expand my methods to participant observation in addition to interviews. Over the course of making the documentary, I spent a great deal of time with veterans from different branches, all of whom were very open about their experiences in the military, the impact it was having on their lives, and their struggles with the political and ethical dimensions of their participation, in addition to the postwar physical, mental, and economic challenges they faced. *Grounds for Resistance* is not about music; however, in my time with these veterans, we listened to and talked a lot about music, and I interviewed some people featured in the film about their musical listening during their deployments and after. The research associated with the film project is integrated throughout the study.

The Internet has also been an invaluable resource. Troops and their friends and family members write blogs during deployments, and many vets continue to blog afterward about their experiences at war and the challenges they continue to face. Combat veterans who are musicians have Web sites, post their music on YouTube, and participate actively on social media sites. These virtual community spaces yielded valuable data and increased my ability to establish contact with veterans and active duty military personnel across the country.

One issue I struggled with was how much information about war to include. I designed my research questions so that they elicited discussion about musical listening and not graphic details about the horrors of what some have come to refer to as "war porn." I did this for a number of reasons. Most veterans who struggle with what they saw and did at war do not respond positively to being asked to discuss these painful memories, and eliciting them can sometimes trigger difficult emotional outcomes. A number of interviewees were very generous in their willingness to share troubling memories with me, and some felt strongly that they should voice their stories in public venues, because they thought it was important for civilians to better understand the real issues at stake and establish more effective resources to support veterans. I decided that some of these details were important to share; the disturbing memories that many have experienced are necessary for understanding the main arguments of the book. At the same time, I worried about being voyeuristic, drawing attention to others' pain and suffering or somehow romanticizing the gore of war. I have attempted to achieve a balance. For the most part, I am either ignorant of or selected not to share much about the actual events that people experienced. I have, however, included limited information about some incidents and memories to give readers enough information to understand the extent of what contributors to this project experienced and are coping with on a daily basis and when necessary for illustration or analytical purposes.

Another issue that arose was how to refer to people. Many of those I interviewed appreciated the opportunity to share their stories and perspectives and were willing to have their first and last names known, while others asked me to use limited identifiers or pseudonyms. Though many interviewees did not mind being identified, for several reasons I have elected to use only first names or pseudonyms when they specifically requested that I do so. The topic of war is sensitive, and one never knows how an individual will feel about something he or she uttered during a conversation in a particular time or space after it is fixed on a page at a later date, when that person may be in very different circumstances and may feel quite differently about the subject. Furthermore, the Internet facilitates the possibility that a reader curious about or angered by something mentioned in the book could track down interviewees for any number of reasons, a possibility that is reduced with the use of only first names. I do use first and last names for those individuals who have a public presence and who gave me permission to do so, for example musicians or activists whose participation in this project was an extension of their public personas and where access to their other activities could expand readers' engagement with this topic.

The reader will encounter many long block quotes and descriptions of personal experience narratives from interviews throughout the text. I struggled with the balance of integrating my voice with that of the people I interviewed. Each interviewee was so articulate, and the interviews were so powerful, speaking so fundamentally to the individual's experience at war, that I felt that my role might be to collect and present rather than interpret these narratives and that readers could think about the narratives in interaction with one another to produce their own analyses and conclusions. After much thought, I opted to write a more standard academic text, though I am still conflicted about the value of the interviews themselves, especially as a folklorist who values stories and storytelling. I have attempted to achieve somewhat of a compromise, in that I integrate many direct quotes and personal experience narratives about war and musical listening, because the people I interviewed tell their stories the best, at the same time that I have used the breadth of my research and scholarly training to try to make sense of and situate their listening within broader scholarly, cultural, social, economic, and political frameworks.

ACKNOWLEDGMENTS

I am profoundly grateful to the many people who contributed to this project in so many ways over the course of almost ten years. I can in no way remember and acknowledge everyone, so thank you to all those who helped by participating directly or indirectly. My knowledge and reflection on this topic continue to grow over time through your generous interviews, casual conversations, and encouragement.

I offer my deepest respect and gratitude to all the veterans who willingly offered me not only their time, but also their stories and thoughts on musical listening at war and after. I am humbled and honored by your trust and willingness to share with me so many profound insights and memories. I am all too aware of the impossibility of truly understanding that which one can only know through personal experience and hope that I have gotten bits and pieces right and that you will forgive my errors. I am grateful to so many of you who put me in touch with others and directed me to relevant resources, making this project possible. To Nate, Peter Chinnici, and Joseph, your generous availability to participate in multiple interviews, answer my sporadic questions, and read drafts of the manuscript has been invaluable to my efforts to gain insight into life in the military and at war. The frank conversations we have had about gender and combat-related mental health issues have been critical to my analysis. My long-term relationships with the veterans involved with Coffee Strong and the antiwar movement have been essential to my attempts to grasp some of the economic and mental health issues faced by combat veterans. Geoff Valle, thank you for your insights and for helping me to launch the project in its very earliest phase.

To my colleagues Jonathan Pieslak and Martin Daughtry, our conference panels on music and war and your scholarship on the topic have greatly informed my thinking. Wendy Beck, I appreciate your patiently reading through chapter drafts, providing specific and clear directives for smoothing my prose. Thank you to the anonymous reviewers who carefully read the manuscript and provided concrete feedback that guided me to produce a clearer and more rigorous book and to the editors, especially Parker Smathers, at Wesleyan University Press for efficiently ushering this project through its journey to publication.

Thank you to my colleagues and students at the University of Oregon, whose creative intellectual insights stimulate my own. Support from the university's faculty research funds, the College of Arts and Sciences, and the Oregon Humanities Center made this project financially feasible.

Finally, I am forever indebted to my husband, John Fenn, and our daughters Anika and Nora Fenn Gilman. I know that my work often takes me away and that I am sometimes distracted or anxious about too many demands. I am grateful for your love and patience and for bringing so much joy and meaning to my life. John, thanks also for being such a great colleague as well as husband and friend.

ONE

Introduction

In the wars in Afghanistan, Operation Enduring Freedom (OEF), and Iraq, Operation Iraqi Freedom (OIF), that were instigated by the September 11, 2001, attacks on U.S. targets, musical listening was pervasive in U.S. troops' experience of war. Recent technological developments enabled listening in many different contexts and allowed troops to carry with them vast amounts of music and easily acquire new music, for themselves and to share with others in their immediate vicinity and far away. War is tough. Regardless of how one feels about war generally, or whether one thinks a specific war is just or necessary, the reality is that in war, no one escapes fear, domination, violence, isolation, pain, and loss. For those troops who fought in the wars in Iraq and Afghanistan as members of the U.S. military, warfare was necessarily fraught with ambivalence. Many U.S. troops may have been proud of their skills and professional accomplishments as well as their contributions in serving their country and protecting its citizens. They may have enjoyed the strong bonds and friendships that developed among members of units and the opportunities to travel and participate in important historical events. Yet most also missed their friends and family members; felt isolated and sometimes dreadfully bored; were uncomfortable with some of what they were required to do; and experienced pain at the loss that surrounded them, both within the U.S. military and what they experienced, observed, and sometimes inflicted on others.

The ways in which those most directly involved experienced these wars were highly idiosyncratic. People navigated the complexities of war in very individualized ways, at the same time that their relationships to their experiences were intricately tied to collective experience, cultural expectations, and widespread political perspectives. Musical listening was one of the few activities over which U.S. troops had control during their deployments and that they could do both privately and collectively. For many service men and women, listening to music provided one of the most salient mechanisms for thinking, feeling, escaping, communicating, connecting, passing the time, bonding, hiding, and grieving.

In his writing on iPod culture in urban spaces, Michael Bull argues that "the use of personal stereos changes the nature of the user's cognition and facilitates the effective management of these states together with a range of strategies (technologies) enabling the successful everyday management of space, place and interpersonal experience." Personal stereo use provides a "variety of strategies that enable the user to successfully prioritize their own experience, personally, interpersonally and geographically." Individual listening devices provide individuals with "a vastly expanded range of management strategies as they go about their daily lives" (2000, 9). Whereas Bull writes about people listening in industrialized cities, this book is about people living within the isolated and dangerous confines of war, where the need for management strategies is especially great. The ubiquity with which contemporary Americans can access and listen to music allowed troops to creatively and ingeniously take advantage of music as a resource available for entertainment, expression of identity, communication, and emotional and physical survival.

Janata Petr and colleagues (2007), Thomas Turino (2008), José van Dijck (2006), and others explain that because music is such a salient part of people's lives, and people often experience life concurrently with listening to music, specific musical pieces, artists, or genres often "evoke autobiographical memories and the emotions associated with them" (Petr et al. 2007, 845). Therefore, it has been especially effective to use questioning about musical listening as my entry point into investigating memories about the experience of war and the process of reintegrating into "normal" life afterward. This study, the result of many interviews, less formal conversations, and ethnographic fieldwork with individuals exploring their musical listening during and after their deployments, contributes to scholarly insights about music and conflict at the same time that it provides an avenue through which to gain greater understanding about what war is like and how individuals survive in the messy webs of conflicting thoughts and emotions that are so intricately part of the moment-to-moment and day-to-day phenomenon of war and the pervasive memories in its aftermath.

MUSICKING AT WAR

I borrow the term "musicking" from the late Christopher Small to emphasize that "music is not primarily a thing or a collection of things, but an activity in which we engage." Musicking includes performance, composition, dancing, and the focus of this study, listening (1987, 50; cf. Crafts, Cavicchi, and Keil 1993). Troops participated in music making. Some brought instruments, which they played privately or in groups at informal gatherings or in more formalized settings, such as religious services. Shannon, a veteran of the U.S. Air Force, remembered that at one point during his time in Iraq, the military shipped a piano from "somewhere," he thought maybe Kuwait, for use during religious services. Others brought with them smaller instruments, such as guitars, mandolins, or harmonicas. With the accessibility of recording and editing technology, some troops recorded instrumental or vocal tracks, some of which were made available to wide audiences through YouTube and other Internet sites or on compact discs (CDs) available for purchase. It was also common for units to create videos to commemorate their time at war or to document specific events, many of which are still readily accessible on YouTube and other Internet sites. These videos tended to be scored with popular musical recordings, creating intersecting forms of expression. These examples of musicking are worthy of study in and of themselves. My focus, however, is primarily on musical listening, the objective of which is experiential—active and passive consumption and engagement—rather than something created for an audience, because listening to music was the type of musicking most readily available to U.S. troops at war.

Like Anthony Seeger, I consider that "listening is as important as making sounds" and that "performance is an exchange in which one side is actively giving performance and the other side is actively reciprocating with attention" (2010, 123; see also Cavicchi 2011). When music is experienced through recordings, audience members are not limited to those present when the music was first produced, but rather expand across time and space, yet always as reciprocal participants in the performance. Listening to music was pervasive throughout the days and nights of troops' deployments, and musicking permeated their day-to-day reality through what Heike Weber refers to as dedicated and secondary listening. "Dedicated listening" refers to people consciously focusing on music, whether or not they are also engaged in another activity, and includes such things as a person choosing to play recorded music, actively paying attention to the music in the surroundings, discussing music, sharing music with others, and so on. Weber defines "secondary listening" as "listening to music while doing something else" (2009, 69). I add to this definition occasions when individuals may not be doing much else, but nevertheless are not listening closely to the music; rather, the music simmers in the background of their consciousness as they contemplate other things. The distinction between the two is muddy; it is relevant here only because of the importance of examining the types of dynamics that occur in all sorts of contexts in which music is present, regardless of the degree of active engagement.

The men and women I interviewed described music as "being everywhere" throughout their time at war. Army veteran Joseph's description in an interview on July 9, 2009, echoed that of many others: "I was always listening to music, I mean constantly. Music was sort of a sound track of my life." Musical listening was an integral part of work and nonwork activities for many, though they all reminded me that leisure time during deployments was not the same as in civilian life. Most civilians leave their physical work environments behind when work is over and engage in leisure activities with different people or at least in other places. During deployments, no such distancing was possible. Troops were largely in the same spaces whether they were working or not, surrounded by the same people, wearing the same clothing, and were always at risk of similar dangers, with their weapons in easy reach. The overlap of work and leisure times and spaces made music especially attractive, because it provided a way to differentiate time and space. Someone needing distance from others usually had no separate place to go or much opportunity for differentiated activity; thus putting on headphones and listening to music privately was often a way to create privacy, what Bull refers to as a "sound bubble" (2000, 2007)—or as Benji, a veteran of the U.S. Marines, explained, putting on headphones signaled "leave me the fuck alone."

Troops I interviewed described listening to music through headphones privately during all sorts of nonwork activities, from resting to sleeping, reading, writing letters, exercising, hanging out with friends, watching movies, and playing video games. They listened to music in collective settings by sharing one side of their headphones with a friend; projecting music through speakers attached to individual listening devices or computers; or when they were available, through CD and other media players. Group listening occurred in sleeping quarters, in gyms, on basketball courts, and on large bases, sometimes at organized events, such as dance nights.

People also listened to music during work activities. Troops reported listening to music on bases in operations centers, clinics, motor pools, and other work environments. Some music in work situations occurred privately, for example when a medic or chaplain played music in a consultation with a suffering soldier, or when a marine on watch listened to music through headphones in the middle of the night to help stay awake. As has been widely documented, troops often listened to aggressive musical forms through headphones or collectively through speakers as they prepared for patrols and missions, an auditory pick-me-up intended to get them into the necessary mental state for the activities to come (Pieslak 2009). Though many reported that they were not supposed to listen to music during patrols and missions, they nevertheless did, though whether or not such listening happened depended largely on whether it was tolerated by a vehicle's command.

MUSICAL TECHNOLOGIES

The rapid pace of technological innovation has transformed the musical listening potential in these wars compared to previous ones. The development of recording technologies in the twentieth century radically transformed people's engagement with music because of the possibility of listening to music separately from the space in which it was performed, which created what Ahahid Kassabian (2001) calls a new mode of "ubiquitous listening." With the availability of recorded sound, people could listen to music simultaneously with other activities, enabling musical listening to blend into the environment. This disarticulation between performance and listening spaces has continued to increase with subsequent technological advances, which have dramatically expanded the accessibility and mobility of musical recording, playing, and listening for U.S. troops at war.

Music has always been an important part of the military and of war, serving as a rallying cry, motivating warriors to charge, entertaining troops during lulls, and providing a means of identity making and self-reflection.[1] Folklorist Lydia Fish (2003) describes the prevalence of musical listening, composition, production, and sharing during the Vietnam War. The Armed Forces Radio broadcast popular music across combat zones, a musical repertory that was restricted and controlled by the military (cf. Baade 2012b). Troops listened to this station at the same time that they created their own idiosyncratic broadcasts through underground and home-style radio systems. State-of-the art recording equipment was widely available, and on reel-to-reel tapes troops recorded themselves playing music, concert nights, and the sounds of war, recordings that were subsequently disseminated across combat zones and eventually within the United States (Heuer 2003). Prior to the advent of portable technologies, when they were in locations where it was feasible troops could also listen to music on turntables, as remembered by ethnomusicologist Frank Gunderson, whose listening habits when he was in the air force from 1980 to 1984 "focused on LPs, played on my PX-purchased stereo" (personal communication to author, January 22, 2015).

People I interviewed who had served in the U.S. military and been deployed in the 1990s described the prevalence of more portable boom boxes in many work and living environments, which enabled troops to listen to music collectively while they worked or hung out. Many people brought individualized listening devices—Walkmans and portable CD players—to deployments, which they listened to mostly during nonwork time. The first cassette Walkmans, introduced by the Sony Corporation in 1979, were revolutionary because they enabled "users to travel through any space accompanied by their own 'individualized' soundworld" (Bull 2000, 3). Yet with portable cassette and CD players, one could only listen to as much music as could be carried on recording media. Though the players were relatively small and portable, they nevertheless took up enough space that it was difficult for troops to easily hide them and listen to music during times when it was prohibited. These devices did allow for private listening and for people to shut out the outside world by creating sonic sound bubbles. With cassettes they could create more individualized playlists through mixtapes, which also enabled music sharing. For example Simon, interviewed on October 11, 2012, who served in the navy from 1993 to 1998, described his personal musical collection at the time as consisting of mixtapes made for him by friends. He enjoyed the opportunity to listen to these cassettes and to spend time with others listening to their music, but his ability to acquire new music or to create new playlists for himself geared to his own mood or musical needs was limited. Music was everywhere on his ship during his two deployments, but he remembered getting bored with his selections very quickly. Troops who served during this period explained that the exchanges (PX), stores on bases, sold CDs, but the options did not necessarily match their musical tastes. They were always happy to find ones that they liked, but many were more likely to count on friends or family members to send them CDs or cassettes in care packages. They also remembered stocking up on recordings when they were on leave.

The timing of the beginning of the wars in Afghanistan (October 2001) and Iraq (March 2003) corresponded with especially significant transformations in the technology of recorded sound. The MP3 format, developed in the 1990s, uses a technique called compression to produce a very small file that can be as small as 12 percent of the size of the original format, for example, a .wav file (Sterne 2012, 1–2). These tiny sound files, which proliferated in the early 2000s, transformed the production, consumption, and distribution of music, and troops benefited because "more music" was "more ready-to-hand for more people than at any other time in human history" (Sterne 2012, 224). The MP3 revolution instigated what Jonathan Sterne refers to as the "age of musical abundance," and it exponentially increased the ability to acquire and share music with others (2012, 224). According to Bull, "for the first time in history, the majority of Westerners possess the technology to create their own private auditory world wherever they go" (2009, 83).

Troops who joined the service before the proliferation of MP3s and served through the transition described dramatic changes in their listening from one deployment to the next. No longer was space or weight an issue, because, as Sterne notes, "MP3s are particularly striking because they are so small but circulate on such a massive scale" (2012, 225). Airman Shannon explained that "in the days of CDs and tapes, those were very hard to bring over to war and especially to trade. . . . In this day and age, war is very different, in that people are able to bring over stuff from home like that, that they did not have in previous wars." A number of interviewees noted that with the availability of MP3 players, part of their preparation for deployment was purchasing individual listening devices with the largest amount of memory they could afford so as to maximize the amount of music they could bring with them and continue to acquire. Some brought portable computers, whose memory potential allowed for enormous amounts of music to be stored. Shannon explained: "Even though we were sleeping in a tent [on] a cot in pretty rough conditions, a lot of people had laptops and were able to utilize all that technology." No longer did troops have to wait for loved ones or Amazon.com to mail them CDs or to be on a base that sold music to acquire music; all they needed was access to the Internet.

Sharing music was also made easy. No longer did CDs have to be borrowed and returned. Tracks could be copied between digital playing devices, allowing multiple people to integrate particular tracks into their private playlists. Access to the Internet and the increase in social marketing made it easier for soldiers to keep up with music trends across the globe. Army veteran Mark enjoyed the opportunity while he was in Iraq to use the Internet to research new music whenever he had access. He could read about bands and listen to sample tracks and then buy any music he wanted right then and there. For Mark, for whom music collecting and connoisseurship were central to his identity, following developments in his favorite musical scenes at home helped mitigate his sense of isolation.

The Internet also facilitated communication between service members and their friends and family members outside the military. Music sharing became an even more important means for troops and their loved ones to commune across time and space. Soldiers sent music on their sound tracks to friends and family members to entertain and express feelings or aspects of their experiences, and loved ones could reciprocate.

Digital listening also transformed the ways that troops could listen to music. Previously, musicians and producers controlled the sequencing of songs on commercial cassettes and CDs. Mixtapes allowed for more individuality, but once the tape was recorded, the song order remained fixed. CD players enabled variation in sequencing, though the random setting gave the user little control over the order in which tracks played. With MP3 players, in contrast, listeners could create idiosyncratic playlists of a single band's music or of particular genres, and random settings made possible unexpected sound experiences to interact variously with what was happening in a person's mental and physical environment. This capacity increased the ability of individuals to tailor their musical listening to their private listening needs and desires and for their experiences to be mediated through their musical listening. A person could create an esoteric sound track through an ever-emergent process of gathering, selecting, and ordering tracks based on individual taste, emotional state, and listening needs at any given moment.

People could withdraw into their own musical listening and enjoy the isolation of knowing that they were alone with the sounds and their own thoughts. Yet these same technologies were inherently social because of the ease with which they allowed one person to share music with others in the immediate environment, for example, by connecting an MP3 player to a computer, stereo, or sound system in a vehicle and thus enabling shared listening. And people could easily communicate with those they either knew or did not know across time and space by sending tracks or links to music through e-mail, phones, or Internet sites. Web sites and social media networks abounded and brought people together in virtual communities through their shared musical tastes who may not otherwise have interacted. In some cases, music may not have been the primary element that brought together a virtual community, but the sharing of music was part of what transpired in the community formation and interaction. The smallness of devices also made it easier for soldiers to bring music with them on a variety of activities and allowed music-playing devices to be easily hidden. Troops could slip an MP3 player into a pocket without it being easily detected by their command. And earbuds could easily be worn under protective headgear without being seen.

IPods in pockets could be turned on and off, increasing the confidence of some that they would be able to complete their job as necessary, turning off the music when maximum attention was needed. And when possible, larger headphones could be worn around the neck rather than over the ears, allowing troops to hear music while moving through space while still aurally tracking what was going on around them. Digital music devices could be easily connected to the high tech sound systems in vehicles intended to enhance communication between units. Troops described streaming music to the headphones of everyone on a vehicle, thus allowing for shared musical listening during intense work activities (see Pieslak 2007, 2009; Daughtry 2012).

The possibilities that contemporary technologies afforded for both personal and public musical engagement at war resulted in music being a profound and effective resource for troops as they attempted to address their own personal needs, obtain support for themselves, help others in need, communicate to others in their immediate surroundings and far away, express their identities, and participate in conflict.

THE PROBLEM OF GENRE

One challenge of writing a book about a broad range of musical listening is the issue of genre. Throughout the study, I refer to many different musical styles and artists that were discussed during the interviews. Understanding the inherent problem of categorizing music into neat generic classification systems, I often use the generic labels given to me by interviewees to help place the music for the reader or provide insight into how the person describing the music identified it. In these cases, I do not question the interviewees' labeling nor try to impose my own. My analysis engages genre more directly in that certain types of music and artists are identified by troops or by the general public as being associated with particular ways of being or thinking, for example, the frequent association of certain types of rap and metal music with articulations of hypermasculinity or of certain country artists with patriotism. These generic classifications and boundaries are fluid and inherently messy. For example, there is no monolithic category of heavy metal; rather, many fans identify subcategories, such as thrash or death metal. Different people identify different musical selections differently, and there is contestation, sometimes outright conflict, about generic categories associated with identity politics, aesthetics, status, economics, and so on.² This study does not intend to engage these conflicts, nor does it claim to accurately classify the vast amount of music that is discussed. Readers will unavoidably disagree with some of the lumping of different music into broad groupings and will disagree with some of my classifications and that of the interviewees. My hope is that readers will recognize the inherent problem of genre in popular music studies and will focus on the arguments made about musical experience rather than on disagreements about genre.

THEORIES, THEMES, AND CHAPTER MAP

This project builds on the scholarship of those working on music in everyday life, namely such scholars as Susan Crafts, Daniel Cavicchi, and Charles Keil (1993), Tia DeNora (2000), and Bull (2000, 2007, 2009). The central premise, inspired by Charles Keil in his introduction to *My Music: Explorations of Music in Daily Life,* is that "each person is unique," and "choices of music and the ways you relate to music are plural and interconnected in a pattern that is all yours, an 'idioculture' or idiosyncratic culture in sound" (1993, 2). "Grounded theory" describes my approach. Rather than analyzing data with a preselected theoretical apparatus, themes for analysis emerged through the process of doing the research. In their overview of grounded theory, H. Russell Bernard and Grey W. Ryan explain the benefits of this approach, which (1) "brings the researcher close to the informants' experience," (2) provides a "rigorous and detailed method for identifying categories that emerge from texts," and (3) enables the researcher to "link concepts to substantive and formal theories" (1998, 607–8). In my research process I carefully analyzed preliminary interviews to determine categories that emerged as substantive theoretical themes. In subsequent research, using an open-ended and fluid interviewing process that engaged the themes I had identified while also allowing new categories to emerge, I developed critical insights based on dominant topics in interviewees' narratives about musical listening. These insights and thematic topics form the theoretical core of the study.

The obvious overarching theme is the relationship between music and conflict, encompassing multiple types of explicit and implicit conflicts, with the most overt being the Afghanistan and Iraq wars themselves. In *The Dark Side of the Tune:*

Popular Music and Violence, Bruce Johnson and Martin Cloonan emphasize that inasmuch as scholars have celebrated the "positive power of music," music is just as much implicated in conflict, and "war perennially provides the most extreme manifestations of the connections between music, identity, and violence" (2009, 2). The musical listening during the Iraq and Afghanistan wars was part and parcel of the war efforts; simply put, troops listened to music in order to engage in conflict, though their use of music expanded far beyond the immediate objectives of war. In the introduction to *Music and Conflict,* John Morgan O'Connell begins his attempt at definition with the statement that "conflict is hard to define" (2010, 2). He then explains with nuance that conflict can be viewed negatively and positively and that by definition, conflict "implies the possibility of conflict resolution" (2012, 3). Correspondingly, this study is situated within numerous, sometimes overlapping types of conflict, from the violence of war to the less explicit and more intricate negotiations of conflict that existed within military communities during deployments and with which combat veterans and their families contended after their return from war. The latter types of conflict were associated with such things as differences in rank, age, personal interest, politics, race, religion, ethnicity, gender, and sexual identity/practice, and very important, especially after troops returned from war, their internal conflicts as they struggled with their memories, the ethical implications of their actions, and their attempts to reintegrate into their families and civilian lives.

As Regina M. Sweeney (2001) argues in her study of singing in France during World War I, studying musical engagement during war takes us from the business of governments and political leaders to the everyday realm of the troops in the trenches. It takes us from official propaganda and information channels to the informal, everyday expressivity and activities of those most directly involved in and impacted by their participation in conflict, thus providing a complex perspective about all those participating in a war effort. Comparing music to language, O'Connell suggests that music may

> provide a better medium for interrogating the character of conflict and for evaluating the quality of conflict resolution. While language as prose tends to delimit interpretation according to the partial dictates of authorial intention, music as practice serves to liberate interpretation according to the multiple views of audience reception. (2010, 2)

It is this possibility for the very individuality and multiplicity of engagement and interpretation that makes musical listening an especially effective mechanism for U.S. troops to contribute to and negotiate conflict in numerous, sometimes contradictory ways (see Ritter and Daughtry 2007).

Music has been used in these wars as an explicit strategy to promote patriotism and support for the war, to motivate troops to engage in battle (Pielak 2009; Daughtry 2012), as part of invasions (Pieslak 2009), and as an instrument of torture (Cusick 2006, 2008). As other scholars who have examined music and conflict in various historical, geographic, and cultural settings have documented, music has played an important role in war efforts because of its capacity to disseminate messages, forge unity, build morale (see Baade 2012b), communicate, and channel a wide variety of emotions (e.g., Pegley and Fast 2007). This capacity has been especially productive for evoking collective feelings of patriotism or shared antipathy for the "enemy." As in situations where people participate in shared music making as a means of forging bonds or expressing an imagined or even forced solidarity, uniting troops through shared listening to music pregnant with prowar or nationalistic messages has been important for solidifying a sense of shared identity and dedication to the mission.[3]

Conversely, different groups within the military identify differently and sometimes in conflict with one another. Certain popular music genres tend to be associated with certain sociocultural categories in the United States, so different groups within the military often listened to particular genres, artists, or songs as a means to identify with those within their groups and thus simultaneously differentiated themselves from others, which sometimes contributed to intragroup conflict within the military (see Sugarman 2010).

In some conflict or postconflict situations people from opposite sides come together and share in music making as a means of bridging and ultimately resolving difference (e.g., Vincente 2012). In the interviews I conducted, troops indicated that they had few or no opportunities to share music with members of the local civilian populations other than the occasional interaction with a child on the street or a relationship forged with a translator or collaborator. Music did play a big role in resolving existing or potential conflict within the military, as troops listened to music across various social boundaries or otherwise bridged differences through participating in musicking, and music is playing a big part in helping combat veterans process, heal, and reintegrate into civilian life (Fast and Kepley 2012).

An important subtheme of music and conflict is the relationship between music and political identity and expression. These wars have been controversial and politically divisive, yet most of us outside the U.S. military hear little about the politics of the people who fight them. As is true of any armed conflict, such wars are inherently political; the majority of people in the military have been involved very significantly as actors in U.S. foreign policy who have little decision-making power about what they were asked to do. Many of those I interviewed described feeling conflicted, either during their deployments or afterward, as they tried to understand their participation in the wars. Music provided an important means for them to think about, process, and sometimes transform their political thinking, in addition to expressing a political identity. Certain musical styles were associated with pro-mission and patriotic stances, and these genres pervaded the soundscapes of war in U.S. military spaces. On the other hand, certain songs and other musical styles contributed to soldiers' reflections about the politics of war, sometimes contributing to their shifting political perspectives, and some soldiers used music to actively express opposition to or engage in antiwar activism.

In addition to politics, one of the most significant sources of conflict for troops during and after deployment has been internal psychological turmoil. Relationships between music and affect have been well studied. In the introduction to *Handbook of Music and Emotion: Theory, Research, Applications,* psychologists Patrik N. Juslin and John A. Sloboda note that "several studies have suggested that the most common motive for listening to music is to influence emotions—listeners use music to change emotions, to release emotions, to match their current emotion, to enjoy or to comfort themselves, or to relieve stress" (2010a). People create, perform, and listen to music to express, feel, control, and alter emotions, such as joy, pleasure, love, sadness, humor, grief, anger, disappointment, and rage (DeNora 2000). The affective dimensions of music are inherently multiple, in that an artist can create or perform a song to express multiple and conflicting emotions. And particular affective states are not fixed to specific musical phrases, instrumentations, or pieces; thus the same music can express and evoke many different emotions simultaneously. The emotional connections that both producers and consumers can form to music are vast, thus making music a vital resource for both articulating and processing emotion. People can listen to music as a form of self-therapy that they associate with a particular psychological state, as a way to express or fully feel that emotion, and they can listen to music to evoke a particular affect, or alternately, to try to avoid or escape an affective state. Furthermore, because people often do not have control over the music that is playing in their environments, music can operate affectively in ways outside the control of the listener.

These relationships of music to emotion are especially salient in war settings, in which all emotion is experienced by most at a higher intensity than in nonwar settings. Living in constant danger, being required to do emotionally and physically demanding things, being far from loved ones, not having access (at least officially) to alcohol and sex, and having no break from their social and occupational environment increases the need for tools to express and negotiate how they are feeling. As will be elaborated on throughout this book, the emotional aspect of musical listening was one of the most widely discussed by interviewees.

For logistical reasons, the research methods used for this study relied heavily on people's memories, and this necessity has in some ways been fortuitous because of the complex relationships between musical listening and memory making. Turino explains that we make "connections between indexical signs and their objects by experiencing them together in our actual lives" and that music "commonly indexes the people and situations where we have heard the music" (2008, 8–9; cf. van Dijck 2006, 363). The association of memory and music is especially heightened in war, where the experiences that will eventually contribute to troops' autobiographical memories occur within the taut emotional state that they described as characterizing their day-to-day lives: the excitement and danger of death lurked constantly; they were aware that every action could lead to either their own or others' survival or destruction, and simultaneously, that regardless of how skilled or prepared they were, they ultimately had little control over whether or not they would survive. Everyone I interviewed had either experienced, observed, or heard of fellow military personnel dying from vehicles overturning, improvised explosive devices (IEDs) expertly concealed on roadsides exploding suddenly, or other war-related trauma. Added to this were the uncomfortable living conditions of crowded spaces, in which individuals lacked privacy; the harsh weather; and heavy clothing, intertwined with the meaningfulness that many felt about what they were doing and its importance for their relationships with those in their units, in addition to their contributions to history in the making. This poignancy of their experiences, so closely linked with their ubiquitous musical listening, contributed to the long-term linking of music with private and collective memories.

In the introduction to *Sound Souvenirs: Audio Technologies, Memory and Cultural Practices* (2009), Karin Bijsterveld and José van Dijck explore why musical compositions are so effective at evoking private and collective memories. They consider the work of neurologists, such as Oliver Sacks (2007), who determined that humans tend to have much more detailed and varied memories of musical sounds than they do of other sounds because of the "intrinsic characteristics of music itself—its complex sonic patterns woven in time, its logic, its momentum, its unbreakable sequences, its insistent rhythms and repetitions, the mysterious way in which it embodies emotion" (2007). Though individuals listen to music selectively and differently, the highly structured nature of the musical dimensions of melodies, rhythms, and tempos can be more easily and carefully stored in human minds than are the unstructured sounds that constitute the background of many of our activities, for example the barking of dogs. According to neurologist David Huron (2006), people's musical memories are so detailed that they can often pinpoint the exact moment in a piece that elicits particular emotions and memories. Bijsterveld and Van Dijck suggest that it "may be the *combination* of the structural exactness of our memory of musical composition and the high variety of individual associations elicited by music that make music recordings such a popular tool for eliciting the past in people's minds" (2009, 13).

This capacity for music to be so intricately linked to memory is a critical theme throughout this study in its exploration of relationships between musical listening and identity, power, and gendered practice. Because music is so tied to memory neurologically and experientially, asking veterans about musical listening was a highly effective way to evoke memories of their war experiences. This strong connection between music and recollection is thus also useful for exploring how music triggers desired and undesired memories. Bull writes about music's role in evoking nostalgia, likening an iPod to a diary, a collection of musical selections linked to memories (2007, 137). Users can choose a musical selection from this "diary" for the nostalgia they hope it will evoke, or music can trigger memories without their control (Anderson 2004, 9). These associations between music and memory are important for how individuals integrate their experiences of war into their autobiographical perceptions of themselves, in addition to how music plays a role in collective memory making for units and the military as a whole during the course of war and in the time and relationships that follow. Music is also significant in the negative aftermath of war, as it can evoke memories of trauma and thus be implicated in post-traumatic stress disorder (PTSD), at the same time that troops use music to subdue memories or evoke positive memories to help them cope with PTSD.

The social dimension of music is also very important in war contexts, much as it is in others. Musical listening is intricately tied to self and collective identity making for most of us. "Identity" refers to how individuals think of themselves in relationship to other individuals or groups and the way that other people classify a person in relationship to social categories. In my use of the term, I understand identity making to be a fluid process that is forever emergent and shifting in relationship to an individual's self-perception at any given moment and any number of factors in the social and physical environment. These social categories can vary greatly and are often based on such things as gender, culture, race, occupation, family, religion, place, class, interests, abilities, sexuality, musical taste, and so on (see Dundes 1980; Berger and Del Negro 2004, 125). Some identifiers are more officially constituted (e.g., U.S. Marine), while others are more informal or fluid (e.g., fan of rap). All people identify and are identified in many different ways, both formally and informally. Our identities are dynamic and ever shifting as we think of ourselves differently. Furthermore, people constantly map identities onto one another in relationship to a whole host of factors having to do with their assumptions about others, an individual's body and self-presentation, and details in the social environment. Identity is thus "*contingent,* different social environments contributing to an internal-external dialectic in different ways" (Robinson and Hockey 2011, 5). Folklorist Richard Bauman (1972) articulates that identification occurs within the twin processes of differentiation; when people identify selectively with others because of some shared quality, they simultaneously disassociate themselves from those without it (see also Stokes 1997 [1994], 5; Johnson and Cloonan 2009, 4). Identity is not static, but rather is an ongoing, interpretive process whereby people are constantly articulating various identities and interpreting their own and others' behaviors based on ideas they have about social categories (Berger and Del Negro 2004, 125). For many, music is important in the performance and negotiation of identities: people capitalize on music to construct strong associations with others, and they "can equally use music to locate themselves in idiosyncratic and plural ways" (Stokes 1997 [1994], 3). Important to this study is that musical taste is often ideologically linked to other forms of identity, such as class, religion, race/ethnicity, or politics (see Connell and Gibson 2003, 15).

In the United States people, especially young people in the demographic of many of those fighting in the lower echelons of the military, display their musical taste through visual and aural channels in order to communicate to others who they are: ethnicity, gender, class, region, politics, educational level, personality, or social grouping. Outside the military, youths wear T-shirts, sport tattoos, don specific styles of clothing, and wear hair and makeup associated with particular identity groups tied to musical listening. Members of the military have just as much reason to express these types of identity, but they have fewer avenues available to do so, especially during their deployments, when their hair and dress are strictly controlled and are expressive of little other than their identity as members of particular branches of the U.S. armed forces. Musical listening thus becomes an important way that troops express their individualized and group identities and forge bonds with others within their units.

These themes thread throughout the text, and each chapter engages one or more of them in its focus to provide descriptive and analytical information about musical engagement during and after war. Chapter 2 provides important contextual information about the demographics of the military, motivations for enlisting, and the nature of life during war. Chapter 3 focuses on additional contextual information, explaining how, before their first deployments, despite their training and the stories they heard, troops generally knew little about what war would really be like, and thus their musical preparation for subsequent deployments was usually more productive than for their first. Once in combat, they listened to music in a wide range of settings in different social environments. As does the rest of the book, this chapter emphasizes the memories of individuals who described when, what, and why they listened to music.

Because listening to music is such a pervasive part of deployment, chapter 4 considers how music mediates experience and memory, and alternately how experiencing something while listening to particular music can impact how a person hears those musical selections in the future and remembers the incident. Chapter 5 considers associations between musical listening and gender, an especially salient social category in military culture, which is typically defined as "masculine" or even "hypermasculine." This chapter examines the role of music in the construction of masculinity and what it means for people not identified by either themselves or others as masculine enough—women, homosexuals, unmanly men—to operate within these spaces. What emerges is a complex analysis of gender in the military, wherein multiple, sometimes competing masculinities (and to some degree femininities) operate simultaneously, despite the projection of a very narrow definition of masculinity in much of the expressive culture that permeates within and about the U.S. military.

In the narratives of musical memories that run throughout this book, the troops interviewed discussed emotional stress and issues with which they struggled during their deployments and after. Chapter 6 explores ways in which people used music to manage their emotions, evoke desired feelings, suppress difficult ones, and communicate with others about their psychological struggles. In addition to managing their own emotions, people also used music to try to help others who were struggling by sharing it with them or creating soundscapes that they hoped would evoke a more positive emotional state.

While chapters 2 through 6 focus on music during deployment, chapter 7 shifts to troops' musical listening after they returned from war. Many of the themes already developed in previous chapters continue to be significant, as veterans used music in attempts to transform themselves from warriors to civilians, which for many occurred while they were struggling economically, socially, physically, and emotionally. For some veterans, making music about war became an important way for them to not only work through their own struggles, but also help other veterans. Some of these musicians developed very active social networking sites that provide vital community for active duty troops and combat veterans, bringing people together to share their perspectives, provide support for one another, and express themselves through both the listening to and consumption of music. For others, music played a role in their complex negotiations about their own political positioning in relationship to their having served as actors in the war effort. For all, the music they heard at war continued to feature in their sound memory as they came to terms with who they were as veterans and in their ongoing conceptualizations and constructions of self into the future. Chapter 8 shifts to the political transformation of some veterans. Though at one time they volunteered their service to the U.S. military, their time at war impacted their thinking so much that by the time of the interviews they had become disillusioned and critical of the government and the war efforts, and some had become antiwar activists.

TWO

Setting the Scene

Musical listening does not happen in a vacuum, especially when one is at war, or as Seeger states, "the important sonic universe for discussion is the whole soundscape, not music itself" (2010, 123). The sound track to war was loud, scary, often deafening. Interested in musical listening in the Iraq war, ethnomusicologist Martin Daughtry (2012) emphasized that music could not be separated from the larger aural setting, in which gunshots, mortar explosions, voices, IEDs, vehicles, and aircraft flying overhead were not only omnipresent, but could not be ignored because they were potentially vital communications. Sounds of war signaled whether circumstances were relatively safe or danger was near and imminent. Sounds alerted people to the need to dash for cover or move into action, or that they could try to relax. Musical listening at war occurred within this soundscape, whether troops were listening to music to mute these sounds or were carefully calibrating the volume to ensure that they could track aurally. And significantly, in the contemporary conflicts in Iraq and Afghanistan, the U.S. military used music as an instrument of war; to give a few examples, music was used as part of the attack on Fallujah in April 2004, the first by U.S. forces to capture the Iraqi city (DeGregory 2004); music has been used as an interrogation strategy (Cusick 2006, 2008); and music was used to calm the injured in makeshift medical facilities, as discussed in later chapters.

Though this study does not engage all these overlapping sounds in its focus on musical listening, this overbearing soundscape and the multiple ways that music was used officially and unofficially made up the sonic context in which listening occurred. This auditory environment, in combination with other aspects of the social and physical reality, shaped all musical engagement. The demographics of the military and the contexts in which troops worked, interacted, hung out, and slept were the additional institutional and physical structures that shaped musical experiences at war and afterward.

WHO JOINS THE MILITARY, AND WHY?

Jason K. Dempsey, a lieutenant colonel in the U.S. Army who holds a PhD in political science from Columbia University, starts his preface to a book on contemporary soldiers and politics with the following:

> We project our prejudices onto people we do not know. We fill gaps in our understanding of others with stereotypes and assumptions. The American army is especially susceptible to this dynamic, as few Americans have direct experience with military service. Because of this, a formation of soldiers can become a blank slate upon which we might imagine the best, or worst, of America. (2010, xv)

This blank slate potential, especially within the context of these two very divisive wars, allows for contradictory narrativizing about the U.S. military within popular discourse, which often uses soldiers as central characters for putting forth a certain point of view. At one extreme, a mythos exists about U.S. troops that homogenizes them into a glorified archetype of heroic and patriotic warrior. In the current wars in Iraq and Afghanistan, troops are the symbolic actors in the master narrativizing put forth by the government and military and disseminated through multiple communicative outlets, including news media; politicians' speeches; movies; song lyrics; reality TV shows; and sometimes soldiers' and family members' memoirs, blogs, and personal experience narratives—part and parcel of what some have come to term "militainment," or entertainment centered on military themes that celebrate the U.S. Department of Defense (Stahl 2010). In this mythologizing, troops are key characters in the discourse about the reasons and objectives for engaging in the wars: the threat of terrorism, freeing Iraqis from Saddam Hussein's oppression or Afghanis from the Taliban, and bringing stability to countries threatened by internal insurgents. Troops of the United States are characterized as heroic, noble, honorable, devoted, unquestioning, courageous, skilled, and selfless patriots willing to make sacrifices to protect the good of their country, the Iraqi and Afghani people, and the world. At the other extreme, for those who for a variety of reasons disagree with war, militarism, the U.S. government, or a host of other related issues, troops are characters in a different set of narratives, in which military personnel may represent the very worst of that which they detest, or they may be presented and interpreted as unintelligent rule followers, blind patriots, politically ignorant, lovers of violence, and at the worst murderers or torturers. And at yet another extreme, troops are portrayed as the vulnerable victims, who to a large extent lack agency and have been manipulated into participating, and as a result are now broken from their participation in the war effort.

In all this narrativizing, regardless of the point of view, troops become part of an imaginary, largely fulfilling a symbolic role that differs depending on the point of view of the one imagining. That each are human beings with their own reasons for having joined the military, their own thoughts about war in general or these wars in particular, and their own personal and political trajectory gets lost in the partisan discourse. The portrayal of U.S. troops as the homogenized trope of patriotic hero or as the blind patriotic follower or victim is inherently flawed, because it would be impossible for the thousands of individuals who make up the U.S. military to all share a single perspective, especially because war is so inherently contradictory. What is too often lacking in these collective memory makings is the reality that these wars are messy business. The people fighting in them are individuals, with their own social, political, racial, gendered, psychological, and economic positions. And throughout the experience and after, each one interprets the war in ever-emergent, fluid, and highly varied ways and develops an often ever-changing narrative that reveal much more diverse and nuanced perspectives on the war experience.

Before the September 11, 2001, attacks on the World Trade Center in New York City and on the Pentagon in Washington, D.C., recruiters marketed military service as an opportunity for young people to see the world, enjoy adventure, and obtain an education. Army advertisements promised the opportunity to "be all that you can be"; the air force sold the chance to "do something amazing"; the navy clarified that "it's not just a job, it's an adventure"; and the Marines emphasized their selectivity with "The Few. The Proud. The Marines." Slogans interacted with visual images and music to convey "two principal messages: military service as a heroic, patriotic, and honorable duty; and military service is a source of action, adventure, and excitement" (Pieslak 2009, 22).[1] Everyone who joined the military understood that they would be trained to fight, and the possibility of war was always there, but many expected that they could end their service without ever having to engage or die in combat. Nate, who joined the Marine Corps in 1996, remembered making his decision:

After high school, I tried out college for a semester, and I didn't make it through one semester. I didn't want to be there. I didn't know what I was doing. I decided to enlist in the Marine Corps. I chose to enlist because at the time I thought I wanted to do something in law enforcement. . . . I thought that going the route of the military would be a good first step toward that. If I wanted to be a police officer, or if I wanted to do something more federal, having a marine background would be great. I thought of it in terms of job training.

Once I got there I started thinking about it as a career and even thought about going back to school and going in as an officer. I enjoyed it. I started out in infantry, which was great. I did most of my training stateside. At that time there wasn't really anything major going on that as an infantryman I'd have to really worry about.

The perception that being in the military was less about war and more about having a job or leading to a profession was bolstered by the reality that "in the twenty years from 1980 through 1999, a total of five hundred sixty-three U.S. soldiers died from 'enemy' fire." To put this figure into perspective, according to statistics obtained by Catherine Lutz from the U.S. Department of Transportation in 1998, "the same number of people die every five days on American highways" (2001, 218).

After 9/11, when the United States invaded first Afghanistan and then Iraq, all those already in the military quickly realized that their participation in war was imminent. When asked where he was when he heard about the 9/11 attacks, marine veteran Andrew responded that he was "down at the motorpool," doing "maintenance on some Hum-Vs at Twentynine Palms," the Marines' base in San Bernardino County in California, when he heard "rumors of buildings blowing up." The troops spent the rest of the day watching the attacks "play over and over and over again" on cable TV in somebody's room. Andrew said that "right afterwards, we all assumed we were going to war." After much waiting and expectation of being deployed to Afghanistan, his unit was part of the initial invasion of Iraq.

Those who joined after 9/11 knew that signing up most likely meant that they would engage in war. Angered by the attacks or concerned about the threat of terrorism to their country and its people, some Americans and foreign nationals were motivated to enlist in the military to help protect the country and its interests. Despite this rise in patriotism, the overall rate of enlistment dropped as the two wars progressed and potential enlistees became concerned that signing up was a guarantee that they would go to war ("Vanishing Volunteers" 2006).

Within the military are people with a wide range of educational, class, race, ethnic, political, and geographic backgrounds, who join for a variety of reasons. John Faris (1981) divides recruits broadly into two categories, those who join primarily for "marketplace factors," for the salary, educational benefits, or job training, and those who join out of a desire to serve their country or because of family tradition (see also Dempsey 2010, 46). Since the end of the draft in 1973, which shifted military service from conscription to voluntary employment, the U.S. armed forces have relied on monetary incentives to attract recruits (Dempsey 2010, 45), and it follows that people with lower family incomes are more likely to join than those with higher ones (Lutz 2008, 184).[2] According to Dempsey, within the U.S. Army, officers are more likely to fall into Faris's second category, and enlisted men and women are more likely to join because of the remuneration. "Educational benefits" was the "most popular reason given by young soldiers and officers" for joining (Dempsey 2010, 46; see also Maclean and Parsons 2010; Bachman et al. 2000). The military provides professional and educational opportunities for thousands, many from lower income families, for whom college or other post–high school education or training is out of reach.

Dempsey's (2010) study revealed that within officer ranks, people who identify with the Republican Party and with conservatism are more prevalent, but at the lower ranks, people identify across the political spectrum. He explains that from the end of the draft through 2000, no data were collected about troops' political affiliations. The few surveys that have been done since 2000 have revealed that a majority are supporters of the Republican Party; however, Dempsey cautions that the respondents were not representative of everyone in the military because they were either overwhelmingly officers or those who had served in the military for ten or more years (2010, 3–5).

Though I interviewed a few officers, the main focus of my project was enlisted men and women in the lower echelons. Interviewees expressed a wide range of reasons for joining, the most common of which echoed the findings of Faris, Dempsey, and Bachman and colleagues, having to do with economics and to some extent social and psychological factors. Many joined right out of or soon after high school. Tina was from southern Oregon and served for eight years as an intelligence analyst. She joined the U.S. Army in 2000 "under the delayed entry program, where high school seniors sign up and then do their senior year and then go after their senior year." Her mother had a rule that after graduating, her kids were not allowed to stay in their small hometown and "get a job and do nothing." Her mother insisted that they had to "go to college or go to the military," because she thought that it was "really important that we experience things." Tina remembered that she joined because she "wanted to get out of town," because her hometown was "kinda small" and she "wasn't ready to go to college," so following her mother's plans for her children, she joined the army. A veteran of the U.S. Marines, Paul enlisted in 2002 when he was seventeen years old, while still in high school. Three days after graduation he headed for boot camp. He explained that he had worked at a grocery store in high school. Though he knew he could continue in that job after graduating, he "didn't want to work in the same job forever" and knew that he "wasn't ready for college." He celebrated turning eighteen in boot camp and twenty in Iraq.

A few people I interviewed explained that they had joined because they wanted to serve their country. Andy, a college student in his late twenties at the time of the interview, joined the U.S. Army in 2004 shortly after high school. Though he had some scholarships lined up to help pay for college, he said: "I turned them down because the war was going on and I wanted to do my part." Mike, a twenty-seven-year-old college student at the time of the interview, was born and raised in a town about forty-five miles northwest of Chicago. He was just a "few days under twenty-two" when "I joined in April of 2003 and that was right after we entered Iraq in March 2003; obviously I wanted to be part of serving, you know, it seemed the armed forces were spread a little thin." Between graduating from high school and joining, he "was at community college for a little while" and "worked for the machine shop." He remembered that throughout high school, he had planned on working in a machine shop, but when he finally did, he "didn't like it." He chose to join the U.S. Army National Guard because it "seemed a good way to pay for college and just get some experience." He was interested in becoming a medic because his father was terminally ill, and he wanted "to help take care of my dad" and eventually get certified to be an emergency medical technician and a certified nurse assistant, which would give him "a good base taking care of my dad."

The motivation of most of the veterans I interviewed had to do with promises of economic stability and the possibility of professional training and funding for higher education. Even Andy and Mike, who wanted to serve their country, were also attracted by the possibility that they could do so while taking steps toward professional goals. Army National Guard veteran Danny's reasons were firmly economic. He began by explaining: "Well, I come from a poor background, didn't have a lot of money and didn't know that school options were there." After graduating from high school in Oregon, he first went to a community college while working full time "with a little bit of financial aid, never knowing that I could go to university with that." He ended up not doing well with his studies and losing his financial aid, which he attributed to his having devoted most of his energy to working full time for a metal fabrication company. He described the work as "brainless" and "mindless," but it paid well. Looking around him at his coworkers, he realized that he "didn't want to be forty-five [years old] like the guys around [him] who were making the same money." He felt that he was "better than that" and "should strive to get something else." He saw a commercial for the U.S. Army National Guard and thought, "I'll get some money to come back, go to school; it sounded like a great idea."

A frequent theme that emerged in the life stories of many of those I interviewed was a difficult childhood, either because of their family situations or because they did not easily conform to the demands of public school life specifically and authority more generally. Several described struggling with their parents and school throughout their youth.[3] Some explained that they were very rebellious and prior to enlisting were engaging in antisocial or illegal activities. Army veteran Mark, for example, described himself as being "pretty messed up." He said he had massive problems with "drugs and alcohol and depression and all that stuff." Marine veteran Benji described himself as being rebellious, especially after his parents divorced. He said, "My rule in life was I have to ask why before I take a single step." He too described alcohol and drugs as having been an issue at the time he joined. Navy veteran Angie grew up in a tiny community in northern California with parents who were struggling with drug and alcohol addiction. By joining the navy, Angie was escaping both physical abuse and a family in which the parents often failed to provide for their offspring's basic material needs.

For Benji, joining the Marine Corps was an act of defiance against his parents, who hoped and expected that he would become a well-respected military officer: "It was a rebellious act for me to enlist in the Marine Corps and join the infantry. I mean, I was a Lewis. I had so much intelligence and potential that I should be an officer, a leader of men." He explained that he was expected to join not the infantry, but something with more status, like "the intelligence department or logistics or something like that." When remembering why he decided to enlist, Benji explained that he was still a kid interested in "girls" and "partying," though the breadth of his musical listening at that point was also indicative that he was a thoughtful youth who was always questioning everything around him. Part of the reason Benji joined the Marine Corps rather than another branch of the military was related to music. He was attracted to the Marines because of the location of the Twentynine Palms Marine Corps Base, which is in southern California, close to where a lot of the bands he was listening to at the time were based. By joining the Marines, he hoped to be able to participate in the music scene.

Each story was different, but what I found striking was that many of these young people had struggled in their youth and in high school because of lack of focus or problems with authority, rules, and conformity, and then they joined an institution at a very young age in which rules and authority dominated and there was little room for individuality and self-expression. For some, the military was just what they needed, a structure in which to operate and thrive. Marine veteran Andrew, for example, explained:

> I knew I wasn't ready to go to college. I wanted to go to college at some point, but if I was going to treat college the way I was treating high school at the time, I knew I wasn't going to make it through. I needed something to give me the discipline and motivation to be able to make it through.

For others, the rigid structure was overwhelming and stifling, to the extent that it led to intense negative personal and psychological repercussions. Benji epitomized the rebellious youth who joined the military and then found himself in the very type of authoritative environment he had spent his teens defying. He said that once in the Marines, he was lucky to find a "group of guys" in his unit with whom he felt affinity: "We never had that pro-unit thing. We were all guys who even thought that school pride was dumb. . . so we never had that unit pride." His friendship group consisted of four core members from a unit that ranged over the course of his service from between fifty and eighty men. He felt that he and his friends were a minority in the military to "come out of boot camp and not be pro-mission or excited." What united these four initially was their musical taste, or as he put it, their "musical dissidence." He emphasized that at this point his feelings about his situation were not political. They were just rebellious youths who were "against military culture, military life, . . . because we all felt that we were smart people [who] didn't need to be led around."

MILITARY STRUCTURES, DEMOGRAPHICS, AND MUSICKING

Army veteran Noah's answer, "a hodgepodge," to my question about what he listened to during his deployments, echoed the answers I received from almost everyone. I met African American army veteran Dave when I was researching in Colorado Springs, home of Fort Carson army base. He was sharing drinks with a Croatian DJ who played electronic music and was listening to reggae on the outside patio of a downtown bar. We arranged to do an interview a few days later, on July 19, 2006. Asked about his musical taste, he responded:

> My choice of music is really diverse. I mean I love everything. Everything that feels good: beats, vocals, all that good stuff. If it hits me, then I like it. There's no really deep style. I love hip-hop. I love alternative. I love house music. I love it all.

In many of the depictions and descriptions of soldiers' musical listening in the news, popular media, and scholarship, the emphasis has been on the dominance of aggressive musical forms, especially heavy metal and rap genres (see Pieslak 2009; Gittoes 2004). Some attention has also been given to the popularity of certain types of music associated with a strongly patriotic and pro-mission stance (see Wolfe and Akenson 2005; Willman 2005; Schmelz 2007). My research confirms the popularity of metal, rap, and country genres, and corroborates much of what has been written about them: troops I interviewed reported listening to aggressive metal and rap music to "amp up" for battle, which is discussed in much greater detail in later chapters, and when socializing. Many listened to country music either because they liked it or because they were attracted to the patriotism in the lyrics of some artists or in songs that had been written specifically to commemorate, comment upon, or celebrate these wars. Yet Noah's remark that he listened to a "hodgepodge" of music indicated a much more diverse and complex engagement with music.

Because the members of the U.S. armed forces comprise a diverse array of the country's population and include a significant percentage of foreign nationals, it would be surprising if musical listening within the military was as limited as many depictions suggest. Four branches of the U.S. military participated in these wars: the army (by far the largest branch), Marine Corps, navy, and air force, in addition to the Army National Guard and Air National Guard. All the branches also have Reserve forces, some of which were mobilized. Members of each branch for the most part have their own bases and train on their own, and units usually deploy separately; units from different branches often collaborate and support one another. Troops were structurally separated from one another depending on their branches, units, jobs, ranks, and so on. And within the social/work grouping in which they were positioned, such things as gender, race, ethnicity, class, region, personality, and educational level all played into social divisions and thus also musical listening.

Percentages of women in each branch of the military vary, with the air force having the highest in active duty, at 19 percent; the Marine Corps the lowest, with 6.8 percent; the army 13.5 percent; and the navy 16.4 percent.[4] Different branches and different rank levels are associated with different articulations of masculinity, and displays of homosexuality were banned until the repeal of "Don't Ask, Don't Tell" in 2011 (Belkin and Bateman 2003). Gender is integrated in the military's social organization and ultimately has implications for musicking, as elaborated on in chapter 5. Men are numerically dominant in all branches and units of the military, creating an inherently gendered environment. According to the U.S. Department of Defense, women comprised 14.5 percent of active duty forces in 2011. Women have been restricted from certain types of jobs and units until recently, for example, those that engage explicitly in combat (Mackenzie 2012). Sexual activity is supposed to be muted during deployments, and sex between unmarried men and women was banned in Afghanistan until 2008, when the ban was lifted, though it was still "highly discouraged" (Brown 2008). Nevertheless, sexuality permeates military life as people find opportunities for intimacy, consume pornography, fantasize, and interact sexually with people physically removed from them; unfortunately, some of this sexual interaction occurs without consent and with violence, as described in chapter 5.

The U.S. military was proud to be one of the first U.S. institutions to integrate across race (1948), and the military is far more representative of the diversity of the U.S. population than are many other institutions in the country. The ethnic/racial breakdown for the U.S. forces in 2011 was 69.8 percent "white," 16.0 percent "black or African American," 3.8 percent "Asian," 2.5 percent "multiracial," 1.6 percent "American Indian or Alaska Native," and .6 percent "Native Hawaiian or other Pacific Islander." Within these categories, 11.2 percent were "Hispanic or Latino." The distribution of people of various ethnic and racial identities varies between branches, hierarchical strata, and units. For example, in 2011 Euro-Americans/whites constituted the highest percentage of active duty personnel in the air force, at 73 percent, while they comprised 61.5 percent of the navy and 69.3 percent of the army. African Americans constituted around 21.8 percent of enlisted men and women in the army, yet only 10.9 percent of the Marine Corps. These fairly general figures are useful for understanding relationships between structural patterns and identity. More detailed demographic information is available on the Web site for each branch.[5] As with any population, these demographics can shape musical listening because of music's frequent role in social life and identity making (Gilman 2010).

Because I live in an area (Oregon and the Pacific Northwest) dominated by white/Euro-Americans and relied largely on personal introductions to make research contacts, a majority of the thirty-five people I interviewed were white/ Euro-American (80 percent) and are in no way a representative sample of the military. My intention was not to provide generalized information about troops' musical listening, but rather to delve more deeply into individuals' "ideoculture," how they use music both privately and collectively (Keil 1993, 2). Four of the people I interviewed were women; the rest were men. Twenty-seven identified as white; three as African American; one as mixed white, Native American, and Mexican American; one as mixed Italian and Latino; one as Caribbean American; and one as Peruvian American/Latino (see appendix). Though I do not have information about everyone's gender identity or sexual orientation, one identified as gay (male) and one as queer. Though not representative, the people I interviewed identify in many different ways and have a variety of experiences and musical tastes. Most served in the lower echelons of the military, as enlisted men and women, and served in the main branches of the armed forces (with the exception of the Coast Guard).[6]

The people I interviewed described their units and work environments as more or less diverse. Craig, who is white, shared that his unit was "heavily minority," including "a lot of Mexicans, a lot of African Americans, and one Russian." About 10 percent of his company were "islanders from Puerto Rico, the Dominican Republic, Jamaica, and Haiti." For Craig and others in similarly diverse units, the military provided the opportunity to develop personal and work relationships with people from a broad spectrum of backgrounds. At the same time, demographics also impacted social relationships; for example, Craig explained that though "the Mexicans" in his unit spoke English well and a lot of other people knew some Spanish, "the Mexicans" "spoke Spanish among themselves," and although the Jamaicans spoke English, they had strong accents that made them difficult to understand, so they tended to spend more time together. In some cases, musical taste extended across ethnic backgrounds and identities and provided the rationale for social groupings. Rap was popular among many people from different backgrounds in Craig's unit, and "people [regardless of ethnic/racial identity] who liked rap would be together with the stereo" in the background while they played card games or dominoes.

Paul, an African American, described his unit in the U.S. Marines as "more white guys than minority." He emphasized that everyone got along, though people told plenty of racist jokes. He took these jokes lightly and explained that "nothing ever got serious." He compared his unit to a family. Conflicts would sometimes erupt, but they never lasted. Within thirty minutes or so, the people with the conflict would be back to "hugging each other" "high fiving each other," just "like any family." Gabe, whose family emigrated from Peru, did not remember ethnicity or race having much impact on his social relations in the military. According to Gabe, his unit members were more concerned about what jobs people had and whether they were skilled and fulfilling their roles than about what a person's ethnic background was.

Mark is white and grew up in Detroit, which he described as being " very segregated." Though he did not consider himself "to be racist" before joining the military, he also had never had the opportunity to get to know African Americans. He explained, "I hated the racism of some of the adults in my life, yet I . . . never was put in a position where I actually knew a black guy." The military was his first opportunity to develop friendships with people from different racial and ethnic backgrounds: African Americans, Latinos, and also Euro-Americans from different regions. He explained that he had never known a white southerner before his time in the army. Everyone in his unit, regardless of their ethnic background, interacted and lived and worked together, though he remembered that he also heard plenty of racist comments when only white soldiers were present. His relationships with people of different backgrounds in the military expanded his musical listening. His friend Kevin was "into this dirty south rap stuff." Though he had not previously been "into rap," Mark was introduced to some new bands, for example Lil Scrappy, that he "started to like a lot." Other types of music "started to grow" on him, for example "a lot of polkay kind of Mexican stuff," which he would not ordinarily have listened to. Phil, an African American whose MP3 playlist during his first deployment consisted mostly of hip-hop tracks, explained that during his second deployment his driver, who was white, hooked up speakers inside their vehicle. They would then alternate listening to "two or three country songs," the driver's choice, and then "two or three hip-hop songs," his choice, and they would "continue that rotation until we got to where we were going."

Other units were less diverse, often paralleling the demographics of the branch or a U.S. cultural geographic region. For example, airman Shannon explained that his unit in the air force was mostly white, though they "did have a few African Americans," guessed around 20 percent, and "not very many Hispanic people." National Guard and Reserve units were even more defined racially and ethnically because of their regional base. Some of this regionalism also shaped the demographics of active duty bases. A National Guard unit from Oregon was dominated by white members more than one from a state with greater percentages of African Americans. These dynamics impacted musical listening in complex ways, in that the diversity in many units increased opportunities for troops to interact with and listen to music that they might not have otherwise experienced. At the same time, the unequal distribution of people from different ethnic and racial backgrounds contributed to certain types of music being listened to more in some units than in others, and the ongoing racial tensions that permeate all of U.S. society played out sometimes through musical practices.[7]

Though there are a significant number of Americans from a variety of ethnic backgrounds—for example, Native Americans, Latinos, Asian Americans—in the military, their music, along with most of their other cultural practices, is at the margins of mainstream U.S. popular culture. Here it is important to realize that musical genres do not exist as an "autonomous artistic form," but rather within a system of genres within a community (Flueckiger 1991, 182–83; Tuohy 1999). Within a generic system, genres are often linked to people in specific social categories that are positioned within hierarchies of status, prestige, and power within a community. Popular music genres in the military exist within a system of genres that maps onto social relationships and divisions within the military. Those genres associated with those who are socially dominant—white and black working-class men—have sonic prominence that overshadows or marginalizes the sounds of those who are on the social periphery.

In the military, where people from different backgrounds live and work together, people whose musical tastes were more at the margins tended to listen to music with others who shared their cultural identifiers or musical taste rather than sharing their music with the wider diverse audience. To some extent, the marginalization of cultural groups in the United States was mirrored in the musical listening in the military. For example, Mexican Americans listening to culturally specific music tended to do so with other Mexican Americans as opposed to their music dominating soundscapes populated by people from different backgrounds. At larger bases in Iraq that have morale, welfare, and recreation (MWR) centers, the diverse music and dance tastes of the military population were acknowledged to some extent, and entertainment evenings were devoted to different types of music, such as hip-hop and salsa. When I talked to troops who had spent time on these bases, they indicated that anybody could go to these events, and no one was overtly excluded who did not belong to the cultural group typically associated with the genre. However, by and large it was mostly

Latinos present at the salsa nights, and mostly African Americans at hip-hop nights. For less-defined cultural groups—those considered to be minorities in our country and also other types of social identities less prevalent among the military population—no such special events were officially designated, which resulted in those people either feeling isolated or finding ways of creating events and spaces for themselves, which held true for those in cultural minorities and those who did not fit into the dominant groups for other reasons. Simon, who was in the navy, explained that his very small social group was "middle-class white guys who liked to climb rocks." He described frequently listening to music with this small minority. However, as previously mentioned, it was common for people living in shared spaces, working together, or who had developed friendships to introduce different types of music to one another.

Age is also linked to the social organization of the military; for example, the lower echelons and combat units tend to be comprised of more young people, while officers and those in certain types of jobs are older, more highly trained individuals. Age is important to musical listening, in that young people tend to participate in musical trends often produced by younger people. As people get older, some continue to listen to the music that was popular in their youth or to follow the same bands, which age alongside them. Furthermore, as people mature their musical and social needs often change. Benji explained that in his teens he listened to bands whose songs were about his biggest concerns: rebelling and picking up women. As he got older, so did the bands, and he listened to more and more political music.

The rigid hierarchies of all the branches also contributed to social divisions that were associated with different types of people and thus with different music listening. Shannon explained: "Officers stayed to themselves basically. In the air force, officers and enlisted [men and women] really don't have much interaction at all. Unless you're higher enlisted, and then you have to report to them." The hierarchies were determined by rank, which was also often associated with age, gender, race, educational level, and class. Thus to be a commissioned officer, one must usually have a college education, and this was a distinction made between commissioned officers and warrant officers; the latter commonly achieved rank by moving up from enlisted to warrant rank rather than because of college education. The inherent class difference has implications for musical listening, in that those with more education may not have done the same kind of grunt work as the others and may identify with types of music that they find superior or distinct from that enjoyed by the lower ranking troops. Army pilot Evan observed that he had "seen more interest in house music from fellow Scout pilots [jobs requiring a similar level of education to his] than . . . from any other career fields in the army." Asked why he thought this preference existed, he answered:

It might not be the case at all. But I think part of it could be the personality of most Scout pilots. I mean we tend to be the guys who tend to like to question things, to be big picture people who execute and act on a tactical scale. I'm just speaking in generalizations, but every air frame in the army has its own personality: the type of people who fly that air frame tend to fit a type of personality, though there are certainly exceptions to every rule. Scout pilots tend to act a certain way. Apache pilots [act] a certain way, and other pilots act other ways.

Evan's explanation brought in personality as well, suggesting that certain personalities were attracted to certain jobs and certain types of music. Also, troops who moved up through the ranks might be more likely to have grown up in a social milieu where certain music dominated, such as country or metal, and thus these genres may have continued to be important to their soundscapes.

These intersecting and overlapping structural and social layers, combined with the emotional needs engendered by combat environments, inevitably resulted in widely variant and divergent musical listening. The playlists of every single person I interviewed—even those who claimed to not be terribly interested in music or who said that they considered themselves to be fans of a single musical style—were eclectic, and they varied depending on the context in which they listened, the music they had available to them, who was around them while they listened, and the need they were attempting to meet by listening (cf. Crafts et al. 1993). Every person I interviewed, people with vastly different musical tastes and ways of identifying themselves, named (or showed me) playlists that incorporated lots of different genres and different artists. Of those who were deployed more than once, many described listening to different music during different deployments and explained that their musical listening often shifted over the course of a single deployment in conjunction with what music was available to them, their moods, with whom they were spending time, the events that happened during their time at war, and their emotional needs.

THREE

Musicking at Work
and Leisure

Musical listening maps onto daily living, especially in settings where one's mobility and activities are limited and restricted. How troops prepared for their musical listening prior to deployment—what musical tracks they amassed and what technology they brought—impacted what music they could listen to in addition to how much more they could acquire while at war. Life during deployment was highly varied for U.S. troops, and over the course of deployments individuals and units often moved to different locations as the needs of the military changed. The type of base, outpost, or living arrangements of troops, combined with the social organization and occupational hierarchies of military units, shaped how, when, and with whom troops could listen to music.

PREPARING FOR DEPLOYMENT

The people I interviewed were in the military for various amounts of time before they received their deployment orders. For some who joined long before September 11, 2001, it was a long time between enlistment and combat. Many people who joined shortly before or after 9/11 received their orders very soon after training for the specific positions in which they would serve concluded, specializations that were assigned after basic training. After receiving deployment orders, members of a unit prepared together to gather everything needed to accomplish the mission, and individuals gathered what they would bring for both their work and personal needs. Those for whom it was their first deployment described their thinking about what they needed as being largely hypothetical. They could only imagine what they needed based on what they had heard and had been told, what they had seen in movies, and what they thought war would be like. Those who were on a second, third, or fourth deployment had more knowledge and could better predict their needs.

Individuals told different stories about how much they thought about music in these preparations. Some were given little notice and were so focused on everything that had to be done that they put little thought into their projected musical needs. Keith joined the U.S. Army in 2002 and served through 2006. Originally from Louisville, Kentucky, he explained that he was deployed to Iraq about six months after enlisting and at the age of twenty-one participated in the initial May 3, 2003, invasion. The second time he deployed, in March 2005, his unit was given very little notice, maybe ten days. In October 2006 he was medically discharged for a knee problem and post-traumatic stress. Asked about his musical preparation prior to his first deployment, he did not recall thinking much about music. Once he was in Iraq, he realized that he could listen to music, so he asked his mother to send him CDs and was able to share music with others in his unit. Those for whom music was especially important in their civilian lives put great thought into amassing music. Gabe, whose family was originally from Peru, joined the Army National Guard in 2001 and served for "about eight years." He described music as being "very, very important to me during deployment" and remembered that he brought to his first deployment recordings of some of his favorite bands, such as Coldplay, Depeche Mode, and Radiohead, because "I like British rock music a lot." He explained: "Music was very important to me, it's part of my life, so I decided to load up my MP3 player with the music I liked best."

Many went to great efforts to purchase new equipment and accumulate as much music as possible. At the time of our interview on October 11, 2011, Evan was a twenty-seven-year-old, white army officer and Scout helicopter pilot. He had a bachelor's degree in history with a music minor and a master's in computer science. He had joined the U.S. Army in October 2003 through its warrant officer flight training program and had deployed to Iraq for a five-month period. Evan started DJing house music when he was in grad school, "mostly doing parties and smaller raves and stuff." Later he moved to New York City and then San Francisco, where he played in clubs. He described music as being very important to him and said that he had been active in music making since high school. When he started thinking about joining the military, he realized that "it wasn't too much of a departure because I knew that I could still DJ when I wanted." Music was such a central part of his life that Evan put a great deal of thought and planning into his projected musical listening prior to deploying:

Before I went, I got a new iPod, and that was my first MP3 player. And I just looked for any new music that I could find. Because usually, I'm pretty satisfied with my FM radio and listening to BBC Radio 1 once a week or twice a week. You know, not necessarily acquiring music to have, but having a constant stream of new music coming in. I'm pretty happy with that usually. But I knew I was going to Iraq, where I wouldn't have satellite radio. I wouldn't have a good enough Internet connection that I could listen to streaming stuff. And so I was just looking for everything I could find. I was recording stuff off the satellite channel and putting it on my iPod and e-mailing friends and getting access to MP3 repositories. I went over with a pretty sizable collection. Not all of it was electronic, probably about 80 percent electronic, 20 percent other stuff. Because I've always enjoyed Bob Marley and the Grateful Dead and stuff like that, stuff that's not dance music. But definitely a lot of dance music.

Most of those who were deployed more than once described a significant difference between their preparations for their first and subsequent deployments. The first time, they did not know what to expect or what their musical needs might be, and for some the technology available had changed. Some described utterly missing the mark, bringing all the wrong music, not what they wanted once there. Experience informed their subsequent deployments. They could plan ahead and foresee what they might need. Benji did not put too much thought into his music when he prepared for his first deployment in 2004: "I got as many CDs as I could put in these CD folders, and I don't remember which specific ones I brought, but I can probably take a pretty specific bet. I remember Bruce Springsteen's [album] *Devils and Dust.*" For his second deployment, he devoted much more energy to preparing for his listening needs. He explained that he spent the month of his pre-deployment leave largely focused on music. As he put it: "It was a huge preparation process. I went out and spent $400 on an iPod. I still have it. I had a forty-eight iPod and I filled it up with forty-eight gigs of music."

Gabe found that the bands mentioned above, which were his favorites at the time, were not the best music for him to listen to during his first deployment: "I felt kind of sorry to be deployed and to be far away from my family, and it was not the type of music that was going to keep me alive." In preparation for his second deployment, he therefore "chose the Beatles": "I thought it would be a little bit more happ[y], happier, I guess."

Even with these efforts, however, many explained that their emotional states were different the second time around, a combination of doing different jobs, being in various places, experiencing diverse events, and just feeling differently. Regardless of what they brought with them, the availability of music from the collections of members of their units and the ability to purchase or otherwise obtain new music made it possible for most to shift their listening.

WARTIME LIVING AND MUSICKING

Some of those interviewed reported living on large bases that provided a wide range of resources, secure structures for lodging and work, gyms, basketball courts, computer labs with Internet access, and MWR units that provided entertainment. Others lived in more remote locations with no Internet access. Marine veteran Phil explained that on his first deployment, he listened to "strictly hip-hop": "I was limited to what I had on my MP3 player at that time because there wasn't any Internet out there for us to download or transfer music freely."

Some interviewees lived in buildings that had been abandoned or seized during a city's invasion, for example, the many luxurious palaces of former Iraqi president Saddam Hussein and his son Uday Hussein, as seen in the documentary film *Gunner Palace* (2004). Depending on the nature of the setting and its location, housing and work environments differed. Usually, several people in a unit shared a space in which they created some privacy through positioning of beds, curtains, and other dividing tactics.

In describing sharing space with the other people in her unit, Tina explained: "We didn't have very much space, of course, about three feet wide, however long your cot was, pretty much." Asked if they put curtains around the cots for individual privacy, she said that they did not, but they did have a separator between the men's and women's cots. Before moving into the sleeping space of the opposite sex, they had to call out "Are you guys decent?" Airman Shannon stayed in tents that fit six to twelve people in what they called "Tent City," which included a chow hall and shower tents. Some of the more secure bases provided more space for private and group activities than others. In his short time at Joint Base Balad in Iraq, navy man Matt had a brand new trailer to himself, and Mike, a medic in the National Guard, shared a trailer in Iraq with one other man, whom he described as similar to him: a white man of similar age. Others resided in less secure bases, a plot of land taken over by U.S. forces, with tents erected or shipping containers transformed into rooms. Yet others, involved in taking over

Mark at FOB McKenzie around September 2004. Courtesy of Mark Leahey.

cities or whose units were attached to other units to provide various kinds of support, moved frequently, changing the nature and type of their residence on a regular basis.[1] Mark's army unit was charged with supporting other units in Iraq, so they moved frequently. They were frequently mobilized, yet they maintained living quarters at Forward Operating Base (FOB) McKenzie, where they "would like pop in and out occasionally throughout the year."

Toward the end of his tour, they spent a few months there. On the base they had "conexes" or "hootches," which were "basically like shipping containers that they turned into living quarters. They put a door in it and then put air-conditioning in it." He shared his with three other men. When on the go, by contrast:

> Sometimes we were living in the Bradleys [fighting vehicles/tanks], sometimes we were living in tents. Like in the summer months, we lived in these tents that had air conditioners. But it was like 130 degrees outside during the day. We couldn't do anything during the day. It was unbearable. We almost always did night missions during that time. The first place we ever went to, a couple weeks after we got there, we were in old Iraq army barracks that had no windows or doors, and everyone got sand fleas in their sleeping bags.

Because those in the same units lived together, people who worked together necessarily also slept in close proximity, and often unit members were the most accessible social partners, thus also those with whom one was most likely to listen to music. Even when they were not deployed, the military encouraged people within the same unit to socialize together because, as army officer Evan explained: "You try to build a lot of unit cohesiveness because those are the people whom you are going to go to war with, you are going to fight side by side with." You may or may not find people in your company with whom you have a lot in common, so as Evan puts it, if you find somebody with similar musical tastes, "that's a bonus." Before and after deployment, the military encouraged members of units to develop relationships with one another to assist in forging strong bonds among members. Evan explained:

> You want a tight-knit group. You want a group that has shared meaningful experiences both in and outside of combat. You have lived side by side with these people or right on top of each other in a lot of cases, and you have to go out, and you have to put your life in the hands of the guy next to you. You tend to form pretty deep bonds.

According to Evan, this need for group solidarity sometimes won out over individual musical taste. On a night of barhopping with other officers in his unit while he was based in the United States, he would choose to leave a club "playing some real nice deep house music, and [would] want to hang out and listen to house music," but he would "kind of have to put that on a back burner sometimes in favor of unit cohesiveness and the relationships" that he had. Because of the way that the social and work spaces were organized, Evan explained, there "may be a guy somewhere in another unit who may have had similar experiences to me and may love the same kind of music that I like," but between the pressure to hang out with people in his unit and the difficulty in finding times and spaces to interact with those outside, the chances of his spending time with this person and developing a relationship were small.

In the organization of spaces at war, men and women often had separated spaces, though the separation could be no more than a curtain, as in Tina's example, or firmer walls. And those at different ranks were housed separately, thus reinforcing social divisions that corresponded to work-time hierarchies. Airman Shannon, for example, explained that everyone who was at E2–E6 ranks stayed in tents together, and everyone who was of higher rank stayed in other tents.[2] "They matched people up with their rank." U.S. Army officer and pilot J. D. similarly explained that music sharing was

> mostly among the pilots with the warrant officers, and enlisted men traded among themselves as well. It wasn't really across the ranks, I don't think. We were all kind of separated in rooms by rank as well. It was more like who was in your room or building and stuff like that.

This hierarchical grouping within units was reinforced through spatial as well as social divisions. It produced a situation in which friendship groups developed in very restricted social settings, which encouraged people to both bond over perceived shared identifiers (e.g., we both like rap or punk) and develop relationships with categories of people they might not otherwise have known, because of the simple fact that they were in constant proximity to and interacting with one another, and there was little or no alternative company. This relationship building across social boundaries and musical tastes is in contrast to what Susan Douglas (2004) documents in her study of radio listening in civilian life as a trend in the United States, in which Americans prefer safe, gated listening, that is, listening to narrowly identified music. In the military, especially at war, because people did not have as much mobility or choice in association, circumstances pushed them out of their gates to interact musically outside typical musical taste/listening boxes. At the same time, the restriction of socializing to certain people and within restricted space created new gates, often not based on shared musical taste, but rather on the circumstances at hand. Andy, for example, was a medical technician who came into contact with a lot of soldiers from other units who had been injured and had the opportunity to interact with soldiers from other units on the base. When I asked Andy whether he developed friendships with people outside his unit, he answered:

> It was mostly just the people within, you know, within our small unit. There's thousands of soldiers out there, that we don't know, that roam around the bases and in the country itself. The patients that came in, I mean we really didn't have enough time to bond with them. We could relate to some of them because they've gone through hardships, but they were out of there before we could really bond with them.

This dynamic resulted in people sharing and listening to music that they might not have otherwise listened to simply because they did not have the ability to restrict their social lives to those with whom they perceived they already had much in common, and it created new structures for listening that sometimes created sonic restrictions for some, because of others' tastes, expectations, or social pressures.

Different types of bases offered different types of musical opportunities. Large bases with chapels sometimes had instruments, such as organs, pianos, and drums, which allowed people to both play and listen to music at worship and on other occasions. MWR units provided entertainment; for example, nightly dances were often scheduled throughout the week featuring different styles, allowing people to gather to listen and dance to hip-hop, salsa, or 1980s U.S. pop music. On especially large bases, State Department–sponsored musical acts occasionally offered large performances. Bases where there were basketball courts or football fields allowed for people to listen to music collectively while playing team sports. Those that had gyms allowed for people to listen to music individually while working out or collectively when music was played over a sound system. At larger bases some spaces were designated for leisure activities. Tina explained that they had an "area upstairs with a TV and a table and some books." She said that so many people had laptops, there was usually music in the background throughout living spaces.

Those who were on smaller bases, such as FOBs, had much less space in which to move around or people with whom to interact. Those sleeping in temporary encampments or in their vehicles had little time or space for any activity other than direct engagement with the war they were fighting. And some were in outposts where they stayed for long periods in sandbagged enclosures with little differentiated space, as depicted in the documentary film *Restrepo,* which Sebastian Junger made with the late Tim Hetherington. Work, sleep, and socializing all took place within a confined and highly dangerous temporary enclosure. Music was often especially important in these settings, because it was one of the few ways to get a little bit of downtime and time alone. Keith, who was in Iraq shortly after the initial invasion, described going months without phones or computers, with no way to communicate with people outside the unit's immediate surroundings other than occasional letter writing. Members of his unit often worked twenty-two-hour days and rarely were able to shower. He described the first eight months of his deployment as "really rough" and said that music was the only "outlet that they couldn't take from us."

Where people slept was one space where individual and group listening often occurred. Those few who had private rooms could enter the enclosure and fill it with sounds of their choice, thus creating an individualized soundscape differentiated from outside both physically by walls or other barriers and by the creation of sound bubbles. The majority who shared rooms with others could listen to music with others in their room or could put on their headphones while lying in bed, sometimes with a curtain around them, creating a private soundscape within the cacophonous setting of conversations, movement, war sounds, and other music playing.

Many described listening to music through individualized listening devices when on watch, and others described listening at places on base where they could simultaneously observe and interact with the world outside. Shannon described running in the desert around the perimeter of the base enclosed with barbed wire while listening to "a lot of punk rock," including the bands Social Distortion, Suicide Machine, and Flogging Molly, "upbeat stuff that you can listen to while you're running."

Spatial arrangements in the navy during deployments differed from land because everyone was confined to the even more finite and restrictive space available on a ship. Navy veteran Simon explained that the sleeping quarters on his ship consisted of six berthings. Each housed anywhere from 50 to 120 beds. Beds were in stacks of three, back to back. Each individual's personal space was limited to a bed with a fan that could be enclosed with a curtain, some storage space under the bed, and a locker to the side. Both Simon and Angie described the amount of personal space on their respective ships as being comparable to a coffin. Lower ranked officers and enlisted men and women slept in the berthings, while higher ranked officers shared rooms in pairs, and the captain had a private suite. Women were housed in separate berthings from those for men.

According to Simon, because of the very limited space in the rather public berthing, people on his ship spent little time in the berthing except to sleep, and some found alternate places to sleep. He explained that the relationship between work and nonwork space was blurred, and that most people on the ship used their work space as leisure space when they were not working. As a medic, he was fortunate to have a private office, which he used when consulting patients. Between seeing patients and after his shift he continued to use this private space to listen to music, read, or hang out with friends. Even those working in more collective spaces used work spaces in similar ways. He described those working in the welding room as hanging out in the space all the time, sometimes even dragging their sleeping gear there. This use of work space for both work and leisure reinforced the bonds with those one worked with, merging occupational and social alliances. People worked together and played together, all in the same space. In contrast, Angie, unlike Simon, who was also in the navy, did not have any place other than her curtained, enclosed bed to enjoy privacy. She described closing herself off in her bed whenever she could to listen to music and write in her journal, which she explained was the only escape she had from others and her work environment.

MUSICKING AT WORK

The degree to which troops listened to music during work activities varied greatly depending on the nature of their jobs, the settings in which they worked, and whether or not their command allowed it. Some explained that they were never allowed to listen to music when working on or off base, because it was crucial that they hear any incoming sounds, many of which could signal the need for a response or approaching danger. Others were able to listen to music through headphones when not explicitly working, though they were not allowed to listen to music while working, either because of the need for auditory focus or because the command did not deem it professional or appropriate. Troops described the presence of background music in many work spaces on bases, sometimes all day and night.

Simon was in the navy from 1993 to 1998, during the era of cassettes and CDs. He explained that most of the work spaces were equipped with boom boxes, most provided by service men and women themselves, not the navy. In some work environments, such as the welding station, people listened to music during work and nonwork times. In others, such as the medic facility where Simon worked, music listening was restricted to nonwork hours. The gym had a big boom box. People listened to music through both boom boxes and headphones in their beds, private nooks and crannies, and anywhere else, though it was not allowed on the decks, where it was deemed dangerous. By contrast, Angie, who was in the navy from 2001 to 2005 and deployed to the Persian Gulf from March to June 2003, explained that music was not part of her work environment in the operations center. The only time she listened to music was privately, while exercising, playing video games, or spending time in her berthing.

Andy served as a surgical technician in the U.S. Army in a unit that was designated as a combat hospital that supported the front line. He described the musical listening in the surgery center:

You know during the surgery, there's really nothing else to pass the time, to get you through seeing some of the stuff we had to see. Some doctors would actually put a playlist on for their surgery time, very interesting variations of music choices. Then the rest of us had headphones for when we were not in the operating room.

Army veteran Tina remembered listening to music through a CD player in the operations office where she worked as an intelligence analyst. She remembered fondly the night shift, when most of the "upper officers were all sleeping and not really checking in" and when "not a lot happen[ed]." The people working night shift organized a regular competition of "Name That Tune." A connoisseur of country music, she often won the rounds in which country dominated.

Jonathan Pieslak (2007, 2009), journalists, and I have written about soldiers listening to heavy genres, especially metal and rap, to get motivated for battle. The documentary films *Occupation; Dreamland* by Ian Olds and Garrett Scott, *Gunner Palace* by Petra Epperlein and Michael Tucker, *Soundtrack to War* by George Gittoes, and *Fahrenheit 911* by Michael Moore all include scenes of troops listening to hard genres as they prepare to leave the wire. Musical dimensions of these genres—driving beat, fast tempo, screaming voices, and often angry, violent, or misogynist lyrics—combine to create a soundscape defined as loud, physical, strong, and dominating. Troops I interviewed described listening to these genres either individually through headphones or as a group over some type of amplifier as they prepared to go out on missions and patrols. Many people I interviewed described listening to heavy genres to psych themselves up for battle, something that is discussed in a later chapter.

Despite how much listening to music to prepare for battle has been emphasized in the media, a significant number of people I interviewed explained that they never did it or saw anyone do it. When I asked Gabe whether heavy genres featured on his playlist, he answered repeatedly that they did not: "That's not me at all." Listening to music while preparing for a mission was also sometimes forbidden; for some troops, as Shannon explained, it was so important to focus and get everything together properly that music would have been a distraction.

Once out of the wire in vehicles, many continued listening to music, often these same aggressive genres, but often a wider variety of music. In some vehicles music was streamed through the sound system, giving the driver and others sitting in front control over musical choices. In others individuals listened to music through headphones. Craig poignantly remembered that before crossing the berm, a ten-foot-high, human-constructed dirt division between Kuwait and Iraq, as part of the initial U.S. offensive into Iraq on March 23, 2003, "We all had hooked up CD players to our intercom systems in our vehicles so that we could play music over the common intercom, so everyone was listening" through the headphones that were part of the communication kit of their CVC (combat vehicle crewman) helmets. He explained that the "music sound[ed] phenomenal" because of the high quality of the Bose sound system that was installed in their vehicles for communication purposes. As they crossed the berm, they listened to Drowning Pool's "Bodies." In this case they listened together to the same music, contributing to a unified experience. In other cases, people in the same space doing the same thing listened to different selections using their individual listening devices, contributing to the differentiation of shared experience.

The leadership in some vehicles did not let the troops listen to music because it distracted them from paying attention to the aural details that surrounded them. Army veteran Chris explained that listening to music was strictly forbidden on his vehicle, but that they could get away with it when a particular officer on his vehicle chose to overlook the policy. His vehicle mates devised a clandestine way to bring equipment on board, which they then could set up and enjoy once the vehicle was away from the commanders who enforced the restriction:

I would take my Zune [portable media player] onto the truck in my sunglasses case. Once everyone had mounted up and the only officer who outranked my truck commander was in his vehicle, I would use surgical tape to tape the headphones of my Zune onto the mouthpiece of an extra radio headset. These Bose headsets had a switch that controlled your microphone. This switch had an off position, an intercom position that could remain constantly on, and a radio position that had to be held while transmitting. The intercom was for communication inside the truck and would be muted anytime someone transmitted over the radio, whether that person was in our truck or elsewhere. So the way it worked was that we could hear the music over the intercom, but if someone tried to radio us the music would be muted and allow us to hear the transmission. If one of us called out using the radio, the threat of music being heard in the background was avoided by only using stereo headphones to play into an intercom headset.

Craig explained that they listened to music through the sound system of their vehicle, but as soon as "there was contact," the music was "cut off" to avoid music interfering with communication or "what was going on." Some listened to music by hiding earbuds under helmets; others turned the music down so that they could hear; others wore their headphones around their necks so that they could listen to music without covering their ears and obscuring other sounds; and others, such as Chris, devised ingenious strategies to mask their musical listening to avoid detection and optimize safety.

Many described patrols and missions as being boring, so they listened to a great deal of music while doing these jobs. The type of music they listened to varied depending on the person, the job, the level of danger, and what else had happened recently. For those working long hours with little action, music helped keep them awake. Paul, who worked in motor transport for the Marines, described listening to a lot of rap that was "real gritty," such as Young Jeezy, Lil Wayne, Juvenile, and Twista, to stay awake, energetic, and aware. He preferred listening to artists and songs whose lyrics he knew, because then he could sing along, which would ensure that he stayed awake. Shannon described listening to music while lying in an aircraft flying over Baghdad preparing for a mission. As the plane landed, he put away his music to focus his full attention on the job at hand.

As previously explained regarding space, wartime was characterized by much less distinction between work and leisure time than was civilian life. Most troops worked in scheduled shifts, with designated times when they were on duty. Depending on the job and the setting, these shifts were more or less distinguished from nonwork time and involved differing lengths of time. Thus someone whose job was mostly on base would have working shifts, and others were scheduled for missions and patrols. Airman Shannon described a regular day:

> We would get up in the morning, go to the shower tent, clean up, put our uniforms on, go to the Chow Hall tent dining facility. You're not allowed to call it Chow Hall. We'd go to that tent to eat, then we'd get picked up, then we'd go to our planes, and then we'd do our missions on our planes for anywhere between 13 hours and 24 hours. As soon as we got back, [we would] eat, go to our tent, and pass out. So that was our daily routine for months.

In some cases these shifts lasted for a designated period, though they could be unexpectedly lengthened or interrupted by any number of occurrences. For those more centrally located in a battle zone, for example those in the outpost in Afghanistan described in Sebastian Junger's book *War* (2010) and shown in the documentary *Restrepo,* the immediate danger and constancy of engagement provided limited distinction between work and leisure; distinctions did exist between when one was on duty and when one was free to engage in other activities, though duty could call at any moment.

MUSICKING AND LEISURE

Leisure-time activities were limited during deployments because of restrictions on mobility and the lack of choices of activity. Troops in Iraq and Afghanistan rarely left their bases unless they were traveling on military business, which meant that they were mostly confined to relatively small and bounded spaces.

It is important to note that some activities that many who share demographics with those in the military enjoy when not working—going to restaurants, dancing at clubs, drinking with friends, picking up potential sexual partners, engaging in sexual activities—were largely nonexistent, heavily discouraged, or outright banned during deployments.[3] Many people I interviewed reported that the restrictions against alcohol and pornography were strongly enforced in both Iraq and Afghanistan out of respect for Islam, though some did describe finding ways of accessing both. These types of activities play a significant role in the lives of young people, in having fun, articulating identity, expressing emotion, interacting with others, letting off steam, and so on.[4] As a result of these restrictions, troops took advantage of anything not restricted that was available, such as cigarette smoking, video games, watching movies, reading, and listening to music.

That these very common activities were for the most part not available during deployments was especially significant because being at war was so emotionally, physically, and socially taxing. If anyone needed a break and distraction from work and the environment, the options were limited, as Shannon explained:

> The fact that it's kind of a bubble over there and you're not able to just go home. A lot of people [outside the military] have their own little spaces that they go to, you know, they go to work, they go to school and they might not like it a whole lot. Then they just go home, like you said. They have that escape, whereas over there there's absolutely no escape. There's no way to get out of it besides dying.

Within this context, music was especially important because it could be listened to often and because of the multiplicity of types available and the diverse functions that it could play.

Though it did not happen during wartime, navy man Simon told me a story that exemplified the extent to which people needed some type of personal leisure-time activity to help give them respite, connect with others, and anchor themselves to some idea of self. Simon noted that when he went to basic training, aka boot camp, he was "basically put into jail." He explained that troops were completely removed from their lives and put into a new environment where they were not allowed to leave, interact with their outside lives, or do any activity, including listening to music, other than what they were commanded. Simon remembered that after "about a month" in boot camp, he and his friends were so starved for music and connection with the outside that they would get up in the middle of the night when they were supposed to be sleeping, to spend time together. They would sit down and each write down the lyrics of favorite songs. For Simon, it was "Come Monday" by Jimmy Buffett, while "Bye Bye Blackbird" by Edie Brickell topped another's list. He remembered an African American peer writing down the lyrics to a "rap song" and another white man writing down a "country song." After writing down the lyrics, they would sing them together. He laughed when remembering that one minute they would be singing an Edie Brickell song together, and the next they would be punching one another.

Some troops who had access to the Internet took advantage of their downtime to explore and collect music. Paul was very interested in music and in pursuing a career in music production after his military service. Though he described his musical listening during work time as being restricted mostly to rap, during leisure time he listened to "everything," including "a little rock, pop, R&B, rap, and gospel." He spent much time in Iraq scouring the Internet for interesting music and building his collection. He was introduced to new music by others in his unit, all of which he added to his two iPods. By the time he came home, he had more than twenty thousand songs.

During nonwork time, listening to music was an important way for troops to have fun and build friendships. People often bonded with others with whom they shared musical tastes. Gabe, for example, gravitated toward Mike and others who were more "into mellow music": "I didn't care for so much noise, you know, hard core rock and rap noise." He enjoyed spending time with people who listened to "more melodic music."

People in units or who shared living space often described listening to music together and sometimes having dance parties. Joseph spent a great deal of time with his best friend Robert, with whom he was deployed to Iraq twice. They listened to a lot of recorded music together in addition to Robert's music making. Joseph described his friend as being really into "pop-punk bands." Robert had his guitar shipped to Iraq, and he said that the two would "sit there and sing these songs that he'd written, and we'd just sit around, like in our room, and he'd play on his guitar and play these songs that he wrote." Joseph explained that these times were really important to him and that he "sort of got into punk music" as a result. Similarly, Shannon remembered that a number of people in his unit "managed to smuggle over guitars," since in the air force they took their own planes and thus had more control over loading them. This enabled them "to get together after missions for some recovery time." In separate interviews, both Gabe and Mike remembered spending time together listening to music and being introduced to the music that others in their units enjoyed. Mike listened to rap and house music, and Gabe remembered being introduced to country music genres, styles he had not listened to much prior to his deployment. Mike fondly remembered Gabe break dancing, something he did a lot. The two shared a room, and he explained that sometimes there were others present, and sometimes it was just the two of them. They "would put on some music; it didn't matter what kind of music it was." Mike would do his "uncoordinated dance," and Gabe would "do his house dance."

Evan, the pilot and DJ, enlisted after others in his unit, so when he deployed the others had already been in Iraq for six months. Aware that he was the outsider coming in, he was tentative about revealing too much about himself at the beginning, hoping to be accepted and to fit in. Soon people realized that he had brought with him lots of new music, which made him especially desirable as a unit mate. He explained:

It's a peer group just like any other, especially when you're coming into a unit that has already been deployed for six months, and you have to, you want to fit in. You don't want to stand out too much right in the beginning. But later on, when people found out that I had been a DJ and that I had all this recorded music, sets that I had recorded, they started passing it around because they were, of course, hungry for new music too. And so, guys who I knew in the troop, but who didn't know me very well, they'd come in and be like, "Dude, I walked into the squadron TOC [tactical operations center], and they were playing some techno on the speakers, and I asked them, 'Who is this?' And they said, 'This is Evan.'" And they were like trading my mixed CDs around, so it was kind of funny. All of a sudden, I got the feeling that a few of them, just by their level of astonishment, were not understanding that this was me DJing, not producing electronic music. If I was producing that stuff, I wouldn't be in the army. But I kind of explained it and let it go at that. . . . It definitely, with a couple of people, earned me some cool points.

When he had some time off and was at a base that had an MWR unit, Tyson, an army officer and pilot for whom dancing was an important part of his identity, enjoyed participating in the dance nights, which were arranged by contractors hired by the army to organize entertainment for the troops:

> I was focused on my job. But periodically when you have off time, your mind kind of wanders and things like that. And when I was back at the larger base. . . . I'd go to the morale welfare building that they had set up for us, you know, just a kind of a rec center, and see what was going on, because sometimes they would have a dance there. And so I would kind of keep my eyes open for posters if they had a Latin night or if they had a country western night. I'd keep my eyes . . . open because, you know, that would give me a chance to do that. And I'd just go and have fun for a couple hours.

These dance events, though limited to the larger bases and not available to most soldiers or very frequently, nevertheless provided a fun diversion from the work environment. Few people that I interviewed ever attended these events. Evan remembered attending some. At first he described them as well attended with about one hundred people, but then he corrected himself when he realized what a tiny percentage that was of the approximately seven thousand on his base. These evenings also tended to draw people who shared certain demographic characteristics, allowing people to bond and socialize with others with whom they identified. Tyson explained that mostly African Americans would show up to hip-hop nights, white folks dominated country nights, and Latinos dominated Latin nights. However, these were not segregated events; anyone was welcome. Tyson said that at the Latin nights, most people were Spanish speaking, and little English was spoken except for the one or two "extra people, white people or a couple of black people that would be invited along as friends." Tyson, who is white, was welcome and known to be an accomplished dancer; people would encourage their friends to dance with him and say, "go and dance with that guy. Even though he's a white guy, he knows how to dance." Tyson explained that the scheduling was confusing; for example, for some time Latin and western nights were scheduled for alternating Thursdays; "after awhile people started losing track of what was what, and you'd just have a mix of people show up . . . and it didn't matter so long as you were out and having fun." These dance nights thus provided an opportunity for shared musical activity and for people who shared musical tastes and/or ethnic identifiers to come together. They also provided an opportunity for at least some people to stretch across military hierarchies and ethnic/racial divisions. Tyson danced alongside those of other ranks and ethnic identities.

Recent developments in recording technologies allowed troops to integrate musicking into their lives throughout their deployments regardless of the deafening din of war and the demands of their challenging jobs. The structures of the military and the organizational systems through which war was orchestrated created social maps that on the one hand brought together people who would not otherwise have interacted in the same work and leisure spaces, allowing for cross-fertilization of musical engagement, and on the other hand let individuals find others with whom they identified, whether because they worked together, shared cultural identifiers, came into the military with similar musical tastes, or just happened to like one another. This ubiquity of musical listening through work and nonwork times and activities resulted in intricate linking of musicking with the multiplicities of experiences of war for individuals and collectives.

FOUR

Music as a Sound Track
of War

With the ubiquity of musical listening, much of what troops experienced during their deployments on a moment-by-moment basis in all different kinds of situations occurred with music in the foreground or background. Their experiences were partly mediated through musical listening at the same time that what was happening around them shaped how they listened to and interpreted music. Following DeNora, I "conceptualize musical forms as devices for the organization of experience, as referents for action, feeling and knowledge formation" (2000, 24). The relationship between musical listening and experience at war could be profound. In Turino's work on the semiotics of music, he explains that we make "connections between indexical signs and their objects by experiencing them together in our actual lives" and that music "commonly indexes the people and situations where we have heard the music" (2008, 8–9; cf. van Dijck 2006, 363). What one was listening to when something significant happened could contribute to the nature of the experience and how a person remembered and interpreted the event afterward. At the same time, what one was doing while listening to a particular musical selection, ensemble, or genre could shape how one listened to, understood, and interpreted that music and how one listened to or thought about the same or similar music later.

These relationships among music, experience, and memory are fluid. As time passes, some memories concretize while others fade and change, for example, when people develop narratives about themselves based on select moments from their past or when a series of recollections repeat themselves over and over in a person's mind, to the exclusion of other things that happened. Music can play a role in this concretization; marine veteran Nate described his life in relationship to a series of sound tracks. He remembered listening to the same musical selections at particular moments in his life as he was struggling with specific emotional challenges. His experiences at those times were mediated through his musical listening, in that the music was part of what he was experiencing and how he interpreted and responded to his environment. After the fact, the sound track for particular periods in his life became part of the fabric of those memories. He explained that when he hears particular music, he does not just listen to it; rather, his mind zooms to the memories that were evoked by the music. Other memories change or shift over time, in that people come to interpret things in the past or the world in general differently, and so the significance of the musical memory or of a particular artist or song shifts in accordance with the new thinking. There is no limit to how often or frequently these shifts can happen, making the relationship of music to experience and subsequently to memory part of the fluidity of how humans navigate their ever-changing relationships to the world in which they live and operate.

MUSIC AS ANTHEM OF WAR

Certain music was so pervasive throughout individuals' military experience generally or wartime specifically that some troops came to associate a particular song, artist, or genre with their war experience. In many war contexts, official songs, such as "La Marseillaise" in France during World War I, serve as the official musical anthem of war (Sweeney 2001), and in some, troops elevate a popularly known song to anthem status (e.g., Baade 2012a). Though official and unofficial overtly patriotic songs certainly served as anthems in the Iraq and Afghanistan wars, those troops I interviewed referred much less frequently to official songs associated with U.S. nationalism than they did to ones that came from their unofficial, individualized playlists. For many the band Drowning Pool's song "Bodies" became an unofficial anthem, a song that was also an incitement to violence (see Johnson and Cloonan 2009). In interview after interview, troops said that if there was one song that immediately evoked their war experience, it was "Bodies," whose most aggressive verse is the following:

Skin against skin blood and bone
You're all by yourself but you're not alone
You wanted in now you're here
Driven by hate
Consumed by fear

The driving chorus, repeated screaming of "let the bodies hit the floor," pounded through sound systems on bases and vehicles and through headphones connected to various individual listening devices. The song became emblematic of who they were as soldiers: strong, powerful, well-trained warriors who evoked fear through their ability to do what was necessary for "bodies to hit the floor." The music—the instrumentation, crashing rhythms, and distortions—was bombastic, loud, driving, aggressive, and violent—just like war. As Pieslak explains, the overwhelming articulation of sonic power in metal resonates with the centrality of power in all things military (2009). Penny, formerly a pharmacist with the U.S. Army, said that even though at the time of the interview in 2012 she was involved in antiwar activism, every time she heard the song, it "trigger[ed] that rush of adrenaline," the feeling that "we're going to go shoot some motherfucker." The song was written before the wars, and according to Dave Williams, the band's guitarist and lead vocalist at the time the song was recorded, was "a mosh pit anthem" about the band's view of the crowd during shows, who would "get in the pit and get it [whatever they were feeling] out."[1] Troops have reinterpreted the song to make it relevant to their situations (Pieslak 2009, 148).

For some, the song came to represent the very worst in attitudes that surrounded them or what they saw and sometimes did, making this song of all songs one of the most difficult for them to hear after their return to civilian life. When Benji, an antiwar activist who struggled with the fact that he had contributed to the war effort in Iraq, heard the song, it reminded him of boot camp, "when they would saturate us with these videos" with "Bodies" playing in the background. He remembered: "They would show us pictures of dead Iraqis and bombs going off in cities, and like, these just horrible videos. That was repulsing."

As an expression of a unit's cohesiveness, many units established a shared culture that featured a theme song. Some listened to the theme song at particular moments, for example, as they prepared to leave for a mission, as a ritualization of these shared activities. Each time that they gathered, systematically preparing what was needed and inspecting their vehicles or gear, music blared in the background, helping them communally enter a shared state of mind—that of confident and fearless warriors prepared to do what was needed across the wire. In Pieslak's and my research, interviewees described their units always listening to the same song as they prepared to exit the wire; examples from Pieslak's research are songs by the bands Slayer, Lil John, DMX, and Metallica, all driving and powerful hard music.[2]

Pete was in a motor transport unit in the U.S. Marines. He explained that as members of his unit prepared their vehicles to move out of the wire, "about a fifteen-minute process," the song "Bodies" screamed out of each of the five or six vehicles that made up the convoy. The song became the unit's anthem, and they continued to refer to it as the "song of Iraq" long after their deployments. Pete had been out of the military for almost five years at the time of our interview, yet he explained that when he encountered the song, he did not hear the music; rather, he was transported back to "every single detail" of what he had experienced and "every single place" he had been during the war. At the time of the interview, he did not seek out this song, nor did he actively avoid it. However, when he did happen to hear it, for example when riding in someone else's car, the memories flooded back. He said that at these times he "starts talking," telling the person about some of the places in Iraq where he had previously listened to the song. Sometimes these moments were calm; however, if they occurred at a time when he was struggling with his war experiences, hearing the song sometimes augmented his anxiety, a topic I return to in chapter 6.

MUSIC AND A UNIT'S VIDEOS

As has widely been documented by military bloggers, journalists, and academics, advances in technology enabled troops to document much of what they experienced in war during leisure times, patrols, missions, and even combat. Still and video cameras had become so small that a soldier could easily carry one in a pocket to take out to document anything that was happening, making these wars some "of the most documented wars in history using participatory media technologies" (Smith and McDonald 2011, 292). As Noah explained, "every soldier overseas doesn't have a cell phone, but they have cameras." In many units, one or more individuals became the informal documenters for the unit, taking photos or video footage of "combat action, routine patrolling, colloquial interaction with Iraqi civilians, recreation in the barracks, and tributes to fallen comrades" (Andén-Papadopoulus 2008, 20). This footage was frequently edited into short pieces that became unofficial documentaries and were almost always accompanied by music, what Rolling Stone journalist D. Sax refers to as a "virtual scrapbook" of the war for a unit's members (2006, 42). Some interviewees described having one such video that they came to consider the unit's iconic video, while others explained that members of their units created multiple videos throughout their deployments, producing numerous multimedia records, documenting anything from combat, to living situations, to fun times, to loss. The music chosen for the sound tracks of the videos depended on what messages the videos were intended to portray.

Though these videos are not the focus of my project, they were a significant way in which troops engaged with music during their deployments and continued to interrelate music with their war experiences afterward, so they deserve some attention here. Thousands of these videos have been posted to YouTube, blogs, social media sites, and other Internet spaces, making them publicly accessible worldwide. They were creative works, a montage of images, still and moving. Some of the visuals came from troops' own documentation efforts and others from other sources.[3]

Some were aggressive, what Christian Christensen (2009) categorizes as "Get Some" videos, packed with footage of flying planes, bombs dropping, and buildings and sometimes people being blown up. "Bodies," as well as other songs commonly listened to, such as "Die MF Die" by Dope and "Hit the Floor" by Linkin Park, were frequently chosen to accompany this aggressive subcategory of video (Pieslak 2009, 42). The frequent use of "Bodies" further solidified the song's position as an unofficial anthem of war for U.S. troops. A typical example that I found on YouTube is the video "Taliban Bodies Hit the Floor," which begins with the text below scrolling threateningly:

> Attention Taliban! You are
> condemned, did you know that?

> The instant the terrorists you support
> took over our planes, you sentenced
> yourselves to death.

It then proclaims the skill and strength of the U.S. armed forces:

Our helicopters will rain fire on your camps
before you detect them.
Our bombs are so accurate,
we can drop them right
through your windows.[4]

The text ends with instructions for how members of the Taliban can surrender in order to avoid these attacks and warns that "doing this is your only chance for survival."

As the text disappears into blackness, relatively quiet instrumental music simmers in the background. The chanting "let the bodies hit the floor" emerges into the sonic foreground as still images of Taliban leaders scroll up, one by one, aggressively implying that these are the bodies that will "hit the floor." The song moves out of the chorus, increasing in volume through the first verse:

Beaten why for (why for)
Can't take much more
Here we go!
Here we go!
Here we go, now!

A montage of quickly transitioning images of varieties of aircraft flying and dropping bombs on targets, buildings exploding, and U.S. soldiers loading guns interacts with the song and the written text to produce an aggressive threat. The chorus returns as more images of what look like Middle Eastern men, presumably more targets whose bodies should "hit the floor," flash on the screen. A recurring visual theme throughout the video is an aerial image of a target as bombs are released.

This aggressive example, similar to hundreds of others, demonstrates how music in interaction with text and still and moving images combined to create a record of war, a memento for soldiers, an expression of patriotism, and a threat to the enemy. The choice of song was especially poignant, not just for its lyrics and sonic qualities, but also because of its pervasiveness in the Iraq and Afghanistan theaters. All troops heard this song repeatedly, and whatever meaning they attributed to it, it came to be linked to the war experience. The video was one more manifestation of this linkage and for many had intertextual resonance that extended far beyond the specific images put together in the video. As Pete and Benji explained, upon hearing the song, memories flooded in on them.

The use of music interacting with often graphic visual images of war in these videos could produce prowar expressions, but also complex criticism of the war and its aftermath. Kari Andén-Papadopoulos, for example, analyzes a video called "U.S. Army, Marines-Iraq War-Kill Insurgents (4th Video Battle)," whose images of the devastation of war interact with the song "Eyes of the Insane" by Slayer as testimony to the "devastating insanity" of war and the resulting trauma for the troops who contributed to it (2008, 22).

Many other videos were thoughtful (Christensen 2009) or less serious, and many were playful and funny. Some referenced boredom, for example, as evidenced by the titles as well as content of numerous examples I accessed on YouTube: "US Army Soldiers Bored in Iraq," "Military Bored," "Bored Navy," and "Hilarious Military Boredom." Some of these may be offensive to some viewers in their dramatizations and parodying of war. Fictionalized depictions of preparing and engaging in battle, murder, and torture were not uncommon, a topic that deserves further exploration but is outside the scope of this study. Others were humorous pieces that played on particular personalities in a unit or juxtaposed musical dimensions, for example cheerful or love songs as the sonic background to the images of the not-so happy realities in which the makers found themselves—the bleakness of the war in the desolation of the endless desert. These examples were more about the friendships and shared experience than they were about military prowess, but again, the musical selections combined with the images in interesting webs of overlapping and conflicting messages.

Others were created to commemorate loss, for example, when a unit suffered casualties. Noah remembered that his unit produced a video set to a sad song that he could not remember, made as a tribute "after we lost one of the guys in our platoon." Tribute videos found on YouTube were set to a variety of music, often more lyrically driven and combined with images of war, devastation, and loss, and often reinforced the need to keep on fighting to defeat the enemy, an affirmation that the loss was not in vain.

Videos of troops dancing to all different kinds of music were abundant: a quick search on YouTube revealed numerous parodic music videos set to popular musical tracks with images of troops in full military garb or bits and pieces of clothing dancing in the desert, interspersed with images of others standing around, laughing, or working. Many of these played on gender norms. A popular trend was for troops to mimic popular professionally produced music videos featuring female recording artists. An example was a video made by a unit, possibly Special Forces, in Afghanistan that parodied a video made by the Miami Dolphin cheerleaders to the song "Call Me Maybe" by the young Canadian singer-songwriter Carly Rae Jepsen.[5] In the video the male marines, most wearing little but their underwear, show off their muscular bodies, mimicking the eye candy of the bikini-clad cheerleaders. They dance sensually, sing lyrically, and at times caress themselves, all a play on the sexualized and objectified femininity of the cheerleaders. They play further on this feminized gender when, instead of emerging happily from a tour bus as the cheerleaders do in the original video, they emerge from a hulking tank, or instead of caressing the delicate fringe dangling from a minuscule bikini swimsuit cover, a marine caresses a massive belt bulging with bullets ever so close to his phallus. This video could be analyzed in great depth for its simultaneous reinforcement and resistance to gender norms, something outside the scope of my objectives in this section. Here I use it as an illustration of how much music in interaction with bodies and visual images and in intertextual interaction with other texts can produce great fun and lots of room for complex expression.[6]

By crafting these videos, the units created records for themselves, a way to cement their shared experiences, much of which felt surreal after the fact, distant memories that haunted them at night and were difficult to come to terms with as something that really happened. The videos not only concretized the memories, but also reified the relationships between those within units, so real and omnipresent during deployments but that slowly receded into the background for many after their return. Watching the videos and listening could remind veterans not only of what had happened, but also of the camaraderie, the significance of their every activity during war, the fun that was had, the boredom, physical pain, and loss. The sound tracks became forever connected to the images, shaping how individuals remembered and thought about not just what was depicted in them, but the embodied experience itself.

MUSIC RESONATES WITH WAR

In *Sound Targets: American Soldiers and Music in the Iraq Wars*, Pieslak explores what it is about the heavier genres of metal and rap that made them particularly prevalent in the Iraq war. He concludes that "the *sound* of metal seems particularly conducive to combat inspiration, resulting from the timbres, performance, style, and musical structure of specific songs" (2009, 150; emphasis added). Jeffrey

Arnett goes so far as to titling the first chapter of *Metal Heads: Heavy Metal Music and Adolescent Alienation,* "A Heavy Metal Concert: The Sensory Equivalent of War." He suggests that heavy metal concerts provide a "sensory intensity" similar to that of war for adolescent males (1996, 14). In heavy rap, by contrast, "soldiers identify with the *lyrical* themes of violence and survival of the fittest" (Pieslak 2009, 154; emphasis added). Listening to these types of music while contributing to a war effort amplified the qualities of power and aggression within troops, inasmuch as the music resonated with certain aspects of their experiences at war. In an environment characterized by aggression, violence, and fear, troops listened to music that was itself warlike, either sonically, in its mood, or in what the musicians were expressing textually. Bombs, explosions, airplanes, violence, and domination inundated troops' sonic, physical, and interactional spaces, and they frequently went across the wire into a threatening environment where the possibility of death loomed, both their own and what they might inflict on others. The aggressive music thus became intertwined with the violence of war; it became one and the same, a tangled part of the experience.

Troops explicitly used songs from these genres as they prepared to exit the wire for patrols and missions, to transform their mental state from whatever they were feeling at the time—lonely, mad, scared, indifferent—to the mental state needed for the upcoming tasks, which required focus, alertness, confidence, and often aggression. Craig explained that members of his unit would listen to the bands AC/DC, Drowning Pool, and Disturbed as they prepared for missions. Asked why these genres, he responded:

> I think it's the aggressive, hard-hitting beat. You can feel the goose bumps come up on your neck. It's almost, maybe the modern war cry, or war drums, I guess. Where the ancient armies had the huge drums that they'd beat moving into war. I guess this might have been our war drum.

Joseph listened to the song "Red War" by the band Probot, which he described as "really heavy," sung with a "primal voice" and "this really primal drumming." He remembered the lyrics, specifically the first verse:

> Red war will fall on my enemies
> Babylon is full of hypocrisy
> You feel the hate is for real
> 'Cause red war will fall on my enemies

Joseph would listen to this song and as he put it, "get so fucking pumped up." He remembered that he would keep his headphones on as long as he could, right up until they "went out the gate." The song fired him up so that "I was ready to go. . . . I was a completely different person."

Inasmuch as violent, aggressive music was part of the experience of the heightened adrenaline that was war, other genres similarly resonated with other aspects of the war experience. Reebee Garofalo argues that mainstream U.S. popular music has served a range of contradictory functions in U.S. history. Before 9/11 it was frequently associated with "rebellion, defiance, protest, opposition, and resistance." At the same time that the 9/11 attacks sent the country into a dramatic political and economic tailspin, "the role of contemporary popular music also changed dramatically as it adjusted to this new political reality." No longer using popular music for protest, artists and listeners shifted to using it in "the service of mourning, healing, patriotism, and nation building" (2007, 4). Garofalo provides numerous examples of popular musicians, many of them white male rock and country artists, donating funds, organizing musical fund-raising events, and recomposing tributes to the lives lost and songs affirming U.S. patriotism (see also Pegley and Fast 2007).

Music's ability to provide an outlet and provoke "the emotional intensity and power of national sentiment" has been widely documented in conflicts across the world (Naroditskaya 2010, 49; see also Sugarman 2010). In the context of U.S. wars, Tad Tuleja traced the popularity of the song "Ballad of the Green Beret," which was cowritten by journalist Robin Moore and Special Forces sergeant Barry Sadler during the Vietnam War. Tuleja explains that when the song came out in 1966, when anti–Vietnam War sentiment pervaded the United States, it provided, "a political touchstone, as unreflectively revered by hawkish patriots as it was unreflectively ridiculed by their detractors" (2012, 249). For decades the song has served as an iconic expression of patriotic fervor for the "fighting soldiers from the sky, fearless men who jump and die." It has been covered by other artists, sung by troops at war, parodied by troops and civilians to produce contradictory messages, and as the sound track to videos created and disseminated by men and women deployed to Iraq and Afghanistan. The song celebrates the self-sacrifice, pride, and loyalty of troops at war, which Tuleja explains "captures the emotional loyalty of the audience" (2012, 251).[7]

The patriotic and pro-troop stance of songs, artists, and genres helped some service men and women reaffirm why they had enlisted and the importance of the job at hand. A number of people I interviewed explained that country music was popular among the troops because many country artists have been vocal about their support for the war (Willman 2005; Sampert and Treiberg 2007; Wolfe and Akenson 2005). Numerous country music artists composed songs after 9/11 whose lyrics were about or directed to U.S. troops and expressed patriotism. A number of people I interviewed remembered Toby Keith's song "American Soldier," whose lyrics are in the first person from the perspective of a soldier and express the protagonist's love for and pride in his country, as is evident from the following part of a verse:

> I'm an American soldier, an American
> Beside my brothers and my sisters
> I will proudly take a stand
> When liberty's in jeopardy, I will always do what's right

The song continues with "I'm out here on the frontlines, sleep in peace tonight," repeatedly stating, "I'm an American soldier." Army veteran Keith remembered that when that song came out, "it was huge." He remembered everyone listening to it and feeling, "We're not totally forgotten. They know we are here." He realized that in his job, he should not expect recognition, so the song was "that pat on the back," that "appreciation that he did not expect."

Another Toby Keith song, "Courtesy of the Red, White, and Blue (The Angry American)," on the album *Unleashed,* released in 2002, pays homage to the soldiers fighting the war and warns those who have put this "nation that I love" under attack that justice will be served:

> And you'll be sorry that you messed with
> The U.S. of A.
> 'Cause we'll put a boot in your ass
> It's the American way

Some of those whom I interviewed, who had not previously listened much to country music, described developing an affinity for it because of its pervasiveness during the war. Gabe explained that he listened to country music in Iraq because of its patriotism, and even though he was no longer in the military at the time of the interview, he continued to listen to the genre:

There are a lot of country songs that are very patriotic, they will talk about the war, and how we will win the war. Before, I was like, country is not really my type of music. I wouldn't probably listen to it. But when I was there, I was even singing country music.

This association of country music with patriotism has become so strong that it can transcend the politics of a musician or a song's lyrical content. This is not surprising, given that as Connell and Gibson (2003) note, a majority of listeners to popular music do not pay as much attention to lyrics as to other musical dimensions, either because the words are inaudible or incomprehensible, or because lyrical content is not what attracts all people to musical selections.

Some soldiers who were critical of the U.S. government's foreign policy and of their own participation in the Iraq war explained that they rejected or disliked country music because of its association with U.S. nationalism (Gilman 2013). Joseph was especially articulate about his dislike of the genre, specifically the songs that were so prevalent during his deployments, and he felt that they were played to reinforce patriotism and support for the war:

> That one song, "We'll put a boot in your ass, it's the American Way," that kind of stuff, that shit irritated me so much. I just felt like it was so blind. . . . I felt like it reflected a particular level of ignorance that was based or steeped in nationalism that I felt masked or veiled some of the misdeeds or some of the acts that America had committed. It sort of acted as a veil, like people didn't want to penetrate that veil. They didn't want to go beyond it. By reinforcing their nationalism with music, they were helping strengthen themselves against some of the attacks coming from people like myself, who were starting to realize that maybe the war was wrong and maybe that America wasn't always right. To me, that music symbolized this refusal to face what was really going on.

Even in these cases, however, patriotic music could still operate nostalgically by evoking positive memories related to their war experiences. For example, though he was avidly against the war and critical of the U.S. government, Joseph explained that during his second deployment, he and his closest friend listened to the song "Letters from Home" by country artist John Michael Montgomery, about a deployed soldier reading letters from loved ones at home. He explained that the song was "totally capitalizing on the pain of soldiers and on some level disgusted me, but I could relate to the song." He and his friend would listen to the song "and get all choked up because it really helped us, reminded us of home." He elaborated that although it was a nationalist and patriotic song, it was not the patriotism he was attracted to, but rather the song's articulation of "the way that it feels to be a soldier at war away from family and having your parents and your fiancée write to you while you're deployed." Similarly, Noah, who was also involved in antiwar activism by the time of the interview, explained:

Toby Keith, I mean that guy was like the spokesman for the U.S. Army and the USO [United Service Organizations]. I remember listening to that, even with my political side, his message was just so, so military. I think that any vet who listens to some of Toby Keith's music is moved.

This association of a whole genre with a political perspective, however, is complicated, because not all country artists support the war effort. For example, the Dixie Chicks, a very popular country band, caused an uproar when their lead singer, Natalie Maines, remarked in London on March 10, 2003, that she was ashamed that President Bush was from her home state of Texas, a statement expressive of her opposition to Operation Iraqi Freedom. When Maines refused to apologize, it cost the group its popularity ratings in the country music charts and CD sales (Willman 2005, 21–54; Rudder 2005). Though many country fans rejected the band following this controversy, two soldiers I interviewed, Tina and Craig, reported listening to the Dixie Chicks when they were in Iraq. When I asked Tina, whose playlist consisted almost exclusively of country music, how she felt about the Dixie Chicks controversy, she answered:

I don't know; I mean, we're really allowed to say whatever we want in America, that's why I like it. But it kind of makes me upset sometimes too because we're over there, we're in the service so that people can say things like that, you know, and I don't know. I mean, I appreciate that we can pretty much say whatever we want and not have to worry about getting thrown in prison or something, but then, when you're over there, fighting for these people who are saying stuff like that . . .

Tina was expressing the irony that on the one hand, she felt she was fighting this war for freedom, including the freedom of political expression, while on the other hand, she felt that Maines used this very freedom to criticize a war that Tina felt was intended to achieve this freedom for Iraqis. Despite Tina's thoughts about Maines's statement, she said that it had not occurred to her to screen the band from her listening. A Dixie Chick fan interviewed in the movie *The Soundtrack to*

War, directed by George Gittoes, was adamant that she really appreciated Maines specifically because she was exercising the freedom that the soldier treasured so much. Craig, an armored crewman in the U.S. Army, described listening to the Dixie Chicks' song "Travelin' Soldier," about a young man who meets a waitress just before deployment, which was number one on the country music charts on March 22, 2003, but then fell off the Top 40 following Maines's London comment (Sampert and Treiberg 2007; see also Willman 2005, 21–54). When I asked Craig whether the controversy affected how he felt about the group's music, he explained that he listened to the song because it reminded him of his fiancée, whom he had met only two months before his deployment: "It just made me think of her, because in the song, it talks about the guy going to training, and he meets this girl leaving town and writes her letters all the way through, and then he dies and she's crying. I met my wife two months before I left for Iraq. And we wrote letters all the way through." Craig listened to the song because he associated his own experience and fears with the narrative in its lyrics, rather than worrying about the band members' politics.

INDIVIDUAL LISTENING, MEMORY, AND DEFINITIONS

Although certain music came to be associated with the collective experience of war, music also mediated individual experience in highly idiosyncratic ways. Because so much private time was spent listening to music, many troops I interviewed explained that music played a role in how they came to characterize their environments and define their experiences. Deployment for many was surreal. Before leaving for war, they were trained in how to be warriors, how to engage in battle, and how to respond to a wide range of eventualities. Yet the targets were dummies or at least not the real enemy, and no one was supposed to actually get injured. Once in the war zone, the ammunition was real, the targets were other human beings, and troops became targets themselves. Being at war was so distinct from almost everything else in their lives that for some, music contributed to their understanding of what it meant to be at war.

Listening to the band The Cranberries brought the war into focus for Keith. He did not choose to listen to this music because of its association with war; rather, he just enjoyed the band. The significance of their lyrics only came into relief when he was listening to them in Iraq. In a phone interview on December 5, 2012, Keith explained that though he was a soldier at war, "Iraq didn't really hit me" until he listened to a Cranberries song. He remembered that he was driving through a combat zone, "up in the turret manning the gun," when he heard the song "Zombie," a song that poignantly evokes the loss caused by war and violence, for example in the lines "Another head hangs lowly / Child is slowly taken / And the violence caused such silence / Who are we mistaking." Another verse personalizes the violence, acknowledging that regardless of which side one might be on, everyone has family and loved ones who suffer when there are casualties: "Another mother's breaking / Heart is taking over / And the violence causes silence / We must be mistaken."[8]

When "the lyrics started talking about tanks and bombs," Keith remembered looking around him at the "tank graveyards and buildings just demolished." He elaborated that "some streets seemed like there was just no way anyone would have survived." The song was still playing "when they went through a village." As he listened to the song and saw what was around him, he started to understand where he was:

> Seeing the kids and how hard they had it, it just starts to add everything up, and you're in the middle of a combat zone looking at what is talked about in this song; whether tanks or bombs or guns, it's all there.

For Keith, listening to this song about the devastation of war—even though it was a very different one, of which Keith had little experience or knowledge—brought what he was doing into sharp focus. The song humanized the experience for him. His perspective shifted as he thought about how the war impacted the human beings outside his tank as well as those inside.

Music also played a part in clarifying for Shannon that he was playing a role in a significant historical moment. He did not listen to aggressive and violent music that felt warlike during his deployment to Iraq; rather, he listened to a lot of Bob Dylan, Lynyrd Skynyrd, and Jimi Hendrix, music that he associated with the Vietnam War. He explained that he liked to match the music he listened to with what he was doing. As he was flying in an aircraft over Baghdad, he said, "You could kind of match which mood you're in and what kind of mission you're into." He listened to "a lot of old rock because it was so appropriate to the situation, especially the Vietnam era type stuff." He explained that after the "Vietnam era," there was not much rock music that was about war, so he did not find the newer music as relevant to his situation. I remarked that I thought it was interesting that so much of the music he listened to was by artists whose publicly expressed opinion or music was explicitly antiwar. He said that for him it was less about the politics, and "a lot to do with the emotion and the psychological aspects that went into that kind of music," and "the realistic emotional stuff that can kind of put your mind in a frame where you really share this experience that is going into war."

Shane Brighton, a British soldier and author, suggests that past tours offer "a potent resource for the imposition of certainties where . . . uncertainty is the only thing of which can be assured." He explains that movies portraying past warfare, such as *Platoon* and *Apocalypse Now!*, both about the Vietnam War, contribute to a "regimental folk memory" that shapes troops' expectations and interpretations of soldiers' own wartime experiences (2004, 51–52). Shannon felt that "in between Vietnam and now, there hasn't been a whole lot of music that focused on those moods [having to do with war]." Whether or not he agreed with the artists seemed to be less important than that the artist and listener were contemplating the same topic, in this case, warfare.

The experience of the Iraq war for Shannon, who was in the air force, was different from those whose missions were on the ground. As he explained: "I had the luxury of having the perspective of mostly flying, so I could kind of be in the situation but detached from the situation at the same time. There's still a threat of getting killed, but at the same time, I'm not down there shooting at people and blowing up people with tanks, so I think I kind of had the luxury of that." Unlike those on the ground listening to music that evoked feelings of confidence, power, and aggression, Shannon's physical and thus psychological removal from the immediate realities of combat led him to select music that was more reflective. Like Keith, who was involved on the ground, Shannon's musical choices contributed to the mediation of his understanding of what he was doing and how to interpret it. Interestingly, much of the music that he associated with the Vietnam War was featured on sound tracks of popular movies about the Vietnam War; thus the intertextuality of the music had multiple layers. Before his deployment he watched movies with captivating musical sound tracks that fictionally depicted previous U.S. wars. The music on the sound tracks subsequently was linked in his mind to these fictionalized visual narratives. He then listened to the same or similar music when he was at war; the music and its association with the movies mediated his own interpretation of what it meant to be at war.

Shannon had an especially poignant memory of a difficult, scary, and sad mission that he continued to associate with listening to a particular song:

We were in Baghdad one night, and we were flying with a bunch of army. And we were doing a particular mission where we were flying into a strip that had just got mortar fired, and about four guys died. I think I was listening to the "Simple Kind of Man" song. I like that song, the new version and the old one, too. I looked at all the other guys. Of course you could barely see them because all the lights were off, but just that particular point in time and situation was relevant to the song. It was a point in my life where you have to judge what you're doing. There are particular points in people's lives where they experience things that can be pretty life-changing, because you really have to judge who you are and what you want and what you're doing and you come to that third person perspective of, "Here's what's going on." You know? Like what we were talking about before, there's not a whole lot of times [when] you're actively participating in something where you can kind of jump to that third person perspective, but I think this was one of those times I just remember: everyone holding onto their weapons, and I was holding onto mine. Of course everyone's in helmets and body armor and landing into one of these situations. It really reminded me of one of those old war movies. Or even one in Vietnam when they're riding in on the helicopter and you've got to judge at that point who you are and what you really want in life, before you get plunged into the mass down below.

In that moment, listening to such a reflective song and thinking about Vietnam era movies, Shannon knew that he was participating in history, something significant, regardless of the politics of the war. The poignancy of this experience and his reflections at that time impacted how he came to think about this event, an important transformative moment in his thinking:

I realized that probably no one that I know will ever have this experience. Whether the ethics behind going into Iraq are good or bad and all of the politics behind it, just . . . . That kind of experience, in a lot of ways, I was thankful for. It gave me the ability to see what other people have seen in previous wars. When I came back to the States, I had had those experiences, and I'[d] seen these people's faces, and I'[d] lived through that. So at that point, I could start studying and researching and doing a lot of things with that experience behind me. So in a lot of ways, that was a turning point. I never really believed in going into Iraq. I really never wanted to be actively involved in any politics. . . . After that point in time, I really wanted to do something about it. When I was in Kuwait and flying into Baghdad that one time. So . . . I think those are points in our lives [when] we come to these conclusions and kind of use those experiences, which is good. I think music plays an integral part in that. Obviously if you're getting shot at and everything, those are experiences, too, but I think if you have the luxury of living through those experiences with music or whether it be with friends or just listening to a CD player or iPod or whatever.

For Shannon, listening to music he associated with the Vietnam War contributed to his deep reflection about the relationship of his role in history, previous wars, and politics.

Listening to music while living at war and observing life around them, even when it was not the drama of combat, could still impact how troops thought about or interpreted what they were seeing. A poignant memory for Craig was sitting on a roof on the military base looking out over Baghdad and watching Iraqi children play soccer while he listened through headphones to music by the Dave Matthews Band. As he sat there, other soldiers sat nearby, ensconced in their own private listening. He reflected that he could imagine that thoughts were "portrayed much differently for the person listening to, um, the heavier genres of music than to say, me, who was listening to Dave Matthews watching these children play soccer." He said that there would often be about ten people sitting on the roof together, each listening to his own music. Asked how the music shaped his thinking, he answered that he specifically remembered listening one time to the song "Busted Stuff," a mellow, lyrically driven love song with the repeated refrain: "I know she's going to leave my broken heart behind." As he listened, he remembered "watching the kids play soccer" and thinking, "you know, even though there [is] a war going on around them, these children are still just out, not really in their yard, but out there, playing a game."

A salient musical memory for Mark was listening to the songs "White Rhino," "Motr," or "Uninvited Guest" by the band Trans Am before leaving for an especially dangerous mission that involved invading a city in Iraq:

I remember it completely. I'm waiting to leave to go up the road to that city that we're about to invade. And I just remember having listened to these songs [the night before] because I couldn't sleep, because we all knew that we were going to go do this. It was the biggest mission we'd ever been on. We left at two in the morning or something. The fight started an hour later when we got there. I remember sitting in my room [the night before] just listening to these two songs. . . . I always hear music, no matter what, in my mind.

He explained that having listened to these two songs as he anxiously awaited the mission, these songs continued to stream through his mind when he was onsite doing the mission:

I would sometimes have these experiences where I was extremely present. You have to put on night sight to drive at night, so we are looking through this telescope thing, and it's all, we don't have the same field of view. We're trying to stay on the road, and it's all like green and black. And I remember having those songs going through my head while staring through this tiny night sight and just thinking, "I don't believe I'm here. I can't believe this is about to happen. I mean, 'how the hell did I get here?'" Just like, this super-present reflection of that exact moment. But I have those very vivid memories of those situations still.

These songs continued to be intricately connected to Mark's memory; as he put it, these songs "definitely shaped my memory of the whole thing leading up to when we got there."

In each of these examples, the men were surrounded by others who were also listening to music through their own headphones. Unfortunately I was not able to interview people who were together on the same occasion listening to different music, but the poignancy of the associations of the memories and interpretations with particular sound tracks suggested that each individual who experienced those same moments was thinking about them differently, partly because of individual perspectives and prior knowledge, but also because of the musical choices each listened to at the time. As Craig explained, another person on the same roof might have been listening to some aggressive music while watching the children play, or the music might have moved him to shift his gaze beyond the children to an explosion farther away, leading his mind to stray into areas of reflection very different than Craig's.

SOUND BUBBLE

The potential for individualized listening provided a mechanism through which individuals could isolate themselves, or at least attempt to, from the physical environment and withdraw into a private mental space, as has been well established by Bull:

Within the enveloping acoustics of the iPod, its users move through space in their auditory bubble, on the street, in their automobiles, on public transport. In tune with their body, their world becomes one with their 'sound tracked' movements, moving to the rhythm of their music rather than to the rhythm

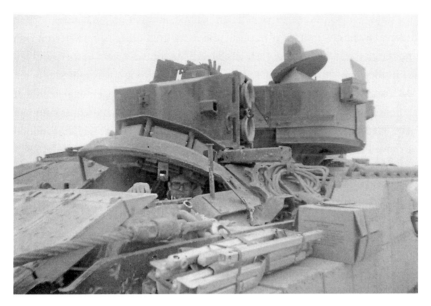

Mark peeking out of the top of the Bradley. "This photo is probably from May 2004. We were on our way to another base to help out some other unit." Courtesy of Mark Leahey.

of the street. In tune with their thoughts, their chosen music enables them to focus on their feelings, desires, and auditory memories. (2009, 84)

When people listened to music, their attention could be drawn to the music itself, or they might meander through a cognitive and emotional journey that took them away from their present physical and emotional being. Turino describes this potential of music to lead to "a feeling of timelessness, or being out of normal-time, and to feelings of transcending one's normal self" as "flow" (2008, 4), following Gregory Bateson's usage. Interviewee after interviewee explained that because of the lack of private physical space, the ongoing emotional demands placed on them, the desire to think or connect with worlds outside their immediate environments, the frequent boredom, and just pure exhaustion, they took advantage of any opportunity they could get to withdraw into personalized space. Often with no physical space into which to withdraw, many described putting their headphones on, a signal to others that they were no longer socially present.

Throughout much of his deployment, Mark was out on extensive missions that lasted days or weeks. When he finally returned to his home base, he shared a room created out of a conex (or hootch) with four other men. He remembered that he would go into this space, lie on his bed, and put on his headphones in order to withdraw into his own mind and away from other people around him and the physical environment. He explained: "As soon as I went in there and put the headphones on, it was like, I didn't even care if anyone else was in the room." Mark often relied on this sound bubble to help him fall asleep. He explained that at these times he listened to Beachwood Sparks: "Indie Rock with a little country-ness." He chose this band because "they sounded so pretty. It was all mid-tempo or slower. It wasn't too loud or anything, so it was easy to fall asleep to."

In an e-mail to me on December 12, 2012, army veteran and musician Jeff Barillaro, aka Soldier Hard, attributed his survival at war to being able to escape by listening to his own and other artists' music:

> Listening to music before a mission and before going to bed was an everyday thing. I listened to the music I created and also music from artists I looked up to, and was a fan of. It literally put me in another mind frame; it put me into another place, other than where I was. I can actually fantasize in my mind as if I was living . . . the music that was playing in my headphones; it's like I was in another world, outside of my body. I can travel to another place, without having to move; all I had to do was close my eyes and press play!!!!

Here, Soldier Hard uses the metaphor of traveling to describe how much music enabled him to transport himself to a different state of mind, to transfer into an imagined other place (cf. Jansen 2009). Heike Weber explains that by listening to music through portable players, "any given spot can be domesticated through a self-selected sound track. Users thus have partially regained control over the spaces they cross . . . by making the unknown territory known through familiar songs" (2009, 79). Listening to music gave Soldier Hard a psychological reprieve and control over his space by helping him feel that he was temporarily mentally and physically removed from where he actually was. In situations in which troops had so little control over space and time, this ability to "domesticate" a given spot was especially necessary. Tina explained that early on in her deployment, when she was having trouble sleeping, someone recommended that she listen to classical music for its calming effects. She tried to "domesticate" her sleeping space by listening to classical selections. Yet she quickly realized that different movements had moods and that some movements were "bombastic" and reminded her of war, bringing her attention fully to her present location, rather than helping to distance her from her surroundings. She then turned to country love ballads, music that she associated with home in southern Oregon and with normalcy and whose sonic dimensions she could count on to soothe her. Listening to this familiar music helped "domesticate" her sleeping space, making it her own and as similar to what she called home as possible.

Many male soldiers described listening to female artists because the music, the artist, and the lyrics were so different from what they were experiencing that they gave them a break. Danny remembered that his girlfriend sent him music by local bands from their hometown, Eugene, Oregon, as well as by artists that she enjoyed, such as Ani DiFranco. When I asked him whether he thought about DiFranco's antiwar politics, he answered that he had not thought about it: "I took it for what it was, there, coming out of the speakers, and that was that it was just something that was not death metal. It was not death."

Joseph remembered that he bought an album by the band

> Evanescence because she [his German girlfriend at the time] had sent me this letter that had the lyrics to this song, "My Immortal," which at the time I thought was like a super deep song. . . . I bought that album because it reminded me of her. It was heavy music, but it also had sort of a softer side because they had a female singer, and they had a couple soft songs on there that were about yearning and sort of longing for this individual.

In this case, this music provided an escape from war for Joseph, because he was connecting with his girlfriend by listening to a song whose lyrics she had sent him and because the vocalist was female, so it had "a sort of softer side."

This idea that music can disassociate a person from current reality, however, is too simplistic. My interviews illustrated that listening to music within a sound bubble that contrasted with the situation surrounding the individual could, instead of providing an escape, put into relief the reality of a person's situation. Even in Joseph's example above, the song was also about "yearning" and "longing," suggesting that the escape was incomplete. The song was emotionally evocative, reminding him of what he was missing. "Traveling" to where he was not ultimately reminded Joseph of where he was and what he did not have.

In some cases the music could be so different from what was happening that it highlighted the reality or at least contributed to the moment standing out in a person's mind, creating an ironic and disjunctive memory. In Bull's research on music listeners on London's streets, he explained that the "disjunction between the sounds in a subject's head and [his or her] perception of the outside can sometimes result in greater concentration" and make the person more "visually attentive" (2000, 23). Correspondingly, Shannon described how surreal it was to listen to music "from home," from "normal" life when he was flying in a military aircraft at night:

> I know just flying around Iraq at night with the lights from the cities coming up and we'd shut all the lights off in our plane so other people couldn't spot us and shoot at us. But I remember flying around that and just seeing all the lights down on the ground and, you know, listening to music that you'd listen to back home, over here. It was very other-worldly, [and] the, of course, the stress of being shot down, is really a lot because people would fire at us, and I think that stress mixed with being in a different country and seeing these alien lights from buildings that were kind of flickering from the ground because of course, Baghdad doesn't have the greatest infrastructure as far as electricity goes.

The extreme contrast between Shannon's association with music "that you'd listen to back home" and what he was experiencing and about to do produced a heightened awareness and reflection of the significance of his situation. This disjuncture, rather than relaxing him, added to his stress because it was "other-worldly," bringing to the fore his knowledge that they could be "shot down" and that "people would fire at" them, concerns he did not associate with occasions at "home" when he might have listened to that music in the past.

Though he was not listening to music privately in the following example, Josh also told a story about how the contrast between what he was listening to put into relief what he was doing. Josh, who had been in the U.S. Army and was an antiwar activist at the time of the interview on August 24, 2009, remembered being on patrol in a Striker (a type of tank) while listening to the Jamaican reggae artist Bob Marley through the Striker's sound system: "At one point, people that were on top of the Striker were shooting at people, while listening to Bob Marley." He was disappointed that he couldn't remember the specific song because that used to be "part of the story." He explained that no one put on that CD because of its ideological associations, but he did remember that his friend turned to him during that particular patrol and pointed out that it was "weird that they were listening to Bob Marley, who is known for his antiwar stance" while they were actively shooting people. Josh told me this story on multiple occasions and expressed that it was a story he frequently told others, indicating that this was a memory that stood out in his mind as being especially poignant, a moment when his musical listening actively contradicted what he was doing.

Though many interviewees described the sound bubble phenomenon in terms similar to those used by the people with whom Bull conducted research in peacetime urban London, the circumstances of musical listening for most troops differed significantly from those of Bull's respondents. Troops' musical listening was often not so private even when they wished it were. During deployments, troops were almost always in unvarying social environments with the same people, only a few places to hang out, limited things to do, and little opportunity to remove themselves into more private physical spaces. In Bull's examples, listeners wandering down a busy city street may have been surrounded by swarms of people, yet they were nevertheless alone in that they did not have social relationships with all those they passed, nor did they have an obligation to interact. Wearing headphones signaled their expressive removal from others, and users developed "ways of auditized looking" that were "inherently non-reciprocal, functioning to bolster the user's sense of power and control in urban space" (2000, 25). In the context of deployment, and I argue in many civilian situations as well, people were similarly surrounded by others and listening to their privatized sound selections; however, they were neither socially nor psychologically removed from those around them. Though their headphones signaled their desire to be alone, the relationships persisted through the listening, in that part of what a person might be trying to escape by receding into a sound bubble could be the very person lying several feet away, who might be buried in his or her own sonic realm. Or a person might be listening to music to process a traumatic event that the others in the room also shared. Even if each listened to different music after such an event in an effort to deal with the emotional aftereffects privately, that they were all together collectively trying to contend with the event individually made the process simultaneously private and public. In this sense, ironically, some type of community could be constituted through shared attempts to isolate oneself in idiosyncratic listening.

Bull explained that "personal stereos tend to be non-interactive in the sense that users construct fantasies and maintain feelings of security precisely by not interacting with others in the environment" (2000, 25). In Bull's examples, people listened to their own playlists knowing that unless their auditory mask were lifted when acoustics seeped out of headphones, no information was available to others about the nature of the sound bubble and individuals' musical selections. They could safely feel that they were removed sonically from those nearby. Correspondingly, many combat veterans said that listening to music was one of the few things they could do that was truly personal and over which they had control. However, they also described sharing the content of their playlists with others or losing that control when they were asked by others what they were listening to. As discussed further in the next chapter, some described being teased or outright chastised for their musical selections. For example, Andy commented that when he learned of people's musical taste, it could surprise and shift how he identified them:

Like we had a guy who had a strong country accent, and we were thinking that this guy is going to come out with some Garth Brooks or something. He ended up coming out with some Britney Spears or something, some really fruity music. We were kind of looking at each other, thinking "Are you serious?" And we'd ask him, "Is that your playlist? Is that your iPod, sir?" And he'd be like, "yeah, you got a problem?" He was really masculine and everything, so you know, you would expect him to have something really hardcore, and they have something soft, or you expect them to be very fruity and kind of reclusive, and they'd have something hardcore on.

This quote highlights how people could use an individual's musical listening to make assumptions about that person's personality and abilities and how much musical taste or just what someone happened to be listening to could be used to place that person in different social categories, for example based on gender, race, or sexuality. It also hints that when the musical preference of someone whose listening deviated from others' expectations was discovered, it could have social repercussions. For example, in some contexts in the military, a man being identified as feminine or homosexual could experience reduced credibility as a warrior and sometimes be harassed or even dismissed, as discussed in the next chapter. Despite their efforts to achieve isolation, troops' private listening could become public, complicating the idea of the safety and the escape potential of the sound bubble.

LOSS, GRIEF, MUSIC, AND SILENCE

Inescapable in these wars was the loss faced by everyone involved. In civilian life, when one loses someone close it is often possible to take time to reflect and grieve. When one is present at the circumstances of or participates in the activity that leads to a death, one often has the time to take a reprieve from that activity, which is important for the individual's own processing of the loss and reassertion of a sense of relative safety. In war, the situation was different. When casualties occurred, whether inflicted on the enemy or suffered in one's unit, sometimes there was little time to stop and acknowledge the gravity of the loss, and when a ceremony was held in memoriam, troops often soon had to return to the same wartime activity that had led to the death. Within these constraints, music once again could be a mechanism through which troops attempted to deal with loss.

Though most interviewees did not describe their own experiences of inflicting casualties, Benji poignantly remembered the first time he was aware of killing someone. A mortar man in the Marines, he and two other men in his crew received orders from their commander through headphones to set coordinates that controlled the trajectory of the mortar that they fired to a destination out of their sight. The first time the crew was successful, he remembered hearing from his commander through his headphones that he had hit the "target" and killed three men. Before he had time to process this information, he was given information to prepare for the next round. It was only much later, while listening to music, that the reality of what he had done sank in.

Andy, who was a medic, remembered an especially traumatic night: "rockets hitting and thirty-something patients came in [for care] at the same time. A lot of my friends died that day." He remembered that Sarah McLachlan's song "Angel" was playing on his playlist: "I don't even know how it got there, but it was playing." In the past, his attitude had been that "this song is corny." After this event, the song became linked to his memories: "Since then, even today, I still listen to it and it just brings back memories."

Music was also used during funerals and became part of the formalized collective soundscape of grief and mourning. In an interview on February 26, 2007, Eric described the rituals that transpired when a U.S. soldier died:

> I'm sure you've seen the pictures . . . where the boots and the weapon is stuck down and they hang the Kevlar on top of the weapon, and they hand the person's ID tags. It's kinda like, I don't know what they call it. Anyway, and then, after everything is said and the 21-gun salute and "Taps" is played, "Taps" is, there's some music I can't listen to.

In this case, the song "Taps" was part of the ritual of shared mourning that allowed those in a unit to commemorate the loss of one of their members. The music, along with the iconic symbolic, ephemeral physical memorial built from the individual's boots, weapon, Kevlar, and ID tags, brought attention to the individual and the gravity of the cost of war for brief moments before everyone had to return to the war effort. As with any ritual, this one was intended to bring members of a unit together and reinforce solidarity and to publicly recognize the loss, which was simultaneously an affirmation of the need to continue to fight the enemy to reduce the possibility of future casualties. For Eric, however, "Taps," did not evoke the intended emotion. Rather than inspiring a sense of bonding, communitas, the song in the ritual acted to separate Eric from the whole. It evoked feelings of anger, resentment, and hypocrisy. The music "Taps" became linked not just to his memory of war, but to the way he felt in and about the war.

Eric described especially intense moments in Iraq as times when there was "no music," suggesting that music was such a regular part of his daily life that when things really shook up, the music stopped. He described a really difficult day for everyone in his unit that was especially traumatic for him because he was a medic. On this day, there were many injuries, and three men were killed:

> But on the day that we had three KIAS [killed in action], or four, but only three of them came to us, there was nothing. At least nothing that I remember. I can't imagine that somebody necessarily would have turned off the music. I just don't remember anything. That was a really hard day. The guys that were killed . . . , I used to be their medic. Just a month before, I had been their medic on the line. The driver and the platoon leader were both killed. And all I can remember about that is silence. Absolute silence.

Music, for him, resonated with a sense of normalcy even within the chaos of war. When it got too chaotic, the music stopped (see also Daughtry 2012, 132–33).

Inspired by Eric's description of silence, I asked Andy, who was also a medic, whether he remembered moments of silence. He answered:

> Um, there were probably a few thousand moments [when] something traumatic has happened, and you're just like, wow. I had a couple of my buddies that got shot, and they were right next to me. And two of them, there were three of them that got shot, and two of them didn't make it. And I was there, you know. In your mind, everything just froze. You know, and you can't hear anything. It was probably from the trauma of it, you know, and also the blast, there was an RPG that hit nearby, and you just, through your head, you just freeze for a couple seconds. And then I'm a medic, so my automatic reaction is I'm supposed to get up. So I did everything I could, and they didn't make it.

Uh, I had one of them alive for a good twenty minutes doing CPR, but he didn't make it. You can, you know, and then you question yourself. You know, if it was your fault or whatever. But, it's, it's, I don't know, there's definitely, and then in the OR [operating room] when I was there, something would be playing and a soldier would die and even though the music's playing in the background, kind of, everything just kind of shimmers out.

Musical listening was tied to many different types of war experiences, and much of troops' reflections about what happened to and around them, was mediated through the music they were listening to, whether it was serving as an anthem of war, a memorialization, a bonding between friends, an opportunity for personal escape and reflection, or an avenue to express a political perspective. The strong associations among music, experience, emotion, and politics continued to play a role in troops' ongoing narrativizing, analysis, remembering, and attempting to forget after the war. Exploring these intricate links among experience, memory, and musical listening is important for combat veterans. Throughout their lives, hearing music either by choice or accidently, that they associated with war and military experiences could generate recollections about details of what occurred, in addition to stimulating thought processes or evoking emotional states. Examining connections between individual and collective music listening associated with particular wartime experiences highlights the ways that experience can be mediated through music and ultimately be connected to memories of war.

FIVE

Music, Gender, and
the Paradox of Masculinity

Of all U.S. institutions, the military remains a bastion of the overtly masculine. The majority of the people who serve in the military are men (83.9 percent active duty), though a significant percentage are women (16.1 percent active duty).[1] Some units and certain types of jobs are exclusive to men. Though women do engage in combat in a variety of situations, until very recently they were officially restricted from direct combat, such as infantry and elite special operations units.[2] In January 2013 the Department of Defense dropped its last remaining rules restricting women from serving in combat, and each branch is currently in the process of assessing what roles women will have in the future, given this shift.[3] In addition to men being numerically dominant and having unlimited access to all dimensions of the military, the jobs and lifestyles of those in the military are associated with societal ideals of masculinity prevalent in the United States (Burke 2004; Enloe 1983, 2000). This gendering of the military is a powerful and effective trope that encourages strong bonds between men, the iconic "band of brothers": men who are physically and emotionally capable of collaborating in the defense of their country and in offensive attacks on enemies, at the same time that they care enough about one another to do whatever is necessary to protect and ultimately save the lives of their brothers and defend their country's citizenry. Some of the strongest resistance to including women in the military, especially in combat units, exists specifically because it is felt they would disrupt this masculine bonding (Mackenzie 2012). Though there have been some changes in military culture since the 1990s, in many cases women in the military are expected to participate in and embrace this masculine culture (see Gutmann 2000; McKelvey 2007). Despite this emphasis on masculinity, the physical and emotional demands placed on troops of any gender who are engaged in warfare produce and necessitate a vast range of emotional and social needs that often explode attempts to control one's gendered being. Music intertwines with nuanced negotiations of gender. It is used to express gendered identities and evoke certain types of gendered emotions and behaviors, at the same time that it can be used in gender conflict and healing.

DOING GENDER

In using the terms "masculine" and "feminine," I am not subscribing to a gender binary that views people as existing in clearly differentiated biological or social categories; rather, I am referring to reified concepts of gender that shape much sociocultural thinking in the United States, not only about differences between men and women, but also about all sorts of things that are ascribed some type of gender, such as behavior, musical taste, and emotion. Great strides have been made in scholarly discourse in understanding that gender categories are constructs, and that in reality gender is messy and is better understood as a spectrum. Most people have a range of qualities, tastes, and abilities that could be considered "male" or "female" using the categories within a constructed gender binary; gender is fluid and flexible and the manifestation of ongoing processes of social construction and navigation (West and Zimmerman 1987). Analyzing social practice in relation to ongoing social conceptions based on a gender binary is only useful because social constructions of gender continue to be reified in U.S. social spaces, though in diverse and complex ways. The culture of the military, because it is so strongly identified as a space for men to do male stuff, even when women are active participants, is especially defined in gendered ways that promote and perpetuate the gender binary within the context of overlapping patriarchal power structures (cf. Pin-Fat and Stern 2005). Jennifer Silva's study of women in ROTC corroborates this point. She found that women in ROTC enjoy the opportunity to break gender barriers and participate in militaristic activities and roles associated with masculinity. They do not, however, typically contest the very notions of gender dualism:

Both the men and the women in my sample drew upon traditional understandings of masculinity and femininity in order to delineate between men's work and women's work, linking masculinity and soldiering in a fundamental and inextricable way that is always in juxtaposition to femininity. While women felt empowered to the extent that they could defy traditionally feminine expectations, none of them questioned the social construction of masculinity or femininity, instead interpreting these concepts as natural, biological and fixed. (2008, 947)

In patriarchal social systems, power is integrally linked to masculinity, and "the common feature of the dominant forms of contemporary masculinity is that manhood is equated with having some sort of power" (Kaufman 2006, 186).[4] As Michael Kaufman explains, this power can be a positive ideal, as in the "potential for using and developing our human capacities." It can also have a "more negative manifestation," such as the "capacity to impose control on others and on our own unruly emotions. It means controlling material resources around us" (2006, 186). The culture of masculinity within the military encapsulates these conceptions of power across the spectrum, though control over one's emotions and over others is often emphasized. Especially at lower ranks, ideals of masculinity in the military are stereotypically based on a very narrow definition of what it means to be male, though in reality many different types of characteristics and personality traits, all of which are typically defined as masculine in the United States or are socially acceptable for masculine-defined men, permeate military jobs and hierarchies. The narrow definition that is emphasized in much military discourse and activity corresponds to "hypermasculinity": "expressions of extreme, exaggerated or stereotypical masculine attributes or traits" (Rosen et al. 2003, 326; see also Mosher and Sirkin 1984). Hypermasculinity is often exemplified by physical strength—sometimes demonstrated with corporal displays of visibly bulging muscles—aggression, violence, confidence, independence, fearlessness, ability to control emotions, virility, and heterosexual attraction to women, and always in the role of sexual penetrator regardless of the gender of a sexual partner. The sexual objectification and denigration of women is often integral to hypermasculinity in the military (Burke 2004; Morris 1996), as is homophobia and transphobia (Belkin and Bateman 2003); gender discrimination has been a widespread problem across the branches (see Francke 1997). This extreme emphasis on masculinity permeates much of military social, cultural, and occupational life, as exemplified in military folklore, which is pregnant with misogynistic and homophobic folk speech, songs, chants, rituals, and folk beliefs that articulate, reinforce, and perpetuate ideas of what is masculine, differentiated from all that is not (Burns 2003; Dundes and Pagter 1991; Weems 2012; Mechling 2012).

When I asked army veteran Joseph how masculinity is defined in the military, he responded: by "traditional masculine norms," which he explained as including the values of protecting one's family and a willingness to go out and fight if the family needs it. He described masculinity as a "rough aesthetic" with an emphasis on being "tough" and "all things that aren't feminine," such as "not being weak" and relating to other men in "ways that all think are masculine." He also mentioned the values of respect, honor, and brotherhood. When asked the same question, Pete explained that "masculinity overall is rampant in the military. It's the big boys club, so there's always a bit of cockiness and strutting, but then again I was in the Marines so it may have just been us." He explained that within the Marines, there were "the normal marines" and then the "G.I. Joes" or the "Secret Squirrel Marines," whom he described as "the guys that buy their own additional armor and gear, carry 20+ magazines, tape their blood type on their boots, and generally are first to go out the wire when deployed. They're the self-styled special forces, ready for anything." He explained that he "ended up like that after the first deployment," but that it was not about how he felt about war, but rather "about being highly trained, always preparing for the [worst], and being ready to go at a moment's notice for anything."

As Joseph's and Pete's explanations suggest, definitions of masculinity in the military tend to correspond to traits important for being a successful warrior. One needs to be physically strong, confident, willing to confront danger to defend and protect others, and able to overcome one's fears to engage successfully in combat. Yet this narrow definition is problematic because many other qualities, which are as much associated with masculinity in popular U.S. conceptions of gender, are equally and sometimes more necessary and celebrated in the military, thus suggesting that the idea of multiple masculinities is more appropriate for thinking about masculinity in the military. Here I am not just using "multiple masculinities" to refer to the fact that masculinity in different social and cultural contexts encapsulates differing constellations of gendered ideals, (e.g., Connell 1993; Messner 1997). Rather, I am considering the multiple, fluid, overlapping ways of masculine identity making that happens within particular moments and contexts, in this case in military cultural spaces. Tony Coles makes the important point that there is not just "hegemonic" masculinity, using the term as developed by R. W. Connell (1987), and then alternate masculinities. Multiple dominant masculinities, with the plural emphasized, exist. Coles gives the example of a "slender, fit, young, aggressive businessman dressed in his designer-label suit," who exudes the appropriate manliness associated with success in his business environment, compared to the appropriate manliness associated with the "working-class pub," where "dominant masculinity may be epitomized by the unkempt, middle-aged man with a large beer belly who can consume vast quantities of alcohol" (2007, 33). In each case the men epitomize masculinity in that environment and as such enjoy dominant positions in those specific contexts. Yet when each moves into the other's domain, his status changes, and even within a single context, status can shift depending on other contextual factors, for example, who else is present, race/ethnicity, wealth, and so on. To complicate things further, even within a single environment, multiple dominant masculinities can exist and be celebrated. When reading an earlier draft of this chapter, Nate pointed out that in Pete's example, "the self-styled SF [Special Forces] grunt's performance of hyperwarrior mask both elevates and denigrates his masculine status dependent on where he's at and who's around, ranging from hero to joke." Regardless of the intention of the person projecting a particular gender identity, the performance can be interpreted by different audiences in multiple ways, some of which may be contradictory. This example raises an important point about the social construction of masculinity. As Jay Mechling emphasizes, "the fragility of the construction, maintenance, and constant repair of masculinity means that the boy and adult male must constantly 'prove' their masculinity" (2005, 218). This ongoing need for affirming gender identity shapes much of the ongoing competition, joking, and harassment that happen in military spaces.

Just as Stephen Meyer (2001) distinguished between the "rough masculinity" of unskilled laborers in the automotive industry and the "respectable masculinity" that arises from the skilled craftsman's traditions, many military jobs requiring the most physicality, danger, and combat are associated with rough masculinity, while those involving less danger and higher levels of education are often associated with "respectable masculinity." Within the military, such qualities as duty, honor, intelligence, discipline, leadership, skill, and coordination, which are arguably often associated with masculinity, are just as important as physicality and aggression, though different gendered qualities are associated with different types of jobs and ranks (Rosen et al. 2003; Morris 1996). Furthermore, some qualities that might be gendered as female—for example, compassion, nurturing, and fragility—are omnipresent in military settings and are sometimes encouraged.

There is also a discrepancy between the ethos of hypermasculinity and the actual structure of the military. As C. Lutz explains, there is a "contradiction between the imperative to be free and autonomous—seen as the birthright of each American, but especially men—and the hierarchy and compulsion of military life" (2001, 230). Though independence tends to be emphasized as one of the most important traits of hypermasculinity, in fact, troops operate within hierarchies in which they are required to follow the directives of their commanding officers rather than exercise individual agency. Furthermore, military structures and strategies are built on interdependence; troops have to rely on one another for their well-being and to successfully carry out missions. As marine veteran Nate explained it, team-building exercises emphasize both individualism and collaboration: each individual has to do his or her part well in order for the group to function successfully. These contradictions between societal ideals about masculine power and the reality are concentrated in the military, yet they exist everywhere and are especially important for considering the gendering of certain musical styles, such as heavy rap and metal genres, whose performers tend to have much less social power than their music making suggests (Walser 1993; Berger 1999; Rose 1994; Lipsitz 1994).

Another complicating factor is that there is great variance in the gender composition of different units and branches within the military; some are all male, while others have varying numbers of women. The air force and medic units, for example, generally have a larger percentage of women than do the Marines or infantry units. The gender makeup of a unit often has an impact on the level of hypermasculinity that prevails, though my interviews suggest that it is always present to some extent (see Rosen et al. 2003).

GENRE, MASCULINITY, AND IDENTITY

Music contributes to the gendering of all sorts of cultural spaces, and the predominance of certain musical genres associated with hypermasculinity plays a large role in the masculinization of military culture. Individual and collective listening, though tied to individual taste and agency, is shaped by and contributes to the constitution of the cultural environment, thus complicating the individuality of musical selections (Walser 1994; Rose 1994). Though in Western cultures taste is often considered to be something that is personal and agentic, I agree with those who, influenced by Pierre Bourdieu's *Distinction: A Social Critique of the Judgment of Taste* (1984), argue that taste is not natural or personal, but is "a means by which social distinctions are made" (Dibben 2002, 123). As in any environment where certain cultural practices and gendered expressions dominate, taste creates pressure on others within the milieu to conform. Listening to the same types of music can reinforce a sense of communal identity, friendship, and belonging, and in this case the communal is defined partly by gender.

Music helps people "formulate and express" individual identities (Hargreaves et al. 2002, 1) at the same time that people use music to communicate to others their values and attitudes. It also contributes to people allying themselves with various social categories, such as age, gender, race, nationality, and so on. As Nicholas Cook put it, "in today's world, deciding what music to listen to is a significant part of deciding and announcing to people not just who you 'want to be' . . . but who you are" (1998, 5). The military is interesting culturally because it comprises a dominant culture—the U.S. service—as well as numerous subcultures based on branch, rank, jobs, gender, ethnicity, class, and so forth. Music is used in the construction of the dominant cultures *and* subcultures, especially during public displays of listening, at the same time that it allows for more individualized and nuanced ways of expressing oneself or feeling about oneself.

The majority of troops, especially within enlisted ranks, are young men, and many listened, at least in public spaces, to music by men that reinforced a particular type of masculinity. Within smaller groups or friendship dyads or trios, people got together and listened to a greater variety of music collectively, and certainly individuals listened to all sorts of music on their own. But in larger collective spaces the listening tended to be more narrowly restricted to those forms associated with the dominant group or with acceptable expressions of masculinity. Aggressive music produced by men, usually with male voices expressing violent content, permeated much of the soundscape of war, thus contributing to an environment that was defined by and encouraged this type of hypermasculinity.

The prevalence of heavy rap and metal genres in the military was partly attributable to their popularity among the demographics—gender, age, class, ethnicity/race—to which a large number of enlisted personnel belong. The two largest demographic contingents in the military are whites—who as mentioned previously made up 69.8 percent of the military population in 2011—and African Americans, who made up 16 percent.[5] The popularity of rap among African American U.S. troops corresponds to its prevalence among African Americans in the country generally, especially those from lower socioeconomic backgrounds, the population from which many African American troops come. The popularity of rap among troops of all ethnic backgrounds is also attributed to its general popularity among youth across race/ethnic categories in the United States outside the military. The dominance of these genres is also explained by the fact that in many ways they resonate with the emotional and physical realities in which people at war find themselves and that these musical styles are popular among the social groups from which many in the military come. As Deena Weinstein emphasizes, "the essential sonic element in heavy metal is power, expressed as sheer volume," and war is about nothing if not power (2000 [1991], 23).

Multiple factors contribute to the gendering of these genres. The majority of the artists are male. Though there are women artists, they are in the minority and were rarely mentioned as being on the playlists of those I interviewed, regardless of gender identity. Though there are plenty of angry people of all genders who do not conform to ideals of manliness and who participate in music making, they were rarely mentioned in interviews. When I asked Penny about her choice to listen to what she called "angry white boy music," which she described as "very masculine, very angry," rather than to women artists, she answered that this was the angry music she was familiar with at the time and that she did not know many angry female musicians. She then elaborated:

> I also think it's the military. They teach you to shun your gender. It teaches you that anything female is weak, you know "you stupid fucking pussy. You can't hack it. Go back to mama."

Asked about her choice to listen to so many male artists, Angie answered that men dominated these and other musical forms: "Isn't just about every music dominated by men? I sure think it is. There aren't that many metal or punk bands with women in them, at least that are good." The dominance of male artists contributes to the genres' masculinization.

In addition to men dominating the scenes as performers, other dimensions of the music also accentuate hypermasculinity. Robert Walser eloquently describes the gendering of 1980s metal:

> Heavy metal often stages fantasies of masculine virtuosity and control Musically, heavy metal articulates a dialectic of controlling power and transcendent freedom. Metal songs usually include impressive technical and rhetorical feats on the electric guitar, counterposed with an experience of power and control that is built through vocal extremes, guitar power chords, distortion, and sheer volume of bass and drums. Visually, metal musicians typically appear as swaggering males, leaping and strutting about the stage, clad in spandex, scarves, leather, and other visually noisy clothing, punctuating their performances with

phallic thrusts of guitars and microphone stands. . . . [H]eavy metal draws upon many sources of power: mythology, violence, madness, the iconography of horror. (1993, 109)

Even when song texts might not correspond to hypermasculinity, the sonic dimensions—the power chord, the heavily distorted and amplified electric guitar, and the driving percussiveness of the music—nevertheless fit hypermasculine music conventions, masking the lyrical content with the dominant sonic frame. And the very name of the genre, "heavy metal," evokes power and potency (Walser 1993, 1; see also Weinstein 2000 [1991]).

In heavier rap genres, song texts are usually far more dominant than in metal, but again, multiple aspects of the performance—lyrics, instrumentation, beat, gender of performers—exemplify the doing of hypermasculinity. As Miles White puts it, aggressive rap performances "create extremely intensified affective investments in malevolence constructed in sound, lyrical choices, story narrative, and gestures of the body that confirm the most egregious discourses around black male deviancy" (2011, 24). In his consideration of these genres and masculinity, White emphasizes that this music not only perpetuates misogyny, but has helped to "(re)construct and (re)define notions of masculinity and ideals of male performance in which misogynistic and homophobic attitudes are encouraged through the rejection of the feminine" (2011, 3).

Bodies and performance are key to the masculinization of these genres. Women in both scenes tend to play the role of fans or sexual partners, and sometimes appear as attractive sexy female backup vocalists or dancers in stage performances or videos, which contributes to the image of the male performers as heterosexual, virile sexual subjects. The lyrics of heavy metal and rap tend to be about subjects that correspond with hypermasculinity (dominance, sex with women, violence, and aggression).

It is not just that the majority of bodies that perform are male, but also what these bodies look like and what the performers display and do with their bodies that is important. The physicality of performers—the musculature of their bodies, gestures, clothing, jewelry, body art, hair styles, postures, facial expressions, movements, manner of handling the microphone, speech, and spatial relationships with one another and the audience—all contribute to idealizations of masculinity. In the case of rap, the predominance of black male bodies is significant because they embody a fetishized (and very problematic) übermasculinity in U.S. popular culture. "For white adolescent males coming to terms with issues of masculinity and identity, the image of the swaggering black male in hip-hop videos is an appealing figure that has become iconic of an authentic and desirable representation of masculinity to be emulated" (White 2011, 23).

The popularity of heavy rap in the military is tied to problematic intersections of race and gender that permeate constructions of masculinity in mainstream U.S. culture. Though there is a long history of a variety of rap genres—some of which feature women artists and much of which is political, with lyrics that are more philosophical and not violent or misogynist—the type of rap that has taken the country, and by extension the military, by storm is what is often referred to as gangsta rap, which epitomizes negative stereotypes of black men (Rose 2008). Its popularity among troops of many cultural backgrounds is therefore not surprising. As White explains, African American men have come to occupy an iconic role since the nineteenth century in U.S. popular culture that has been "central to the formation of masculinity and working-class identity and that reached an apotheosis with hip-hop culture and hardcore rap music beginning in the 1980s" (2011, 4). The mainstreaming of hip-hop culture idealizes the "the idea of a hard man—a revisitation of the black brute who is immune to physical and emotional pain." This fetishization of a particular idea of black male masculinity has had a "transfiguring effect on contemporary constructions of masculine performance . . . for males of all racial and ethnic groups" (2011, 4)(see Bryant 2003). This "hard man" image is exactly the persona celebrated by many in the military. Troops of any ethnicity, race, or gender can perform masculinity in their public displays of listening to these musical choices. From veterans' accounts, African American troops are more likely to listen to a wider variety of rap genres, whereas white/ Euro-American and others are more likely to restrict their listening to those genres that correlate with hypermasculinity, such as "gangsta rap."

Other musical styles are equally aggressive and could have but did not compete with aggressive metal and rap to be the violent music of choice for service men and women, such as some varieties of punk rock, Goth, industrial techno, and narco corridos. These styles are associated with populations not at the center or top of the social/power hierarchies of the military. Though some interviewees described listening to a lot of punk, they generally explained that they were in a minority and that rap and metal tended to prevail.

Country music genres were also pervasive in the soundscapes of these wars. As with metal and rap, their popularity was partly attributable to the demographics of the military. A significant percentage of white troops came from southern states and rural areas, places where country genres are popular; for some, listening to country music at war was an extension of their prewar musical taste. The category of country music comprises numerous subgenres associated with a variety of types of performances, sounds, and gendered articulations. Though the sonic qualities, usually much slower paced and lyrical, do not express masculinity in the same ways that the heavier rap and metal genres do, much country music is nevertheless steeped in masculine ideals epitomized by the southern white working-class male (Malone 2002; Saucier 1986; Fox 2005).

As in rap and metal, male country music artists are numerically dominant and overall enjoy more commercial success and exposure than female artists, though there are plenty of very successful female country performers. Within the context of the cultural milieus in which country music is popular, male country artists and fans fit squarely within masculine expectations, for example the frequent displays of alcohol consumption and woman chasing that permeate both country lyrics by male artists and the public portrayals of the lives of some of the most famous musicians (cf. Saucier 1986). Within these wars, the popularity of country was attributable to a combination of the large numbers of people serving who came from regions and cultures where country is especially popular and the fact that country music has largely been deemed the genre of patriotism (Willman 2005; Sampert and Treiberg 2007).

The lyrics of the overtly patriotic country songs do articulate a masculine ethos celebrated and encouraged throughout the military. Though they may not sonically be deemed hypermasculine, some of the pro-mission country songs' lyrics conform to the aggression expected of war. A number of people I interviewed remembered Toby Keith's song "American Soldier," mentioned in the previous chapter. Unlike the rap and metal music, this song's sonic dimensions do not shout manliness: Keith's voice rises above the instrumentation to produce clearly audible lyrics that speak to troops and their families. The rhythm is slow, and the instrumentation is not distorted, loud, overlapping, or daring. The song text itself, however, reinforces a masculine ethos that is very important to military culture; in this case, the type of masculinity emphasized has to do with honor, courage, and dedication to service. It portrays troops as those ready to sacrifice their lives for "you"; they take a stand, they are proud, they are dutiful and honorable. The song acknowledges that there are men *and* women in the military and that they stand up together, yet the idea of people taking it upon themselves to courageously do all that is necessary to defend the freedom of their country and fellow citizens has typically been coded as masculine.

Keith's song, "Courtesy of the Red, White and Blue (The Angry American)," is more overtly aggressive and conforms to ideals of hypermasculinity. As in "American Soldier," the lyrics dominate in this song, though it has a faster, driving rhythm and features more electric guitar than the previous example. The aggressiveness of the singing style increases significantly when he comes to the "boot in your ass" line. The song text clearly articulates a spirit of domination and overtly masculine sexual imagery of penetrating the enemy.[6]

MANLY MUSIC, MANLY MEN (AND WOMEN)

It has been widely documented that many troops listened to musical styles associated with hypermasculinity right before exiting the wire for patrols or missions. In the next chapter I discuss the emotional dimensions of this practice. Here, the relationship between the gendering of the music and the gendered expectations for troops deserves attention. Many of those I interviewed explained that they listened to these types of music when the characteristics required of them corresponded to those amplified by the music. Prior to entering the war zone, where being assertive, aggressive, confident, fearless, and potentially violent was necessary to the survival of everyone in their unit, many listened to very aggressive, "masculine" music. When I asked why they listened to this music before going out on missions, many explained that it was similar to listening to aggressive music to motivate them when they exercised or prepared for a competitive athletic activity. These explanations were not framed in gendered terms, though they relate to gender in that men and women listened to music associated with aggressive masculinity in order to enhance that quality in themselves. The music served to focus and direct their energy toward the task at hand or that was coming. Sometimes consciously and sometimes not, troops listened to manly music to charge their own manliness.

The contradiction between ideals of hypermasculinity and the structures of the military extended to the dominance of these hypermasculine genres. As White reminds us, the fetishization of heavy rap and masculinity is based on "representations of black masculinity that depend upon and perpetuate the imagined malevolence of black males generally." In addition, the gendered representations associated with heavy rap are "historically marked by notions around criminality, deviance, and pathology" (2011, 23). While aggressive metal genres are steeped in different social and historical imaginings, like rap, the masculinity celebrated is one of deviance and pathology (think of makeup and costuming, mosh pits, and violent lyrics) (see Arnett 1996). This association of criminality and deviance with the dominant masculinity in the military is paradoxical because it contrasts so markedly with the official culture of the institution, which is highly structured, emphasizes conformity, punishes deviance, and is charged with controlling others within its population and in the populations where it stages its missions. Leaving the wire, moving into "enemy territory," blurred these demands for lawfulness. Though the military emphasizes hierarchy, following orders, and promoting lawfulness, what was required "downrange" was a confusing combination of this control and a willingness to defy typical "lawfulness," for example, driving large vehicles quickly across spaces, breaking down doors, and shooting at people. Nate explained that "what most infantry units are tasked with, for example, clearing a structure, is very much like what is required of any 'lawful' police exercise (set-up, entry, tools for entry, etc.), except ROE [rules of engagement] allow for what stateside would be illegal (whether violence against targets or "contaminating" the crime scene/ pilfering property, etc.)." Listening to music that exuded badass masculinity helped troops navigate their own contradictory positioning and activities, as well as helping to push their emotions and thoughts about what they were doing into the background. And as considered in the next chapter, at the same time that these genres reinforced the masculinity that defines the dominant culture of the military, thus reinforcing the status quo, they also provided outlets for resisting the hierarchies by offering opportunities for feeling rage, expressing criticism, and otherwise rebelling via socially sanctioned avenues.

The expectation was that all troops had to be manly in order to survive and appropriately serve in their capacities as service men and women (McKelvey 2007). This pressure to be a specific type of gendered person could impact musical listening, in that people often felt some pressure for their musical listening to conform to that of others in order to not have their masculinity questioned. Inasmuch as a person could display listening to hypermasculine music to perform masculinity, someone who listened to music deemed feminine could be interpreted as performing femininity, something that was not celebrated nor often acceptable. Leo Braudy (2003) suggests that masculinity in the military is defined through its opposition to what it is not, feminine; thus troops of all genders frequently performed a masculine identity by distancing themselves from what they were not supposed to be, or in this case, what they were not supposed to be listening to, "girly" music (see Mechling 2005). For women, there was an expectation that they would be feminine, so there was less policing of their listening. Men, on the other hand, could be derided for their musical selections. When Gabe chose to listen to more "mellow" and "melodic" music, his roommate chided him for listening to "gay music," and many other interviewees similarly remembered people criticizing them for listening to music that they labeled feminine or homosexual: by inference their gender identity and sexual orientation (mandatory heterosexuality) was put in question because of their musical selections.

Danny, who listened to Norah Jones and Alanis Morissette, described people making fun of him, for example, saying, "What, you listen to girl stuff? Like are you gay or something?" He also "got a lot of crap" for listening to Dave Matthews. His friend Eric described similar experiences:

A lot of people thought I was cheesy, you know. There's this separation between infantrymen and medics. And it's—you know, a lot of my infantry guys would probably harass me for saying this, but there's just this different mentality. They're just as educated as I am—well not all of them, but most of them are. The intelligence level is there, I mean, obviously infantry is, does have the lowest requirement for entrance into the job, whereas medic has the highest, you know so there is that. But for the most part, that's just something you wanted to do. You've got people who like to hunt, people who like to shoot guns, think all that stuff's cool. Where there's me, I'm just doing it because I don't want to die, I don't want you guys to die, you know. Whereas some of them, it was like playing GI Joe every day. So they thought I was a little cheesy. Something bad would happen and I'd be, "Oh why don't you come back to my room. Let's talk, do a little debrief." I'd turn on some kind of music, and they'd be like, "What's this crap?" "Oh, you know, it's just something I like to do, is listen to music that's mellow, something where you can just sit there and get lost in the words, and forget about it for a couple hours. All of a sudden you find yourself, you've fallen asleep and you've actually been able to rest before the next mission."

Eric said that though others in his unit "thought he was a dork," he also proved himself, presumably as a heterosexual man, in other domains, lessening the social stigma associated with his musical taste. He explained:

I do feel that they considered me to be one of them as far as, you know, they saw me do everything that they did. I never backed down from any of the things that they had to do, nor did I take any time off that I could have taken or anything like that. So I worked to earn their respect and whatever, but they still thought I was a dork.

Craig similarly was sometimes chastised for listening to the Canadian singer-songwriter Sarah McLachlan. He frequently listened to her album *Surfacing* at night for its calming effect. Though people gave him a hard time, he said that a number of other men in his unit regularly borrowed the CD, indicating that even in contexts where rough masculinity dominated, individuals nevertheless embodied more complex articulations of gender: a man could both be a gunner on a tank and listen to a woman's soothing singing, as long as he had proven himself to be a highly effective gunner. Craig, Eric, Danny, and other men I interviewed chose to listen to women artists specifically because they felt these artists were clearly distinct from what they were experiencing. Eric explained that he listened to Ani DiFranco, whose music he had not been previously familiar with, because "it was totally different from what I was going through, which was what I was looking for."

Some were able to balance an identity that was masculine enough to be acceptable while also listening to "girly" music or otherwise demonstrating qualities deemed feminine. Others suffered greatly from being labeled less than adequately masculine. Shannon, for example, explained that in his unit, there was a man who was "an absolutely amazing" concert pianist who was treated very poorly by his unit mates. Shannon explained that he was recruited to be an engine mechanic, which is the position for the "real rough necks of the air force." Not conforming to this toughness, "he just got absolutely, basically spit on [by] the other guys in his unit." One wonders whether blaring "Bodies" or busting out a rap would have mitigated the abuse he received for being a girly pianist.

MUSIC, POWER, AND HIERARCHIES

Collective spaces, such as gyms, cafeterias, TV rooms, or arcades, were used by men and women, but again, men usually dominated numerically, and men's musical choices and male artists usually dominated the soundscapes. Work spaces were coed and often dominated by men; thus my description of masculine culture and collective listening is relevant to a great extent for the musical listening environments of women as well as men. The only real places that were dominated by women were sleeping spaces, usually segregated by gender, but the extent to which they were divided based on gender varied from situation to situation. Some women had a closed off space to themselves, while others, such as Tina, mentioned in previous chapters, shared a physical space with men that was divided only by a curtain or other material that was permeable to music.

Because there were fewer women overall, there were also fewer areas in which women resided together in a segregated space, which limited the diversity of possibilities for alternate musical listening. Men could segregate into smaller groups and spread into the more numerous sleeping and work spaces to listen to a variety of music in small groups. Women, by contrast, tended to be congregated in fewer spaces, thus giving them fewer options for diversifying where they spent their nonwork time. In Angie's combat ship of 350 people, there was one berthing for women. This means that a man could listen to music with other men in his own berthing or in any of the other ones. A woman, by contrast, would have only a single berthing for her single-sex musical listening. And because there were fewer women, there were obviously fewer women listening to less music, thus reducing the chance of meeting others with shared esoteric tastes.

The situation varied greatly from unit to unit, but what I surmise from my interviews is that in addition to there not being a lot of single gender spaces for women, women often tended not to aggregate among themselves to the same extent men did. Angie explained that in her unit the women were basically nice to one another, but friendships with men were more important to them than were those with other women. My sense was that small groups of women might have been friends and might have listened to music together, but that by and large, women tended not to forge bonds because of gender and create social spaces that were distinct from men. Women befriended other women and shared music in more private ways, listening on collective listening devices in restricted space (rather than dominating a large soundscape) or listening together on headphones. Tina, for example, described listening to music with her best friend, each listening to her own headphones with her own selection while simultaneously talking to one another. Because women were negotiating belonging within very male-dominated spaces, there was an added incentive to keep their musical listening more private, unless they were playing music that emphasized masculinity.

Sexual and gendered hierarchies impacted power and musical choices. The politics of who selected music for public listening was influenced by gender. As with musical listening spaces everywhere, usually some people were either trusted for their musical taste or had more social power in a given situation and were thus the ones who selected the music. In the military context, this hierarchy could be a product of rank. Craig explained that his whole company would do PT (physical training) together in a company football field while two men sat on the roof overlooking them with machine guns "guarding everyone." "Mild music" often played in the background. Asked who selected the music, he answered, "It would depend on who was the highest-ranking person out there." As he put it, they "kinda forced it [their musical selections] on everybody," usually "either classic rock, rap, or R&B."

Similarly, Andy described working in a medical unit:

ANDY: Well, the surgeon's the main man because they're doing all the, they're the highest-ranking person aside from anesthesia. They're the man, so we have to let them, you know, we can't have our music on. If, for example, my music was playing, it happened several times, they would just be like "turn that off!" They're not used to that kind of music or whatever I'm playing. They have the upper hand in the military, it's rank says all, so you kind of just say, "Okay, sir." But when they weren't in there, it was whoever, it was free game for anybody pretty much.

AUTHOR: So would you say that they'd come in and you'd say quickly, "We have to turn this down?"

ANDY: Pretty much, yeah, or they'd come in, and we'd rebel. We would usually rebel and just have it playing, and then they would come in and have us turn it off. The worst thing that can happen is the music going off.

AUTHOR: Did you ever leave it on when they said turn it off?

ANDY: No.

AUTHOR: Yeah . . . .

ANDY: Because they'll just make things horrible, and there is a patient there, and that's what matters at that time, so no.

AUTHOR: So your rebellion could only go so far?

ANDY: So far.

Similar types of dynamics emerged in less formal relationships of power. As in many mixed-sex environments, men often had more social clout than women, especially when it came to determining what dominated the soundscape. Tina did not remember ever having made a selection, nor did she think the other women she worked and lived with usually did, "so it was mostly male music." The reluctance of Tina and other women in her cohort to air music from their playlists could also have been related to being women in a male-dominated environment. When asked whether women ever made the musical choices in his work environment, Andy could not remember that happening. He explained that the women in his unit would usually "just listen to whatever we [the men] listened to, or if they had an objection to it, they would say so, like 'that song is too violent for me.'" He elaborated:

> Especially for rap songs. They would be like, "What is this?" Others would just go along with the flow because there were a lot of males in my section. I don't know if they felt that they should hold back and censor their thoughts, but they never really said too much.

He remembered only a few times when particular female surgical technicians, who outranked the medics, "would use their music, until somebody said it was bad or something." I asked if he remembered what these women played, and he answered "a lot of girly songs, like I don't know, trance music and Britney Spears type stuff, that's what we would call everything as a genre, we've kind of made up the 'Britney Spears type stuff.'" He remembered:

> When that Colby girl came out, Colby Caillat, she came out on MySpace. They [the women in his unit] were all talking about her. "Omigod! We love her voice!" And you know, we are all these hardcore guys looking around, thinking "What are you talking about?" So the soft side for us was buried. For them, they were still just living it up.

The derision of the "Britney Spears type stuff" by the men reinforced masculinity: people in male bodies derided people in female bodies listening to music performed by people in female bodies that corresponded to their ideas about femininity. This chiding was part of the constant need to assert and reaffirm masculinity, which often also involved undermining others' manly status. The subtext was that if I teased you for listening to Spears. I did not listen to that music and thus proved that I was more of a man than you.

Andy's memories highlight divisions between conceptions of masculinity and femininity and how they were tied to both female and male bodies, but also to different musical choices. In the quote above he suggested that men do have a "soft side," but that it was buried deep, especially in this environment, whereas women had more freedom for "living up" that side of themselves. Though these divisions existed, and there was a lot of pressure about what was appropriate listening, there was also a degree of acceptance expressed in Andy's description of this incident. Yes, he and the other men rejected the women's music and teased them for listening to it. But much of the criticism happened through joking. Though the men made up a generic label for the women's music, calling it "Britney Spears type," and harassed them for listening to it, the women nevertheless continued to listen to their music and to do so where they could be heard, thus suggesting a level of comfort and acceptance of the women by the men. This example is illustrative of how even spaces heavily defined as masculine are generally far more complex and allow for greater gender variability than is sometimes evident. There was a heavy emphasis on performing masculinity and often repercussions for doing otherwise at the same time that there was tacit acceptance of a much wider gender spectrum.

Because Andy presented this musical listening in such gendered terms, I asked him whether he thought any of the men who publicly displayed their listening to "hard stuff" and publicly rejected the "girly music" might have listened to some of this more "girly" music privately. Andy answered, "I'm sure they did, and even myself. I found myself emotional sometimes after listening to a corny song." His answer acknowledged that he and other manly men in his unit had a "soft side" and exemplified far more complex gender identities than was suggested by their more public articulations of hypermasculinity.

Hierarchies of musical dominance also existed within single-sex working or living arrangements. Angie explained that in her berthing she did not mind, and even enjoyed, listening to the music that was playing, often selected by the African American women in her unit, though she never chose music for the group. Similarly, among the men I interviewed, whether they did or did not make the musical choices depended on the group they were with. Mark, for example, explained that though he had little control in other domains, he tended to dominate in his living quarters, the shipping container he shared with four other men. He remembered that he "was like, 'I want to listen to this. I don't really care what you guys think.'" Though he joked about his musical domination, he also described listening to a lot of music enjoyed by the others in his sleeping area. However, he also remembered that one soldier in his unit was very much disliked by the others because he made their lives miserable, so they "didn't allow him to do anything," including selecting the group musical listening.

Musical dominance and power to select also emerged in manifestations of conflict. Though the emphasis in much scholarship on masculinity has been on male and female relationships, there are also hierarchies of masculinities among men, and music is one way that hierarchies were expressed and negotiated at war (Coles 2007, 33). Andy explained that people in his unit grouped together based on friendship and work bonds, but also based on cultural identifiers. Here he describes the ethnic divisions that characterized his unit:

I was in charge of all the lower soldiers, so there were twelve soldiers in that bay. And these guys were, you know, like the black guys in my unit, they kind of moved into their own corner. They had their own music playing all the time very loud, and it bothered a lot of people, so there were dislikings because of music choices and volume. I told them, "Hey, get a pair of headphones and you can listen to whatever you want, you know, but everybody else here, you need to have respect."

This example highlights differential masculine identities played out based on race/ethnicity; the black male soldiers arranged their sleeping quarters together and listened to music that Andy and his white cohort found invasive, thus contributing to a sonic division between the men. Power dynamics were also evident in this example, in which Andy described his often futile attempts to exert the authority he had over these men by encouraging them to listen to their music through headphones; they in turn used music to exercise their power despite their subordinate status. Though he was in the structurally dominant position in terms of the military hierarchy, the black men in the unit were in the dominant position when it came to control of the sonic environment in the sleeping quarters, suggesting that they probably successfully exerted power over their white peers in other domains as well.

MUSIC AND HETEROSEXUAL INTERACTION

During deployment, troops were physically isolated from a "normal" social world, and the military had an official policy that discouraged unmarried men and women in the military from engaging in sexual activity with one another, though this policy was not always followed (Brown 2008). Sex was therefore on the minds of many throughout deployments. Sex permeated conversations, musicking, joking, letter writing, e-mailing, Internet activities, video games, and movie watching. Because of rampant homophobia and the official "Don't Ask, Don't Tell" policy—which prohibited service men and women from admitting to being queer and was not repealed until after most of my interviewees returned from deployments—heteronormativity dominated the public displays of sexuality; music was one more avenue for expressing oneself sexually. Songs often referred to sexual or romantic liaisons with people of the opposite sex, and artists whose music troops interacted with performed their heterosexuality through the song lyrics, corporal performances and displays, and public commentary. By flooding the soundscape with this heteronormative music, troops contributed to the reinforcement of a heteronormative culture regardless of their individual sexual proclivities.

Music was also used to engage more directly with sexuality. People shared music selections to establish a connection with others based on shared taste, and it could be a form of flirtation, for example, when a person played a song that had sexually provocative lyrics in the presence of another to communicate attraction or as a sexual advance. This could be friendly and flirtatious or aggressive and harassing, depending on the lyrics and context. And sharing music was often an important activity for those in relationships. Even when not overtly sexual, music provided an avenue for physical intimacy, for example, when men in a unit danced together, sometimes suggestively, or took on roles of the opposite sex in musical performances or play for the sake of entertainment or veiled romance.

In addition to navigating sexual tensions and relations with others with whom they served, for troops music was also a way to engage with sexual and romantic partners far away, such as when troops sent to or received from their current or potential partners back home tracks or musical suggestions. An irony about hypermasculinity rooted in heteronormativity is that there is a "soft" side to men attracting women (and for that matter anyone) that does not correspond to hypermasculine qualities of aggression and sexual dominance. Most men who successfully romance women do not do so through aggressive displays, but rather through less "manly" strategies such as charm, warmth, and attention. Intimate and private interactions between heterosexual men and women or between men often include plenty of tender moments that contrast markedly with common assumptions about what it means to be a manly man. In other words, plenty of sexual interactions are not just about aggressive, virile men penetrating, but about a very contrasting gentleness. Men's public posturing can emphasize hypermasculinity, while the private exchange can integrate soft vulnerability.

These contradictions play out in people's musical listening. In my interview with Andy, for example, much of his discussion of gender in the military reinforced stereotypical ideas about hypermasculinity. Yet when discussing how music was tied to memories of home, he remembered listening to music that reminded him of love and intimacy, as did many other men I interviewed. For example "that Mario song, 'Let me love you,'" which he said came out as a big hit in Miami, where he lived before he joined the army:

It would remind me of being home. I'd think about being home the whole time I was there. And every day, I'm thinking about what I'm going to do when I get back. You know, how the first hug is going to be, and all that stuff.

The song, performed by a man, is directed to a female love interest, who is in a relationship with a man whose behavior conforms with hypermasculine ideals: he sleeps with other women, dominates the relationship, and lies to protect himself from her learning of his infidelities. The singer admonishes his competitor's behavior and pleads with his love interest to leave her boyfriend and choose him instead. He promises her that if he were "her man," he would treat her much better:

> You should let me love you
> Let me be the one to give you everything you want and need
> Baby good love and protection
> Make me your selection

While the song does embrace the idea of men protecting women, the singer is vulnerable, desirous, and not in control of the woman, but rather trying to convince her to switch from her current partner to him, a man who is presumably softer, gentler, and more respectful. Though an active participant in hypermasculinity, Andy listened to music such as this song in these moments to connect with his girlfriend, not to fantasize about sexual conquest, but rather about sharing a tender hug.

The heavy focus on aggressive sexuality within the military, not this intimate, gentle hug stuff, especially during war, is something that the women I interviewed discussed in great detail. On the one hand, many women experienced the military as a place that allowed them to resist traditional femininity and extend their gender identity because they were engaged in activities and cultural spaces that were identified as masculine (Silva 2008). On the other hand, regardless of their training as warriors, women continued to inhabit their female bodies in an environment where objectification and domination of women characterized the culture. The music that dominated their airspace often celebrated sexuality as domination and conquest, which largely correlated with how they were treated by at least some men in their units. In the minority in their units, a characteristic of their time in the military was that many were very sexually active, developing different types of sexual and emotional relationships, often with men in their units. In her memoir about her deployment to Iraq, Kayla Williams explained that as "a woman at war: you're automatically a desirable commodity, and a scarce one at that. We call it 'Queen for a Year'" (2005, 19). Some women enjoyed all the sexual attention; for others it could be oppressive, and for some it was a combination of both.

Many women enjoyed and participated in the sexual attention, taking advantage of the sexual opportunities readily at their disposal. Williams starts out her book by explaining the double bind for women in the military. According to her, there were two options: "If you are a woman and a soldier," to be a "slut" or a "bitch." She illustrated the difference by reciting an "old joke" frequently told during her deployment: "What's the difference between a bitch and slut? A slut will fuck anyone, a bitch will fuck anyone but you. So if she's nice or friendly, outgoing or chatty—she's a slut. If she's distant or reserved or professional—she's a bitch" (2005, 13). Williams goes on to describe in great detail her experiences in Iraq, which included both positive relationships with her male counterparts as well as the sexual harassment she received from some men, including an attempted rape by a man in her unit, and the power struggles with both her male and female superiors that she endured.

Angie explained that during her time in the navy, especially during her deployments, she was harassed constantly. Throughout her days there, men made comments about her body and whom they claimed she was having sex with, and she frequently heard men say that she would be raped. Though she fortunately was not raped, she lived in constant fear because of the never-ending threats. She recounted that one day she was dragged out of her bed into the hallway by a man; he did not rape her, but neither did he suffer any consequences for the physical assault.[7]

In Angie's case, what she described as never-ending harassment contributed to her suffering from severe depression and anxiety, which is addressed in the following chapter. Many other women in the military have come forward with stories of repeated sexual abuse by men in their units. At the time of this writing, the U.S. Department of Veterans Affairs (va) was screening all veterans seeking medical services, inquiring whether they had suffered from any form of sexual violence while in the military. One in five women and one in one hundred men responded that they had. These figures indicate the extent of the problem, though they reflect data only from those veterans who sought care from the va and those who were honest in their responses.[8]

Not every woman (or man) experienced so much sexual predation, though the one woman I interviewed who did not explained that in her unit the women were more fortunate than women in other units because the men in the unit took it upon themselves to be their protectors:

> The males in my unit were pretty protective of us. There were only about forty females on the base in total. So it could have been a really dangerous situation, which it wasn't for me, but it was for some of the other companies and units. The guys [in my unit], if they thought we were getting, like we were at dinner one night and this guy was over there bothering me, one of the guys was like, "Are you okay, sweetie?" So you know, that was kind of nice. It was really, really, really close knit.

Tina interpreted her more positive experience as being the exception in this sexually aggressive environment. Significantly, she attributed her more positive experience to men's agency—not only did the men in her unit choose not to harass the women, but they took it upon themselves to be their protectors. Even this more positive example nevertheless reaffirms that women were in danger from their "brothers in arms" and thus required protection from other brothers; the idea that men are the protectors of women is obviously a common trope of masculinity.

Sexual aggression toward men was also prevalent, though harder to discuss because of the stigma surrounding homosexuality (Hoyt et al. 2011). It was often harder for men to acknowledge to themselves and others that they were victims of sexual violence because of the double stigma of having been penetrated and not being man enough to have defended oneself. The contradiction between gender identity and experience could be especially profound in the military because of the heavy emphasis on hypermasculinity and heteronormativity.

The connection among sexual violence, gender harassment, and music is loose. I am not arguing that people listened to aggressive and misogynist, homophobic music and then proceeded to sexually dominate others. Rather, I am suggesting that in this hypermasculine environment, people listened to a lot of music that resonated with and reinforced particular ideas of what it meant to be a man or woman and what it meant to be a gendered sexual being, and that this culture was defined by what to some might be positive and negative values. On the one hand was the emphasis on honor, protecting, and caring for others. On the other hand was the emphasis on aggression, domination, and sexual conquest, which created an environment in which homophobia and sexual violence were rampant and largely condoned.

MUSIC AND HETERONORMATIVITY

Sexual orientation was also a part of this gendered culture. Under "Don't Ask, Don't Tell," the policy that ostensibly restricted military service to heterosexual men and women, people with alternate sexual orientations (what I will refer to generally as "queer") could serve as long as they kept it top secret. Under this law, which was repealed on September 20, 2011, heteronormativity was not only the social norm, but service members who revealed themselves (or were revealed by others) to be homosexual had to be fired from the armed forces (Belkin and Bateman 2003, 5). My research suggests that in some units, heteronormativity with its twin homophobia dominated, putting a lot of pressure on both queer and heterosexual soldiers to outwardly perform heterosexuality in order not to be suspect, not just because of concerns about being discharged from the military, but for fear of the social repercussions. As Pete explained, in his unit, "mimicking gay behavior or calling someone homophobic slurs was almost constant." Gay army veteran Noah remembered going to great lengths to try to pass as straight. He had a photograph of a female friend that he presented as his girlfriend, and he did much to try to hide the letters and interactions he had with his male partner, who lived in the United States. He was never found out, but he said that he was always fearful because people would get suspicious. While others had multiple photos of their female partners and acquired more throughout their deployments, Noah only had the one, raising suspicions about how attached to her he really was. For some queer troops, musical listening provided a covert means to identify with and express their sexuality. Noah remembered that he listened to the music of a band whose show he and his male partner had attended together as a way to connect with him and remember. Listening to this music was a transgressive act, because it was a direct engagement with his forbidden sexual relationship, yet it was an act that was easily masked, as no one had to know the significance of his musical selection.

Even under "Don't Ask, Don't Tell," some interviewees explained that in their units, homosexuality was not a big concern and that some people were known to be gay or lesbian and no one seemed to care. Pete, who identifies as heterosexual, did not know of anyone in the military who was gay, but he assumed that he probably served with some who did not reveal their sexual orientation. Though heteronormativity and homophobia dominated the culture of the military, my interviews, all conducted with people who were deployed before the revoking of "Don't Ask, Don't Tell," suggested that the acceptance of homosexuality was greater than is often portrayed in the media. As gay marine veteran and folklorist Mickey Weems put it, "in the intimate sphere of the squad bay, barracks, and hangar, men learn all kinds of things about each other, including sexual orientation" (2012, 154).

Pete said that he personally did not care about anyone's sexual orientation; what was important was whether he was "confident in their willingness to go down fighting to win the battle we'd face." Angie, who identifies as heterosexual and was in the navy, explained that some women in her unit were lesbian and that one man was very effeminate and flamboyant and open about being homosexual. Simon, who identifies as heterosexual, similarly remembered a very flamboyant gay man in his unit who was largely accepted and that many men who identified as heterosexual participated in playfully flirtatious banter with him. These examples suggest several realities. In some units people were not overly concerned about homosexuality. And even in contexts characterized by homophobia, sometimes an individual who was charismatic was able to pull off being flagrantly homosexual, even while others who were more subtle and less overtly expressive of their sexuality would be castigated. The man on Simon's ship was a large and strong African American whose sexuality was not associated with reduced masculinity, at least as far as his ability to physically meet the demands of his job, even if the object of his sexual desire did not conform with "hypermasculinity." Simon remembered one incident when the man was flirting with a heterosexual navy man during a task that involved lifting very heavy boxes. Angered at being the object of male flirtation, the recipient of the attention called him a "fucking faggot." The gay man quickly and aggressively threw a heavy box directly at the other man, demonstrating his physical prowess, and then immediately assumed a stereotypically gay male effeminate pose, with his hand on his hip, and asked, "Who's the faggot now?" This anecdote suggests that the reason this gay man was accepted was not only his charisma, but also his physicality and his high level of confidence; thus he proved himself to be adequately manly in domains other than his sexual orientation.

With the emphasis on hypermasculinity, men who exhibited less than masculine qualities ran the risk of being teased, ridiculed, or in some cases emotionally or physically harassed. What emerged from my research is that this dynamic did not happen equally across the board. Some men had a lot of license to express a variety of gendered ways of being, and they got away with it either because they were already well liked, charismatic, and respected, or they had proven themselves to be adequately masculine in other domains. For whatever reasons, these men were more likely to be left alone or at least only teased in friendship. Others became targets and were subjected to regular abuse. Someone with less confidence about his masculinity and sexuality, less physically capable, or more introverted would be more likely to be the target of homophobic comments and acts, ironically in some cases, regardless of his sexual orientation.

When I discussed these dynamics with army veteran Joseph, he thoughtfully provided three examples of men in his unit:

(1) "A" was gay and also often scared and cried in front of others. Joseph explained that he was "at the bottom" of the social hierarchy and received a lot of hazing and was often picked on with lots of misogynist and homophobic insults.

(2) "B" was heterosexual, but he was very "effeminate," with "small feminine features and a high voice." He identified as Christian and because of his religion, he wouldn't participate in all the manly stuff, such as listening to heavy metal, drinking, smoking, or picking up women. Despite presenting himself as heterosexual, he was derided for being "feminine" and "gay."

(3) "C" was gay, but he was a "really good soldier," what they called "high speed." Even though people knew he was gay, he was not the object of hazing, nor was he derided as feminine or gay.

Reflecting on these examples, Joseph concluded that if a man was considered to be "less than a good soldier," he was considered feminine and gay regardless of his sexual preferences. On the other hand, to some extent, if someone was a good soldier, he was often accepted regardless of his sexual orientation. However, how individuals who were queer or labeled so by others were treated clearly differed between units and contexts.

COMPLICATING MASCULINE SPACES

A theme that is emerging from this discussion of gender is that despite an emphasis on hypermasculinity, all of the people participating in this heavily masculine setting were individuals with their own complicated gender identities, emotional needs, and musical tastes. Furthermore, inasmuch as manly music was prevalent in the soundscapes of war, clearly no one, male or female, was manly all the time, and most people have experienced a wide range of emotions and gendered qualities throughout their lives, including during the terms of their deployments.

The military's heavy emphasis on manliness created conflict, whereby people felt the need to find ways of exploring and asserting other aspects of their being that could be in conflict with the dominant gendered expectations. Because of its expressivity and the ability to participate in listening publicly and privately, musical listening was an important avenue for alternative ways of being. Examining smaller group listening to some extent, and individual listening especially, reveals far more complex manifestations of gender.

My research certainly suggests that some men suffered abuse because they did not conform to ideals of masculinity, either socially or in their ability to effectively do their jobs as warriors. Paradoxically, it also reveals that despite this heavy emphasis on masculinity, the culture of interdependence, community, and "brotherhood" also meant that many men exercised compassion and care, qualities often attributed to femininity, and were ultimately looked after, and others in their units helped compensate for their "less manly" unit mates. When I asked Pete if there were men who did not meet the standards of masculinity in his unit in the Marines, he clarified that he differentiated "masculinity" from "proficiency." There were some men that he considered to be "proficient" yet less than manly; for example "there were guys that put sleep masks on at night that would be my first go to in a firefight if I had to choose someone." Those deemed more "effeminate" yet proficient were treated better than those deemed more "manly" yet not as competent. In Pete's words, "we picked on the less proficient, and picking on them to emasculate them was one of the funnier ways to do so." Yet he clarified that "we had guys hide out during ambushes or duck back into the truck. We even had one guy drop his weapon and run into a storefront during a firefight because he didn't know how to handle the stress." He explained: "We made fun of them and gave them hell." Yet he also said:

> We kept them more protected throughout the rest of the time we were there. Some can't handle it; some can. We made fun of them and gave them the treatment (lots of words I probably shouldn't use here, ha ha) but at [the] end of [the] day, we were all family.

Pete's explanation demonstrates this paradoxical combination of hypermasculinity with a "feminine" sense of compassion and responsibility for one another. Inasmuch as these men were supposed to be studly warriors tearing down the enemy and strutting their masculinity in front of one another, they were often simultaneously caretakers, nurturers, and responsible community members.

Correspondingly, individuals' playlists, as evident from examples already given, tended to represent much more nuanced identities, in which hypermasculinity either was not dominant or was only one among many different types of ways of being and thinking. A number of people interviewed described listening to certain music in private in order to protect themselves from being ridiculed for not being adequately manly, yet they often followed this statement by indicating that though they were teased for some of their musical selections, other men asked to borrow their less-than-manly music for a variety of reasons, as described earlier in this chapter.

Though there were women on bases in Iraq and Afghanistan who served a number of different roles, and there were certainly plenty of women among the Iraqi and Afghani populations that surrounded them, the voice of a U.S. or European female artist could transport someone of any gender out of the war zone because of the very femininity associated with voices like Sarah McLachlan's—a type of femininity that some felt was the polar opposite of the combat environment that surrounded them. For those troops who had close relationships with women outside the military—mothers, friends, sisters, girlfriends, wives—women's music, sometimes given to them by these women, evoked memories, nostalgia, joy, and sadness, again all emotions and memories that contrasted markedly with their current environments. The content of the songs, for example lyrics about love and friendship, was attractive because these were concerns shared by most soldiers. The music provided a distraction from the concerns of war and brought them to think about other things in their lives or to be nostalgic for the time when they could share with loved ones what they were thinking and how they were feeling about these things. That it was women expressing these things through songs made their music especially compelling. Plenty of male artists sing solemn songs about love and friendship, and certainly people listened to these male artists. But for many, there was something about a woman's voice, so distinct from the masculine military culture that surrounded them, that made it especially attractive. In contrast to the hypermasculine, the feminine was associated with nonaggressive emotion, soothing, kindness, and softness. Though the military culture emphasized hypermasculinity, troops also have these feminine qualities, or at least those who eschew femininity want to be around women and women's "stuff" sometimes for comfort, warmth, and to remember that there is a different world out there.

My interviews are in no way representative of everyone in the military, but it is noteworthy that it was the men I interviewed who described listening to women's music as an escape, maybe because for them the experience of war was so clearly enmeshed in masculinity: their own physical bodies, the masculine culture that surrounded them, and the type of war activities—combat—that were restricted to men. For men, women, especially "feminine" women, might have been the ultimate antithesis to war. For women the situation was more complex, because they were women fighting in war, so women musicians may have been less likely to represent something symbolically removed from the military experience.

It is also significant that not all troops listened to hypermasculine music, and some actively rejected it. Some I interviewed did not listen to heavy metal or rap specifically because they did not like the aggressiveness of the music. Mark, for example, said that the men in a unit that his unit was often paired with listened to "a lot of Metallica and similar bands, but I've never liked that stuff at all. It's just too brutal, too aggressive for me. I like more melodic stuff." Similarly, Gabe explained that he never listened to these genres, though a lot of other people in his unit did:

> I guess they relate hardcore music and hardcore rap with being pumped and ready for, you know, to defend yourself. But for me, it's kind of like that type of music will actually make you more aggressive, so I don't want to be aggressive. I want to defend myself, but not to be aggressive.

Gabe's explanation points to the idea of multiple masculinities. He understood that people interpreted war as being about aggression, and that people listened to aggressive music in the hope that it would make them more aggressive. But for Gabe, war was not about aggression, but rather something required in order to achieve greater peace in the world. He felt that there was the need to be strong and "defend myself," but because his ultimate objective was peace, and he did not consider himself to be an aggressive person, he shied away from these genres.

One of the ironies about war is that it evokes some of the most "nonmasculine" activities and qualities for men. In the military and in these wars, the relationships between men were very strong and the "brotherly bond" was very intimate. During deployment, small groups of men spent enormous amounts of time together. They served as each other's friends, workmates, confidants, and entertainment partners; there was a lot of physicality and sexuality expressed in everyday interaction in all-male military spaces. Men slept in the same room, showered together, shared pornography and stories of sexual exploits, sometimes engaged in sexual acts together, and often playfully interacted when they were scantily clad or not clad at all. Music played a part in this playfulness when men in a unit danced together to popular music, their pelvises grinding into the behind of another in the highly popular "booty dancing," or when men in a unit produced a jocular video, as in the case of the men who showed off their sexy bodies while sporting only their underwear, described in chapter 4. Troops often pulled erotic pranks on one another that involved genital contact between men, for example, the ever-popular "mushroom stamps," described to me by several veterans, in which a man put a substance on his penis and pressed it against the body of a sleeping man so that he awoke with evidence of having had another man's genitals pressed against him (see Mechling 2012).

Many troops I interviewed described their reliance on others in their units and others in the military as the only people to whom they could openly express emotions that are commonly deemed feminine or at least not manly, such as sadness, weakness, fear, neediness, and so on, that dominated their psyches. Male interviewees expressed intense emotion, the kinds of emotion that manly men were not supposed to express. Pete explained it well:

> We all go through hell, so we know what it's like and there is a time and place for everything. Just because you're a wreck about the wife and kids back home doesn't mean you can't handle business overseas. We all worked through the problems (and ribbed each other over it as usual), but it was never looked down on as feminine, besides the jokes of course.

The jocular physical intimacy could extend to emotional intimacy as well. Joseph explained that before deployment, he did not remember much intimacy between members of his unit. He explained that masculinity and "nonintimacy" were "really big" in basic training when they were being socialized into military culture and that going "against standards of masculinity" was not accepted much in this context. He remembered from his basic training that "a guy cried because he was homesick at boot camp," and that the others derided and made fun of him. During deployments there was more room for intimacy, but for Joseph, only with his best friend or within small groups. Joseph developed a very close and intimate friendship with another man in his unit, whom he referred to as his best friend. With this friend, he remembered talking about his feelings, his homoerotic sexual explorations as a child, his fears, and other topics that would have made him vulnerable with a wider audience. He recalled only rarely shedding his protective shell with others outside this friend. Rarely did he and his unit mates discuss fear, though he remembered that they would sometimes "joke about being nervous," especially after having "just drunk four red bulls [a heavily caffeinated beverage] and listening to heavy metal."

Joseph did remember some intimate moments with small groups after upsetting incidents. For example, a member of his unit got upset after his equipment had been used to shoot down a U.S. Air Force jet, and he felt responsible for the accident and subsequent loss. The man "got drunk and cried about it." Joseph remembered that rather than deriding him, everyone listened. They did not, however, affirm his sadness by letting him know "we know you feel sad because we feel that way, too." They supported him by listening and then by trying to get him to stop him crying by reassuring him that the accident was not his fault. Joseph explained that they avoided insulting him or making fun of him for crying, but they did not want to hang out and encourage him to express his feelings, either.

One interviewee who was sexually abused as a child remembered experiencing intimacy during his various deployments. He explained that he shared his stories with other marines during deployments and found that many in the Special Forces units to which he was attached had similarly been victims of childhood abuse. They knew each other's stories, accepted and supported one another, and often integrated these very personal and difficult intimacies into their joking. As the interviewee explained, people would jokingly ask him how many times he had been sodomized as a child. This joking did not alienate him, but rather let him know that they accepted his history enough that it did not need to be hidden away for all to pretend that it did not exist. He would retort with a similar joke about personal information he knew about others. The joking thus served to strengthen their bonds around communal acceptance of their shared experiences and survival of childhood sexual abuse.[9]

Male troops and veterans sometimes revealed to one another that they cried and that some cried a lot, and it was mostly only with others in the military within their "band of brothers" that they felt comfortable crying or sharing their pain. These manly men relied on other manly men for support and sharing when they needed to express their less than manliness and to be the humans they were: people who could be simultaneously strong, aggressive, sad, and needy. Humans who hurt about what they had seen and what they had done. Humans who were angry and pissed off at the world and whose pain and disillusionment were experienced with sadness and loss.

To this day, when Nate remembers, he climbs into his Ford truck, a vehicle that he knows is an ultimate sign of masculinity. "Just look at the ads," he says.

He gets in his manly truck and drives far into the mountains to cry, because in the confines of the masculine barrier, with music blaring, he is free to remember and sink into his solitude. Keith closed himself in a room, gun in hand, finger on the trigger, ready to pull, but fortunately, and he does not remember how or why, he serendipitously found a song on YouTube by fellow combat veteran Soldier Hard, the first time he had ever heard his music. He put down the gun and listened to the song over and over, tears streaming down his face for hours. It was another vet, another man, understanding and sharing his hurt, his pain, who gave him hope to hang on for at least a little longer, and he cried, the act so often emblemized as the antithesis of manliness.

SIX

"Music Doesn't Judge"

MANAGING FEELINGS AT WAR

Pete, Nate, and numerous others whom I interviewed explained that listening to music helped them exist or even survive war and its troubling aftermath. Impressed upon to be manly men or women who can engage in dangerous, difficult, lonely, terrifying, and often profoundly sad activities, most rarely shed a tear, shared their emotional struggles with others, or obtained professional psychological care. Fortunately, many had their ever-expanding playlists and music players readily available for their personal and collective listening and for offering musical solace to others. As Bull explains, MP3 players permit users to be more attentive to the vagaries and changes of mood, seeking either confirmation of mood or transformation into an alternate mood via their choice of playlist. Individuals "create playlists precisely to cater for a wide spectrum of moods or times of the day" (2007, 128). Acutely aware of the intrinsic capacity of music to influence how they felt, troops described highly customized and complex strategies, made possible through the digital music revolution and the portability of MP3 players, of using music to regulate their own emotions as well as helping others manage theirs.

The relationship between music and mood is well known. Psychologists have determined that certain types of music can have calming effects and that others can evoke anger or excitement (Juslin and Sloboda 2001, 2010a). Warnings that listening to certain music, including heavy metal and certain rap genres, make listeners aggressive abound in discourse about youth and deviance (e.g., Miranda and Claes 2004; Litman and Farberow 1994; Johnson et al. 1995; Arnett

1991, 1996). Alternately, youth in the United States are advised that listening to certain Western classical music soothes and calms and enhances certain cognitive processes (e.g., Rauscher et al. 1995). What has been given less attention is how individuals use music consciously and subconsciously in highly idiosyncratic ways to impact their own moods, sometimes productively—for example, as a means to motivate themselves to achieve objectives—and sometimes in less productive ways—for example, to enhance a mood that may negatively impact them, such as when a person who feels sad listens to melancholy music to sink into an even more depressive state (see Van Goethem and Sloboda 2011). In their efforts to foster healing and improve people's well-being, psychologists have emphasized the positive effects of musical listening. My emphasis in this chapter on music as self-therapy confirms that music can have these positive impacts, but it also importantly highlights that inasmuch as music can evoke emotions that might be deemed positive—for example, relaxation, healing, soothing—it can also unconsciously trigger and be used consciously to evoke emotions that might be deemed negative, such as emotions associated with violence, aggression, depression, or isolation (see Johnson and Cloonan 2009).

MUSIC AND MOOD REGULATION

Psychologists interested in relationships between music and affect have conducted numerous studies to better understand what happens cognitively when people listen to music. Some of these studies suggest that certain types of sonic qualities evoke specific types of emotional responses. For example, in a study on musical listening, John Sloboda found:

> Tears were associated with melodic or harmonic movement through the circle of fifths. Shivers were associated with enharmonic changes and other harmonic, textural, or dynamic discontinuities. Racing heart was associated with syncopation, and other forms of accentual anticipation. These effects were insensitive to style, and examples of all these effective structures were found in both classical and pop-music. (2005, 169–70)

Sloboda's study suggests that at least part of the emotional power of music for troops derived from the structural features of musical selections.[1] What is evident from my research is that the sonic dimensions do not explain everything. Musical selections can have very different affective impacts on different individuals, as well as on the same individuals at different times depending on their own aesthetics, previous experience with a musical selection or genre, musical histories, and so on; thus, as DeNora so cogently argues, we "cannot presume to know what music causes, or what semiotic force it will convey, at the level of reception, action, experience" (2000, 31). Musical materials do not act as "sole agents or stimulus" for a person's emotional self-regulation. "On the contrary, the music's powers are constituted by" the individual; "they derive from how she [or he] interacts with them" (2000, 41). Music's "power" to regulate affect derives from a combination of the intrinsic qualities of the music itself and the ways that individuals appropriate the music, the things they bring into it, and the context in which they listen (2000, 42).

As were the women who participated in DeNora's ethnographic study of everyday musical listening, the participants in my study were "explicit about music's role as an ordering device at the personal level, as a means for creating, enhancing, sustaining and changing subjective and cognitive, bodily and self-conceptual states" (2000, 49). Troops and combat veterans used music for its capacity to impact emotion, for example by evoking emotional states, giving them outlets for expressing emotion, enhancing mood, helping them relax, distracting them from what they were thinking or feeling, drawing them into introspection, or helping them cope with challenging feelings (Van Goethem and Sloboda 2011; Bull 2007).

Of particular importance, given the extent to which troops had to deal with various types of suffering, was the therapeutic value of musical listening for physical and emotional pain and trauma. The result of experiments by Laura Mitchell and Raymond MacDonald (2006) on patients' use of music to mitigate physical pain suggested that the selection was less important than the research subjects' control over their musical listening. Thus it was less a matter of individuals listening to specific types of soothing music that would relax them and more about whether they were able to exercise control over their musical listening and make selections based on their preferred choices. Correspondingly, in my interviews person after person described in great detail how she or he used music, one of the few things over which that person exercised control, to address emotional and physical challenges, and each was highly idiosyncratic based on the ways in which he or she associated particular musical selections with memories, relationships, identities, and thoughts of how it might impact his or her affective state.

FEELING AT WAR

Those who have fought in wars described emotions as being especially taut. Constant danger and fear tangled with excitement and adrenaline, increasing the poignancy of knowing that one's activities were intricately tied to life and death. Dread and sadness about what one did and the hurt one saw done to those around intermingled with the utter boredom of so much time spent sitting around waiting until the next rush into the unexpected. Courage and pride wrestled with insecurity, joy, frustration, fun, and loneliness, all of which had to be frequently muted to focus on especially demanding tasks. Everyone at war suffered the ongoing danger of attack or being present at an explosion. Yet the degree of danger varied among those who had different jobs and were located in different settings, and with what was going on in the war at any particular time.

Aside from troops' dramatic experiences, there was also the isolation and constancy of limited activities and companionship. In attempting to explain the feelings of isolation he remembered, Shannon said, "the most similar circumstance I could put it in is like jail or a prison where you just absolutely cannot escape. There's no way to go outside of the barbed wire." When they did go out, it was usually as part of a mission on which individual agency and control was limited, or more likely nonexistent. The word "prison" echoed in many interviews. Mark, for example, said:

> Well, whenever I started to think about my situation, it felt really confined. I felt that I was in prison. That was basically what it was. I knew I had to be there for a specific amount of time. The only way I was going to leave was that I was dead, or I got blown up, or I stayed there for a year plus.

All these fraught emotions exploded in an environment explicitly defined as "hypermasculine," with its associated ideas that men, and by extension women in men's jobs, do not, or should not, feel or express emotion because feelings could interfere with the male tasks associated with making war (Petrie 1982). Yet as Kaufman reminds us, though men are encouraged to "suppress a range of emotions," the suppressed emotions do not disappear. Men "continue to experience a range of needs and feelings that are deemed inconsistent with manhood" (2006, 189). Those of all genders at war were generally discouraged from expressing fear or sadness, paradoxically in an environment where there was great need to be brave and withstand a lot of emotional pain in order to survive, at the same time as there was much about which to be fearful and sad.

This idea that emotion is feminine, rooted in the Enlightenment's opposition between reason and emotion, is undeniably linked to gender: men are assumed to be rational, while women are emotional. In addition to being a construct, this binary is grounded in a selective definition of "emotion." In this conceptualization, emotion refers to such things as sadness, fear, and sentimentality, which are linked to ideals of femininity. Other emotions, for example anger and emotions associated with aggression, are common tropes of manliness. Control over everything, including one's own emotions, is also emphasized; thus a man should be able to control outbursts of emotion, whether sentimental tears or outrage. Yet as previously noted, conceptualizations of hypermasculinity often emphasize and celebrate expressions of emotion when they are about power and control over others. Thus, expressions of anger are common tropes of hypermasculinity at the same time that discourse about emotion being feminine is pervasive.

Within the context of war, varying ideas about emotion intersected with the multiple types of masculinities that were expected and celebrated: different types of masculinity and thus relationships to emotion were expected from those doing different jobs and at different ranks. Being cool, focused, and in control were often considered "masculine" traits that were exemplified in certain military positions, such as pilots and commanders. This type of masculinity required the control of most emotions, including fear and anger. At the lower echelons, especially among combat troops, though fear and sentimentality were to be controlled, other emotions associated with aggression and anger could sometimes be useful for the job. Some especially emotionally charged, heavy musical styles were pervasive in the public soundscapes of war because the music evoked this aggressive emotionality for "warriors." Yet because the emotional needs of troops were so much more complex and layered, troops engaged with more diverse musical styles associated with a broader range of emotional associations privately and in small and large groups to meet a variety of their psychological needs.

MACHO MUSIC, AGGRESSION, AND FEAR

The use of music to amp up for battle has been portrayed and discussed relatively uncritically in documentary films and in journalistic and scholarly writings, perhaps implicitly suggesting that these genres are obvious choices for soldiers who themselves by definition are loud, strong, and dominating—to be otherwise would result in utter failure, at least for those in the enlisted ranks of the military. My many interviews revealed more complicated insights into this type of musical listening. On the one hand, as previously mentioned, these musical styles were popular among the demographics that dominated these levels of the military, so it comes as no surprise that these genres were pervasive. And it makes sense that people who were involved in a job that required them to be tough would listen to music that was associated with toughness. Talking to troops complicated these common assumptions. Part of the experience of war was that a person had to be confident, controlled, and dominant—to be otherwise could cost one one's life and put others in danger. Yet at some point they all felt scared, vulnerable, insecure, tired, or lacking in motivation as they geared up to leave the wire. Many of those I interviewed explained that they sometimes consciously chose to listen to these aggressive styles in an effort to transform their mental state, as some put it, to convince themselves that they were indeed warriors, especially when their emotional state was far from what was required for them to fulfill this role. This corresponds to Arnett's study (1991) with adolescent males about their listening to heavy metal genres. Many of his respondents explained that they often listened to music because it produced in them a heightened level of energy. Pete explained that listening to loud, "heavy" music gave him a boost of adrenaline; took the worry out of the situation; and allowed him to "put a face on" that projected strength, to not "let his problems get in his way." In his description of listening to Drowning Pool's "Bodies" before crossing the berm during the initial invasion of Iraq, Craig explained:

> Yeah, well, it was a very scary situation. I compare it to going to the gym and trying to get pumped up for the physical task that is coming and trying to make yourself get behind this thing that you have to do, even though you don't know how you feel about it.

Mark listened to recordings by the band Trans Am. He explained: "I don't even like to describe myself doing this, but like pump myself up, or make myself feel like I was powerful, or more powerful than who we were going to fight, then I would listen to that stuff." He remembered more specifically listening to this music a lot as they prepared for an especially dangerous invasion. Similarly, Joseph explained that he found music particularly helpful for getting himself into the proper state of mind, even more so during his second deployment, when he was already avidly against the war. He explained:

> But I still had to get myself up to that level. I would listen to a lot of really heavy, angry, like visceral music. At that point in time, I was listening to Atreyu.

Atreyu was like really big for me at that point in time. I loved them, they had two albums out, one was called um, um, *Suicide Notes* and *Butterfly Kisses*. . . . I listened to this band called Probot, which has got Dave Grohl who used to be the drummer for Nirvana. . . . I would keep my headphones in as long as I could until we went out the gate, so I'd just be like, as soon as we'd left the gate, I'd take them off and then I'd just be ready to go, you know?

Joseph relied on these selections to put him into the mind-set that he felt he needed to muffle his feelings and thoughts and overwhelm himself with a different state of being. He kept the headphones on up until the last possible second, suggesting that he was afraid that if the music faded too soon, the aggressive façade would crumble right before it was most needed. By the time of the interview, Joseph was struggling with his memories of how he felt after being amped up by the music. He remembered one time when he was getting his equipment ready while listening to music:

Somebody saying, "you're going to fire off any more warning shots today" or something like that. And, I was like "fuck no, I'm going to hit somebody." And he was like "What are you going to do?" And I was like, I actually said, I can't believe I ever said this, I said "I'm going to shoot a pregnant woman so I get two kills in one" or something like that, but I was completely antiwar, like, it was completely, I was like a completely different animal like, you have to be, like I felt like I had to be that way. I feel really, really guilty about saying. . . . I can't believe I ever said that because of the way that I am now. I almost feel like, I feel like I don't understand why. I don't understand why I even deserve to speak out against the war after saying some stuff like that sometimes, but um . . . .

In this poignant memory, Joseph remembered the intense and disturbing conflict between what he thought intellectually about what he was asked to do as a soldier and the emotional state that he felt he needed to be in to fulfill the expectation. He tried to attain a state of mind largely through music that even at the time, he would have rejected intellectually.[2]

What is clear from Joseph and others I interviewed is that some troops used music consciously to create an alternate state for themselves, either at specific times or throughout their deployments, to allow themselves to be present and do what was required of them. Their physical environment and daily activities were so removed from and discordant with those of their identities outside of war that they had a difficult time reconciling the two. They thus engaged in activities that helped them be the people they had to be at war and distance themselves from the people they thought they were in other contexts. In an interview on August 10, 2009, Seth explained that he went to "great lengths" not to think about his family. He would call and e-mail them regularly, but he expressed that he felt he "was absent even when I was doing that" and that he "was also trying to downplay the level of violence that was taking place." He found strategies for psychologically separating who he was as a soldier and who he was in his civilian life, a husband and father:

> I had to put a lot of things away when I was there, including my feelings about my ideals, because I wanted to survive. . . . I had a shoebox full of pictures of my family that I just had to put away because I couldn't exist in both those worlds at the same time. I couldn't have pictures of my family up and be an effective soldier. I just couldn't, couldn't exist in those two worlds simultaneously.

Listening to music that they associated with what it meant to be a warrior enabled many to remain in the persona of being a soldier. Listening to other music could risk putting this identity into question, and could also put the person in an undesirable state of mind that made it difficult to maintain this psychical division.

Whether or not people felt a need to amp up also depended on the nature of their jobs. Those going out on the ground, where the dangers were imminent and the possibility of their observing something traumatic or inflicting pain on others was more immediate, were more likely to listen to aggressive music. By contrast, Evan, who was a pilot and usually physically removed from combat, explained that "it always became much more routine. Like, oh, we are going to fly circles around Talafar for four hours and maybe we'll get shot at and have to shoot back. There wasn't ever that sense of like, you know, . . . impending; it wasn't something that I felt like I had to psych myself [up] for every single time." He elaborated that his preparation for missions as a pilot required something very different than it did for the infantry: "Our job is such a progression of tasks that are performed, some of them from muscle memory and rote memorization, and some of them, we have to be very clear thinking and able to make quick decisions that could have a very big effect." Making sure they had everything required and in good order took a great deal of concentration, so they chose to either listen to music that aided in their focus or not listen at all.

Returning from missions required another dramatic shift in emotional state. As Dave explained:

You can't just go out there and get into the madness and everything, and suddenly come back and sit around and do nothing. We're still human beings. We're still people. We're Americans, and we're not in our own country. We're in a crazy situation. We'd all come back and play cards, listen to music.

Most people I interviewed described using music to slowly calm down. Some had routinized their listening, usually listening to the same artists or tracts to bring them down, while others selected different music depending on their mood and listening desires. Some preferred to isolate themselves and listen alone, while others enjoyed group listening for this purpose.

MUSIC AND ANGER

Aggressive music could also be a mechanism for expressing or managing anger in an acceptable way. In his study with adolescent boys, Arnett (1991, 1996) asked respondents whether there was a mood in which they were most likely to listen to heavy metal music, and the most frequent response was when they were angry. They explained that listening to metal when they were angry gave them an outlet to express their anger, had a purgative effect, and helped them calm down and otherwise feel better. In my interviews with troops, anger was a commonly described emotion, though the objects of the anger differed widely. Living in tight, enclosed spaces without a lot of privacy, with people who were brought together somewhat randomly, it was common for soldiers to have conflicts and be angry with others in their units. Many also remembered feeling frustration and anger with their immediate command, the decision makers in their branches, and leaders of the U.S. armed forces or the government. This anger could be about details in their work or living environments or about the fact that they were fighting the war at all. Anger toward "terrorists"—the generic term often used to refer to all those perceived to pose a threat to the United States, the people responsible for the attacks on U.S. targets on September 11, 2001, and the reason for which these wars were purportedly being fought—was rampant. Much anger was also felt about and directed at Iraqis and Afghanis, the insurgents and enemy they were fighting, but also the civilians whom U.S. troops came into contact with regularly on their missions and patrols. Anger toward family and friends at home was also common. Anger at girlfriends, boyfriends, husbands, and wives, sometimes because of jealousy or infidelities, at other times because of the distance and lack of understanding, were prevalent.

And many projected their anger at having to be in a situation so difficult and demanding onto any other thing to which they could direct anger. Anger toward oneself was also common. Some were angry with themselves for having joined the military at all, for their perceived weaknesses or failures, for what they did to the enemy or what they let happen to their friends, or for feeling weak and afraid or being too aggressive.

But as previously explained, troops had few ways of resolving their anger. They could not leave the environment or people that angered them, go off and get drunk and dance off the emotion, go home and resolve the issues with their partners, or for the most part, express their frustration with their command or others making the decisions that impacted them the most. Arnett determined that although "metal heads" seek out metal music when they are in a dark mood, rather than inflaming the anger as he had expected, "heavy metal music characteristically has the effect of *calming them down*" (1996, 81; emphasis in original). Troops interviewed explained that there were some outlets for their anger, such as playing video games, watching aggressive movies, working out, real or pretend fighting with one another, and for some, engaging in violence during combat. Music also provided a means with which to deal with anger, sometimes to ignite or fuel the anger, to sink into it and feel it fully, or to calm oneself, as Shannon explained:

> You know, sometimes when I was like, really angry or whatever, I'd listen to punk rock, a lot of screaming. That's a good way to vent your frustration, because there's not a lot of ways you can vent your frustration when you're in the military. You're already firing a gun, you're already working . . . . On my planes, I'd have a hammer and I'd be hammering my plane and I'd still be really pissed off at things, because you know, either we were behind deadlines or there's someone just really annoying. So you're already kind of in a situation where you're kind of stuck. There's not a whole lot of escape from that.

Shannon did not have a place where he could scream and shout, nor other ways of venting his anger. Listening to "punk rock, a lot of screaming" was a vicarious outlet for his own feelings.

Joseph remembered realizing that he lacked much power or control over his daily activities. Exercise was one outlet for his aggression. He remembered that he worked out as much as he could and was stronger than he had ever been, especially during his second deployment, when he was so angry about his situation. While exercising and throughout his days, he listened to a lot of aggressive music. He explained that "infantry guys" who are "knocking down doors" need to feel "invincible" and "invulnerable." Listening to music like the song "Cowboys and Hell" by Pantera and "Angel of Death" by Slayer, which have "intimidating lyrics," could create a "wall of security around yourself in order to survive what's going on, but also to survive what's going on internally. You know, you're still there, a very vulnerable core."

INDIVIDUAL LISTENING AND "INVISIBLE WOUNDS"

Part of the reality of war is that fighters experience significant trauma, the kind that can immobilize a person emotionally, sometimes for days, weeks, years, or a lifetime. Terri Tanielian and Lisa H. Jaycox (2008), in the summary to their *Invisible Wounds of War: Psychological and Cognitive Injuries, Their Consequences, and Services to Assist Recovery,* a study by the RAND Corporation, explain that mental health issues have been especially great in these wars in comparison to previous U.S. conflicts. Because of advances in medical and armor technologies, physical casualties have been less frequent than in previous U.S. wars. However, what they call "invisible wounds," mental health conditions and cognitive impairments, have been greater, which they attribute to a combination of these wars' characteristics, including longer deployments, common redeployment to combat, and infrequent breaks between deployments. The study focuses on invisible wounds associated with PTSD, major depressive disorder and depressive symptoms, and traumatic brain injury (TBI), all three of which can affect mood, thoughts, and behavior. Because these casualties are not visible as are physical ones, they often go unrecognized and unacknowledged.

On its Web site, the U.S. Department of Veterans Affairs explains that PTSD can occur after a person has been through a traumatic event, though not everyone who experiences trauma suffers from PTSD. The four types of PTSD symptoms are outlined on the site:

1. *Reliving the event (also called reexperiencing symptoms)*
   You may have bad memories or nightmares. You even may feel like you're going through the event again. This is called a flashback.
2. *Avoiding situations that remind you of the event*
   You may try to avoid situations or people that trigger memories of the traumatic event. You may even avoid talking or thinking about the event.

3. *Negative changes in beliefs and feelings*
   The way you think about yourself and others may change because of the
   trauma. You may feel fear, guilt, or shame. Or you may not be interested in
   activities you used to enjoy. This is another way to avoid memories.
4. *Feeling keyed up (also called hyperarousal)*
   You may be jittery, or always alert and on the lookout for danger. Or you
   may have trouble concentrating or sleeping. This is known as hyperarousal.[3]

The frequent use of IEDs has made TBIs a significant concern in these wars. The
symptoms of PTSD, depression, anxiety, and TBI can be similar, making it difficult to appropriately diagnose and treat the problem(s). All these conditions
are widespread; PTSD is the most prevalent. According to the RAND study, as
many as one-third of those who have previously deployed have at least one of the
conditions, and 5 percent report having all three (Tanielian and Jaycox 2008, xxi).

Though I use the term PTSD because of its frequent usage, many veterans
reject it because they feel that the word "disorder" is pejorative, suggesting a
long-term, untreatable condition rather than something that can be overcome or
integrated into a healthy life. Many therefore prefer "post-combat stress" to PTSD.
A further problem is that because of the restricted definition of PTSD, involving
the four categories of symptoms listed previously, some combat veterans who
suffer from deep emotional distress as a result of combat are not diagnosed as
having PTSD. The broader and more vague term "combat stress" is sometimes
used to encompass all types of emotional and physical duress experienced by
troops during their time at war and afterward as a result of their war experiences.

Though the pervasiveness of these "invisible wounds" is well known and
documented, many troops suffering from them are not receiving the treatment
they need. According to a study conducted by Tanielian and Jaycox, of those
reporting TBI, 57 percent had not been evaluated by a physician. Of those per-
sons reporting PTSD, only about 53 percent were seeking treatment (2008, xxi).
When they do, "too few receive quality care." And "of those who have a mental
disorder and also sought medical care for that problem, just over half received
minimally adequate treatment" and the "number who received *quality* care (i.e.,
a treatment that has been demonstrated to be effective) would be expected to
be even smaller" (xxii).[4]

A number of those I interviewed referred implicitly or explicitly to their
struggles with these "invisible wounds," and several complained that not enough
was being done to help them. They also referred to cultural factors in the mili-

tary that created barriers to their seeking care or even admitting to themselves, much less others, that they were having problems. A study by M. Jakupcak and colleagues (2014) examined relationships between "toughness" and PTSD among male veterans of the Iraq and Afghanistan wars. The authors define "toughness" as "extreme self-reliance and the suppression of outward displays of emotional distress," which they attribute to core traditional gender norms for males in Western culture. Their findings ironically revealed that those male veterans who most highly embraced toughness were also more likely to screen for PTSD. While toughness could be useful for healing from a physical injury, it could "actually exacerbate emotional distress and delay treatment-seeking for mental health concerns" (2014).[5]

Pete explained that a critical ethos of the military was that everyone was part of a team and that everyone's efforts and commitment were required for everyone's safety and for the successful completion of all missions. From boot camp on, it was inculcated that no one wants "to be the weakest one on the team." Mark, who described himself as completely out of shape when he enlisted in the U.S. Army, explained that "no matter where you are in the military, if you're weaker than someone else, it's like this Darwinian mentality where everyone just attacks." He explained that people in his unit did not like him, that his drill sergeants would single him out, and that he felt he was treated with "this kind of horrible behavior," reminiscent of how "my father treated me when I was growing up." Many veterans I interviewed felt that psychological distress was a sign of weakness and that admitting to it would be an acknowledgment that one was the "weakest one on the team."

War was a setting for men and women who were trained to be warriors to suppress their individual needs for the welfare of others in the military and of their country. Even acknowledging that one was having mental health problems was excruciating for many, and seeking help was worse, not to mention that mental health resources during deployment were relatively scarce. Add to that the strong sense of commitment that most in the military felt to others in their units, it could be really difficult for someone to make the decision to get help if doing so meant not being able to continue to contribute to the well-being of the whole unit.

Keith remembered that during his second deployment to Iraq he started struggling with "extreme PTSD," but he explained that there were no programs to treat it while he was abroad. Fortunately for him, a platoon sergeant recognized the symptoms and evaluated him for PTSD. In Keith's words, the sergeant then "forced him to get help." He was sent back to the United States, but he wanted to return to Iraq to continue to fight with his unit. Many others I interviewed also struggled with mental health during their deployments, but either did not understand that what they were experiencing was a result of combat or did not have the resources they needed to even find out how to seek help for their problems.

Most at war had neither the luxury of physical removal from the setting in which the trauma happened nor the time to rest, think, feel, or get the professional attention to process and heal. Combat medics and chaplains provided some support. Yet the medics I interviewed had little mental health training, and in general, people did not have the time and space for the type of focused therapy they needed. Many thus used whatever means were available to help them endure the tasks before them, and make it through their deployments. In addition to music's capacity to impact mood, it could be especially useful in these trying circumstances, because it was something that a person could do privately without divulging to others, even doctors, what he or she was listening to or feeling and thinking. Tyler, who suffered from PTSD, explained it well in an e-mail in December 2012, writing that although he had been in "one-on-one therapy" after his deployment, he preferred "music, because I feel I am being judged by doctors and the music doesn't judge anyone."

Though the focus of this book is on musical listening, some attention to the music making of Jeff Barillaro, aka Soldier Hard, during his deployments is relevant, because inasmuch as making music helped him therapeutically, numerous veterans subsequently listened to his music to help themselves, as I discuss in the next chapter. Jeff served in the U.S. Army from 1995 to 2001 and again from 2005 to 2010 as an armor crewman. During his deployment in 2009–2010, he brought recording equipment with him to Iraq and produced music in the genres of "R&B and hip-hop." In an e-mail exchange on December 4, 2012, he explained that music "played a huge role" during his deployment. It was "my escape from the harsh realities of what we were faced with." As with the sound bubble created for some through MP3 players, "many times" throughout the "process of making music, I would literally forget everything, even where I was at, in a combat zone. It was my escape! Literally!" He explained that he made music prior to his deployment, but that "the music was different, it was the typical hip-hop same topics." After his second deployment, his music changed to being exclusively about "military topics."

When I asked Jeff if he had specific memories of how music making helped him, he related the following story:

We just got off a horrible mission where three brothers of mine was blown up due to two 155 IEDs in the road that went off on their GUN TRUCK, and what I saw with my own eyes stunned me. And when we got back off that mission, I had to talk to someone, I have to get things off my chest. So I talked to the microphone, and just let everything out. It felt good to put what was on my mind and in my heart into a song. I was OK from that moment on. Music saved my life and still does.

Jeff shared the therapeutic possibility of making music with others in his unit. He explained that "several soldiers" in his unit "didn't make music but wanted to try it, to get things off their chest." He opened up his studio to them, and

for that three hours we stayed recording WE WERE LOST, ALL OF US, especially them, they too forgot where they were and got lost into making music, speaking out what their feelings were. After that, I saw the smiles on their faces.

He explained that it was during this experience, "It hit me I have to keep doing this to help people, but how can I do it on a larger scale?"

Soldier Hard was very articulate about how making music functioned therapeutically for him:

Music to me is ALWAYS therapeutic NO MATTER how I feel . . . . [T]he music itself, i.e., the rhythm and melody, all have to match what I am wanting to talk about, so if I am depressed, for . . . example, I['m] gonna pick music that has a very dark and lonely feel to it, . . . [I]f [I'm] happy [I'm] gonna pick a more upbeat, motivational sound with a happy vibe to it. For an example, I have a song called "ROAD to Recovery," I wrote and recorded this song from start to finish and it only took a total of 45 minutes. I was feeling depressed, anger, defeated, and motivated to get better all at the same time. And so I picked music to match the same feel; the music has a sad organ sound to it, it has an anger bassline feel, and the snare and claps has a motivational sound to it, and well it was [a] perfect match for the feeling I had, and what I did was write lyrics on how I felt using the music as a [guide]; I picked up the pen, played the music, and spill[ed] out my heart into the song. It came out more th[an] what I thought it would, and even till this day when I listen to the song, I get a lil choked up, it's a really deep song, many people relate to it so much, and to think, it only took 45 mins. from start to finish. That's the most beautiful thing about making music, you can just let everything go, let all the feelings you have, and throw it all on the table and have a lighter burden to carry! The recording studio is my best therapist, and I am luck[y] to have it in my life.

After Soldier Hard returned to the United States, he continued making music for a largely military audience, greatly helping many others cope with their war-related issues, which I elaborate on in the next chapter. His music is available to thousands through the Internet and CDs sent to other troops at war, thus adding to their musical listening possibilities. In an e-mail exchange in December 2012, Amy explained that her husband Sean, who was in the army, deployed first to Iraq (2009–2010) and then to Afghanistan (February–October 2012), where his unit was under regular attack and engaged in intensive combat. Sean witnessed multiple casualties within his unit and among members of the Afghan population who were supporting the U.S. troops. A final "UGL round, also known as under-slung grenade launcher," hit "right beside him," causing his third concussion. He was subsequently medevaced out of Afghanistan and awarded a purple heart for this last injury. His wife, at home with their two children, discovered Soldier Hard while her husband was in Afghanistan. She remembered that she "bought and sent him Soldier Hard's newest album *Therapy Session*." Sean and Amy sub-sequently both listened to him and other veteran artists of the Redcon-1 Music Group, a virtual community of veteran musicians, including Jeff, whose mission is to "help control symptoms of PTSD for our warfighter community through music and making music."[6] According to Amy, her husband's favorites when he was in Afghanistan were "If I Was KIA," "Dear PTSD," and "Road to Recovery." Amy shared that Sean listened to this music mostly during his downtime, when he was relaxing, and going to bed. He told her that it helped him "focus, realize he's not the only one that has been through this, and that he has the strength to overcome the fears and the pain and to keep pushing on."

Many others who did not make music themselves relied on musical listening to help them cope. Eric, an army medic who went on one to two patrols daily, explained that upon returning from outside the wire, he

would drop all my gear, you know, the first thing I'd do was just lie down on the bed and try and wind down, you know . . . wash the blood off or I would just try and escape back into something that was less nerve-racking, less intense, you know. Things like Norah Jones has a soothing voice, or you know, Jour-ney's love ballads or whatever. I mean there is nothing dangerous or anything about any of that.

Eric's explanation of his musical choices referred to both the structural features of the music and its lyrical content: Jones's "soothing voice" and music that has "nothing dangerous" about it. Unlike his description of listening to aggressive music to amp up, here he listened to music that contrasted as much as possible from war in order to emotionally withdraw from his environment.

Army pilot Evan remembered purchasing speakers for his MP3 player at a local flea market that came to his base in Iraq on a regular basis. He described listening to music to relax after missions, often reading at the same time:

> I would listen to a lot of Bob Marley just because it's so soothing and relaxing. And it was just sort of to make a lot of the turmoil and uncertainty that was going on day-to-day seem less an issue, you know. . . . I would listen to, the house music that I was listening to was much more on the deep end of the spectrum. I don't know how much you know about house music, but there are a lot of sub-genres, and there are a lot of styles. There is house music that is like all about peak hour in a club, and you know, getting the crowd to go nuts. And then there is deep house that's all about the quality of the music and listening experience. So I was listening to a lot of deep house just because it was very relaxing and definitely helped relax my mind after a chaotic day.

While listening Evan read books, and he explained that he chose not to read books in any way related to the military; instead, he enjoyed reading books about music, such as about the garage music scene in New York. Reading about one type of music while listening to very different music allowed him to relax and separate himself from his environment. His explanation exemplifies the importance of control and also of knowing one's playlist. Evan's longtime, deep engagement with music prepared him well, because not only was he aware of his listening options, but he also knew what kind of impact they typically had on him. After a "chaotic day," he could select "deep house," which in the past had been effective at helping relax his mind. Evan remembered that the music he listened to for its calming effects changed as he became more settled in his environment, and he explained that toward the end of his five-month deployment, he "was more comfortable there, so I was listening to more of the jump up, like peak hour stuff, like DJ Dan." Evan's musical listening shifted as his emotional state stabilized.

Mark explained that early in his deployment, he was "so worried about everything"—for example whether he was going to return alive or dead and how his wife, whom he had only recently married, was coping with their newborn child—that it was "becoming a huge problem for me." He realized he "needed to try to compartmentalize" different aspects of his life and put his worries "out of his mind." He remembered listening to music that "reminded him of his situation" and "how horrible and depressing it was," but that at the same time gave him a reprieve because "it's still enjoyable to listen to good music. So I would get a lot of good feeling out of that." Mark's explanation is interesting because he suggests that unlike Eric's and Evan's experiences, the music did not help him disconnect from his environment; rather it "reminded him of his situation." Yet because he enjoyed certain music so much, the aesthetic pleasure helped him to feel better.

Music was a way for many troops to connect with past lives and people, and alternately for them to know that they were in the minds and part of the lives of their civilian friends and family members. Gabe remembered listening to The Beatles a lot during his second deployment. It was hard for him to be away from his family, especially because his wife was pregnant. Gabe suffered a TBI during his second deployment and continues to suffer memory loss, so he had difficulty remembering details during the interview, including the name of a song by The Beatles that was especially important to him. This song and others by the band gave him consolation because "the theme of some of their songs is about going out in life. Even though you feel tired or whatever, you have to go on, and something beautiful is coming soon." While he was at war and thinking about his family so far away, this music brought him comfort that "something beautiful" would hopefully follow. Later in the interview he remembered listening to a song by The Beatles whose title he could not recall, with the word "honey" in it, of which there are at least three, all of which are about love and reminiscing about tender touches. This song "reminded me of a new day, a whole different day, you know, being away from all that violence."

Those fighting for their country were well aware of how removed these wars were for most Americans, who continued to live relatively untouched while troops were immersed in the bleakness of battle. Songs by artists about the wars and soldiers were very meaningful to some, because it let them know that civilians were thinking about them and that they were not alone. Army veteran Keith remembered that when Toby Keith released the song "American Soldier," "it was huge" for him and his unit mates. He remembered that they all listened to the song and "felt that they were not forgotten. They know we are here." He said that part of his job in the military was to do what was needed and not to expect recognition, but he felt that the song was a "pat on the back," an expression of appreciation that he was not getting otherwise.

Marine veteran Pete was depressed and struggling with PTSD during his second deployment to Iraq. His crumbling relationship with his wife exacerbated his emotions. Though he listened to a lot of "rock" during his first deployment, in his second he remembered listening to a lot of songs by the band Nine Inch Nails and by Johnny Cash. He described both as "depressing music" that "flowed with how life was going for me." He did not remember that the music itself affected his emotions in any way; rather, it was the lyrics that drew him. He explained that he was so depressed at the time, he "wasn't too concerned about coming back," or returning from his deployment alive. He remembered listening to the song "Hurt," which was written by Trent Reznor, songwriter and vocalist for the band Nine Inch Nails. The song was first recorded on the album *Downward Spiral.* Johnny Cash covered the song on his album *The Man Comes Around,* released in 2002. Following are the first few lines. The refrain "Everyone I know, goes away in the end" is repeated throughout the song. The following verse exemplifies the tone:

> I hurt myself today,
> To see if I still feel,
> I focus on the pain,
> The only thing that's real

Pete remembered listening to this song and thinking about how someone like Johnny Cash could feel so much like he did, isolated in a war zone. He would think about how Cash, who had had such an "amazing life," was successful, and had so much money, could feel as badly as he did "alone and overseas." He explained that "in a way it furthered the depression," because it made him feel that even if he were elsewhere and in different circumstances, "was a millionaire" like Cash, he would probably have the same problems.

Some of those who did not engage so directly in combat nevertheless experienced significant stress and trauma associated with the realities of the social and living conditions of their deployments. Angie struggled emotionally throughout her time in the navy and especially during her deployment to the Gulf, when she was confined to a small combat ship with about 350 other people. From the combination of constant sexual harassment, described in the last chapter, long work hours, isolation, containment in a small space, lack of escape, and especially the sense of lack of control over herself and her environment, Angie suffered from severe depression. She explained that because of the intensity of her work schedule, she had little time to herself. She remembered that she would escape by going to the arcade and playing video games while listening to the band Guns

N' Roses through headphones over and over in order to "forget about everyone." She explained that, distracted by the absorbing video games and the pounding music throbbing through her head, "it made me feel a little better because Guns N' Roses is a bit more gut rock poppy sort of thing. I could kind of forget about things for awhile."

Angie's other outlet was to enclose herself in her coffin-sized sleep bunk with the curtain drawn. She would put on headphones and listen to music while writing in her journal. Asked what she listened to, she answered:

> I remember that I was super addicted to, this is going to sound really cheesy, but I remember listening to 4 Non Blondes a lot because [there are] some really sad songs on there. I would just lie there and listen to them and cry.

While listening to this music, she would think about killing herself. She explained that she was a "really bad self-mutilator," which she said was not uncommon among women in the navy. She would cut her arms and wear long sleeves to try to keep it a secret. She described that she was cutting herself "all the time," sometimes as much as twice a day. She wrote frequently in her journal and she would "imprint the blood" on the pages. Then, "I read about it to try to get an understanding of what I was doing." Asked why she thought she chose these songs, she answered:

> I think I was probably listening to it to have something or someone understanding what I was going through. I wouldn't say it was feeding my depression. It was not really to alleviate my depression. But, maybe just understand my depression. Keep in mind, I didn't talk to my parents, I didn't talk to my mom for six months at one point. I would sometimes not have communication with anyone. Because, if the Internet wasn't working, I had nobody to talk to. That's why I wrote in my journals all the time. I just talked to myself. That [music] was the only way that I felt that there was another consciousness able to relate to me.

For Angie, whose explanation resonates with that of others, the songs' texts were what was significant. Listening to songs about someone else's sadness and depression could help a person not feel alone, and also provide a means through which to try to understand how one was feeling. Though Angie says that the music did not feed the depression, she also explained that she would listen to the music and cry. Music was a big part of her process of closing herself into the only space where she had some control over what she could express emotionally. Ensconced in her bunk, she could think and feel. She could choose to listen to music that would invoke tears, a contrast to the rest of the day, when she worked hard to control and ignore her sadness, anger, and frustration. While listening, crying, cutting herself, and writing in her journal, she could feel and express her despair. Angie, who had been out of the military for seven years at the time of the interview, still had the diaries she kept at that time and occasionally read them.

MUSIC AND HELPING OTHERS

Danny, a medic in the National Guard at the time of the interview, provided especially poignant accounts of how he used music as an informal form of therapy to contend with emotions triggered by his experiences in the military. In 2002 he deployed to Iraq with a platoon (usually around thirty men) for which he was the only medic. Though he described the training that he received before his deployment as inadequate, Danny worked hard and took great pride in the important service that he was able to provide the men in his unit. As a medic, he took responsibility for both their physical and mental well-being. The men also had access to a chaplain, who served in the role of counselor and was available for the ecumenical spiritual needs of the platoon. Danny explained that some of the men who were not religious were reluctant to seek help from the chaplain because of the religious dimension, so they would come to Danny instead. Danny felt that he did all he could to help them: "I felt I did a good job. None of my guys, I felt, went without help. I tried to provide as much as I could."

Medics were supposed to accompany patrols and missions so that critical health care could be provided in the event of a casualty. At the beginning of his deployment, Danny's platoon went on missions as a single unit, always with him. He explained that after awhile his platoon was not able to "cover all the areas that were assigned to us," so they broke the platoon in half so that they could go on twice as many missions. Since he was the only medic, he had to go on all the missions, which meant that he did not benefit from the downtime that others in his unit had.

Though this took a toll on him physically and mentally, Danny also expressed a strong feeling of responsibility to the men in his unit because he realized how important it was for him to be there for them. He explained that when this change occurred, "at first I was asking [my]self, 'Why? This is just bullshit, I'm just another soldier.'" But then he started thinking about the implications of his not going: "Who is going to be there if something happens?" He remembered one incident when he was not present:

> There was an instance where something like that did happen. One of the first times our guys fired on somebody. . . . And these guys were young and scared and I wasn't with them on this mission. I guess a van got a little too close and they just, the gunners that were in the back of the truck turned—because that's what we were riding around in, trucks pretty much—turned around and laid into this truck. And they [in the van] stopped, and our guys had to provide aid for them. . . . I sat down with my guys and talked to them about that and asked them how they felt. A lot of them were really hurt by it, really confused. I mean, to deal with a completely bloody body . . . their first time. And they asked, "Why weren't you there, doc, why weren't you there?"

This incident reinforced the importance of his being on all missions and patrols, and Danny accepted the added stress as a necessity.

Danny described using music as a strategy in providing counseling or emotional support. He framed part of this discussion by explaining how gendered the military is. Danny, who was proud of being a good listener, felt that the men trusted him enough to express their emotions to him and to talk about how they felt. As a medic, he had to examine parts of people's bodies that made them uncomfortable. Building trust was important for making them feel comfortable with the intimacy of his physical examinations as well as when he was helping them with emotional issues. Having a private room allowed him the opportunity to use music to create the mood that he thought was most appropriate for building trust:

> When I was trying to console somebody, I would put on a little bit of mellow music. When I had to talk to somebody or when I was giving exams or stuff like that in my room. Because I had a private room, I could shut the door. I would put my music on. I didn't want to make anything uncomfortable for them, especially if I'm having to look at certain parts of their body which they're not really comfortable with me looking [at].

Asked if he remembered what music he used, he related a story about someone in his unit who was mentally unstable. Everyone was very frustrated with him because it was not clear whether the physical problems he had were real or were as extensive as he claimed, especially when they prevented him from doing something that created more work or risk for others. Despite his frustrations with this guardsman, Danny's job was nevertheless to provide physical and mental support for him. He explained:

> I had my CD player there. It was on a random mix of . . . what was I listening to at that time. I had just gotten some new CDs. I guess it was something that was calming to me uh, Tom Waits. I listened to that a little bit. . . . . And that's kind of what I was trying to do with [name], is get his mind off the situation. Because he felt like he was alone. He felt like he was getting shit on. He felt like nobody was listening to him and he's got an attitude problem. And so during that time I laid him out in bed, stuck an IV in him, tried to make sure that he continued to stay hydrated, gave him some Tylenol . . . .

Danny provided for this man's physical care by giving him medication. He treated his mental health by providing him with a relaxing space away from others, listening to him, and playing relaxing music. He explained that he was "trying to set a mood for him with music and having him lie down and just say, 'Don't think about where you're at. Just lie here. Get better. Get some sleep.'"

Danny was not trained as a mental health expert, nor was he given information about how to use music therapeutically; rather, he was extending his own experience with music in order to help others. Note that he did not use classical music, though he mentioned listening to classical music at other times, so it was an option available to him, or other music that professional therapists have determined is effective for calming. Rather, he selected something from his playlist that he had found to be effective for himself and others.

Danny's decision to use music to create a relaxing and trusting atmosphere in his room during consultations and examinations differed from Mike's description of his experience working as a medic in a clinic environment. I asked Mike whether music was played in the clinic, and he answered, "we didn't have music there. Looking back on it, I definitely would have changed that." The doctors and physician' assistants, the top of the hierarchy in the clinic, were the ones who made decisions about the soundscape in the clinic, so a medic like Mike had little say. He explained that going against the hierarchy would not be appropriate, and that it was necessary for the people in charge of complicated procedures to make decisions that best facilitated their work. Thinking back on it, he felt that music could have been beneficial to both the medics and patients.

Troops' ongoing access to diverse musical selections for individual and group listening, combined with their ability to control what they listened to depending on the situation and their emotional needs, was critical for many as they struggled with multiple conflicting emotional demands. Inasmuch as troops could listen to music to bolster their strength and confidence when they left the wire, they could select other music, which "does not judge," to relax, express themselves, or contend with the intensity of their taxing emotional and physical environment. Many whom I interviewed continued to use these strategies that they had developed at war, using music for mood management in their postwar emotional struggles. Yet it is because of this entanglement of musical listening with experience and emotion that certain music could also ultimately trigger difficult memories and evoke troubling emotions associated with trauma.

SEVEN

Coming Home

In an e-mail to me on February 15, 2013, Pete explained that at war, he felt "intense, scared, excited, and vengeful" and that he "hated it and loved it all at once. Now, back in the civilian world, he said, "I miss that feeling everyday. [The] USA is so quiet, I feel lost in the humdrum of daily life; it sucks but it's what I get to do nowadays." In the introduction to *Post-Conflict Cultures: Rituals of Representation,* Christina Demaria and Colin Wright explain that for survivors of conflict:

> The post-conflict situation might be considered more conflictual than the violence of the conflict itself. The discourses and actions of conflict are focused, and therefore reassuringly simplistic (aimed at territories, directed against bodies, justified by clear and rational objectives). Post-conflict discourses, however, are rendered more complex as the more ambivalent and drawn-out battle for hearts and minds goes on. (2006, 6)

For troops returning from war, this observation is especially true. As demanding as deployments were, and as much as troops yearned for home while at war, returning for short leaves and after their deployments was one of the most emotionally fraught and intense experiences that veterans had. During their deployments, they had no doubt about what they had to do on a moment-by-moment basis, and whether or not they were ambivalent about what they were doing, they also knew that their activities were critical and that neglecting their duties could cause harm to themselves and others in their units. Whatever difficult issues people faced, the immediacy of their environments, the importance of their activities, the constant high level of adrenaline, the excitement, and the comradeship kept many going. Once home, they were faced with a radical change of pace and the reality that their daily activities were no longer intricately tied to life and death and often felt relatively free of value. Many described finding themselves in what they felt was an overly quiet and meaningless space, where they had little sense of purpose and where they had too much time to think and feel. As things slowed down, they had the time and space to begin to process; all that they saw and did engulfed them. Many struggled with the feeling that now surrounded them, and for most, civilian friends, family members, and colleagues could not comprehend where they had been or what they were going through. Most returning troops faced varying degrees of postcombat physical and emotional stress.

As mentioned previously, Bull describes music's role in evoking nostalgia and compares an iPod to a diary (2007, 137). Users can choose a musical selection for the nostalgia they hope it will evoke, or music can involuntarily trigger unsought-after memories (Anderson 2004, 9). Because music was so intricately tied to so many of the soldiers' war experiences and thus was linked to their memories, it was involved in enabling many to remember and process what had happened at war, but it also evoked difficult memories and emotions and thus was tied to ongoing trauma. Inasmuch as music was used to manage emotions during deployment, it continued to play a big part for many once they were home. In addition to listening to music by civilian artists, some veterans found that listening to music produced by other veterans who had engaged in a war experience could be especially important for helping them address issues and reintegrate into civilian life.

HOME ON LEAVE

Depending on the length of deployment, most troops were given short breaks, time when they could leave the wars in Iraq or Afghanistan to go somewhere of their choice for a respite. Some whom I interviewed did not get leaves during deployments, but they were given leaves right before and after, when they could go visit family members or enjoy some rest and relaxation with friends. The promise of leave kept many going during wartime, and many spent a great deal of time dreaming and fantasizing about all they would do and whom they would see when they finally returned to their civilian lives, what many referred to as "normal." During leaves, some took the opportunity to go on vacations in different parts of the world, while some went "home" or to someplace they had lived before or where their family or friends lived.

The people I interviewed who went "home" described looking forward to leaving war and thinking about seeing loved ones as being almost painful. For those in dangerous zones, many worried about whether they would survive and still be alive in time to take advantage of leave. They looked forward to seeing loved ones, but many also worried whether their girlfriends, boyfriends, wives, or husbands had been faithful or would be there for them when they arrived. Their friends and loved ones were usually similarly excited and anxious about spending time with returning troops, making sure that they had a good time, expressing their support appropriately, and sometimes assessing them to see how they were doing emotionally and physically.

Many shared that though they were excited to see their friends and family members, they were also acutely aware of how short their visits would be and that they would soon have to return to war. Mark remembered:

> I can't even describe it. I mean, it's, it's just so weird. The whole thing is weird. Because no one there understands anything about what you've been going through. And that's just a regular, normal life that they're living. And then you get thrown into it all of a sudden for just two weeks. It's not even close to enough time to get used to it. But you're so happy to have made it to that point. But then the major fear that is constantly there, right in the back of your consciousness, almost ready to break through from your subconscious to your conscious, is that "I might die. I might die in a horrible way."

Mark explained that while at war he was very preoccupied with everything "that you have to do when you're there. It's easier to put it out of your mind." When he was working a fourteen-hour day and was so focused on what was required of him, he had little time to think about the fact that he could be killed at any moment. Back home with his family, "sitting at home watching my one-year-old" son, who had been born shortly before the deployment, he found it much more difficult to distract himself from these thoughts. Yet he also felt the pressure to be happy and enjoy his time and make sure that his family felt he was enjoying being with them and that he appreciated their efforts to make his leave special.

Troops on leave came out of the intense environment of being confined to some type of military base in a war zone only to be surrounded by civilians whose concerns did not seem overly important. Many explained that at war, it was vital that everyone was well-trained, prepared, and present to do their job in order to maximize the well-being of everyone in their unit and the success of the mission. Momentarily back in civilian life, they found it difficult to take seriously the concerns of those around them. The disjunction between the immediacy of life at war and the mundane monotony of civilian life left many vets feeling that civilian life was empty of meaning. Questions like what to eat for dinner or who would wash the dishes, or children fighting over toys, seemed trivial by comparison, and they found it hard to participate in these dynamics without being judgmental.

Some expressed feeling very anxious about the well-being of others in their units who were still at war and sometimes guilty that they were not there to contribute their part. They worried that something terrible would happen in their absence and that they should have been there to help or at least to support others. These feelings were especially amplified when there were casualties during their absence.

Many people I interviewed had married very young, not long before their deployments, and some had young children with whom they had barely spent any time. Many described marrying in a rush before the relationships had time to mature. Separation, usually hard in any relationship, was even more challenging given how young the relationships were, how rushed the marriages sometimes were, and the stress that both parties were under during the separations. Determining the state of the relationship and commitment of each party and working through issues dominated many people's leaves. Even when relationships were strong, the couple barely had time to readjust to being together before the warrior had to depart again.

After months of isolation from stores, soldiers could go shopping for new music, iPods, computers, speakers, and other accessories for music listening and making. They had access to the Internet and time to download new music, and they had opportunities to talk to others with whom they shared musical friendships about new music that might interest them. And many went to shows. These musical experiences on leave added to their memories, often giving them something to listen to when they returned to war that would connect them to home. These experiences then added to the associations of music and events in their lives. Songs could bring up memories of special times or people, or a soldier might remember a concert to connect him or her to a place. Lovers might share songs that subsequently became part of their special musical bond, something that could affirm their connection despite physical and psychical distance, as in the example given in chapter 5 about Noah listening to music from a show he had attended with his boyfriend during leave.

Listening to music during leave could assuage fears and be used to express frustration, anger, and disillusionment, or alternately, could be used to reaffirm family members' and troops' belief in the important contribution they were making to the mission. Pete never had leaves during his deployment, and the period between his two deployments was less than one year long. He remembered that during this period he felt enraged and vengeful because he had lost a close friend in his first deployment, and he was therefore anxious to return to Iraq because "leave was a 'delay' in me getting back there. I was really pissed about what happened to him and wanted to get back in the thick of it and get them back for them getting one of my guys." He remembered that he spent a lot of time during this leave "in a room at the ex-wife's family's house" watching "videos from my first tour and videos of my buddy that had just gotten killed so I had pretty much made up my mind I wasn't coming back, this was going to be the raging hell that ended it."

Pete's musical listening stood out in his memories of this time. He explained that up until then, he had listened to "all rock, but funny enough right before the second time I pretty much listened nonstop to *The Inspiration* by Young Jeezy." Though he did not consider himself to be a rap fan, a friend gave him a copy of this album and, he said:

> I could relate to a lot of the street life because it's what I was doing before I got my head on straight; listening to music about death in the streets, shootings, and drugs psyched me up for the next pump because I could see what I was doing and then here I am about to go for round two with guys way more passionate about fighting and killing you than anyone I ever met in life up until then. The feeling of I was a POS [piece of shit] and now I'm about to go back into Fallujah for round two against a formidable enemy had me feeling pretty high on life.

Pete's description of how he felt was not uncommon and was indicative of the heightened mind-set of troops during war. Though they might be physically removed from war during breaks within or between deployments, many were still psychologically situated within war, which made it especially difficult to contend with civilian life. Pete used music during his leave as an outlet for expressing the rage he felt and also to maintain his violent mind-set, a psychological state that he deemed was necessary for his return to the war zone.

"TRAINED FOR COMBAT,
BUT NOT TO COME BACK"

The feelings of troops waiting for the end of their deployment were often similar to what they felt waiting for leave, in that they experienced similar excitement and anxiety, and many of the issues they faced were similar and often amplified.

While at war, troops described yearning for home, counting the days, hours, and minutes until they could return to their lives, friends, favorite activities, and loved ones. They had spent months living and working in an intense environment that put a lot of demands on their time and attention and where they felt that what they did mattered in an intense, life-or-death kind of way. They had spent months in a heightened adrenaline state, knowing that at any time something could happen that could change their lives forever, or worse, end their lives or that of someone close to them. They had spent months wearing the same clothes, being told what to do, not being allowed to go out on their own, and carrying a gun. Though they craved a return to so-called normalcy, that return was a very significant and often challenging transition. Over and over in interviews, veterans described a sense of dislocation, feeling numb, not being able to connect with friends and family who expected them to return to "normal," feeling like their time and activities had become meaningless, and feeling guilty about those who were still involved in war.

A common pattern among recently reunited military families was that at first everyone was excited to be reunited, but the reality was much more difficult than the fantasy. For those in families, the returning service members may have been ready to reassert their role in the family. However, the family had learned to cope without that person, and the returning person may not have necessarily been in an emotional state to take on the role, which caused stress and tension. Young children often did not remember the parent or may not have felt emotionally close because of the long separation. Mental health issues from PTSD, TBI, and other psychological stressors were common, further contributing to the challenges of the transition (Laser and Stephens 2011). Family members, especially spouses, were often frustrated and disconnected when the returning veterans were unwilling to share anything about their experiences at war or how they were doing emotionally (Young 2012).

Many of those I interviewed explained that for a long time after returning, they went through the motions of life, but part of them was still at war. Many veterans felt isolated and confused, and they had few outlets to deal with their psychological, physical, and social needs. Many also suffered from a variety of physical ailments, from serious injuries to hearing loss and headaches. A number of people featured in this book are officially retired from the military with lifetime disabilities, even though at the time of the interviews they were still very young; most were in their twenties. The physical problems contributed to the psychological issues, in that they augmented the challenges veterans faced as they attempted to make it through the present while they created a future for themselves.

In his song "Hero," army veteran and musician Leo Dunson, who was a sergeant in the U.S. Army, expresses a problematic reality for many troops: that they were "trained for combat, but not to come back." Ritual theory, as posited by Arnold Van Gennep (1960) and subsequently developed and adapted by Victor Turner (1969) and many others, at its simplest stipulates that rituals serve an important purpose when people transition from one social category into another. Focusing on rites of passage—such as graduations, quinceañeras, and funerals—Van Gennep identified three types and three phases in rituals—separation, liminality, and incorporation—that serve the social function of moving an individual out of an existing category into a betwixt and between space and then incorporating that person into the new social category. The process is intended to help the individual and those in the two social categories involved to understand, come to terms with, and accept the transformation. Rituals of transition are not restricted to rites of passage, but extend to many other situations in which people move from one status to another, for example initiations into organizations, including the military, and inaugurations into political office. Within the military, basic training serves this important ritual function: individuals are removed from their daily lives (separation) and spend time in "boot camp" (liminal), which is neither civilian life nor a full-fledged military one, where they are put together with other neophytes for physical training and symbolically laden activities, after which they will be ready to join units as fully fledged members of the military (incorporation). Individual branches and units have official and unofficial rituals of incorporation to integrate new members into their organizations (Bronner 2007; Burke 2004).

The U.S. military has put great energy, time, and expertise into figuring out this process for creating a warrior out of a civilian. However, adequate, appropriate rituals do not exist for soldiers returning home to successfully reintegrate them into civilian life, ritually helping them to transition from the status of warrior to that of civilian. At the time of this writing, military bases did organize welcome home ceremonies for units upon their return. What happened during these ceremonies varied. They were usually around two hours long and were opportunities for the command to formally welcome back the troops and for family members and friends to reunite with them. Fort Campbell Army Base in Kentucky posted the following description for family members and friends who planned to attend one such event:

After the Soldiers deplane, they will form up outside of the facility. Soldiers will then march into the facility for a brief (3–5 minute) ceremony. At the conclusion of the ceremony, the Soldiers and families will spend about 20 minutes together. Following that, Soldiers will go back into formation to board buses. While they are boarding buses to go to their unit to turn in weapons and other sensitive items, families will be briefed on reintegration issues, and then returned to their vehicles. Strip maps will be provided, showing the location of the unit area where the Soldier can be picked up once weapons turn-in is completed.[1]

These ceremonies were very important to troops and families members, as their service and return were ritually celebrated. The timing and details of these events were not, however, adequate for fulfilling the ritual reaggregation needed by most troops. Note the brevity and timing of the ceremony. The official ceremony was combined with the logistics of troops' returning weapons, being transported where they needed to go, and so on. Upon their immediate return, troops were jet-lagged, anxious to see their loved ones, often overwhelmed by the striking difference in their environments, and not yet mentally ready for the social transformation from warrior to civilian, the ritual function that the ceremony was intended to serve. Similarly, family members were anxious to be reunited and often overwhelmed by the return and not yet prepared to process the significance of the social transformation the veteran would need to go through to readjust to life "at home."[2]

Furthermore, these ceremonies were problematic for some because they were monologic; they presented and supported only a single viewpoint and perspective for interpreting troops' service. Returning troops were celebrated as heroic patriots, certainly something appreciated by many. But this celebration did not address the ambiguity of the war experience and the ambivalence that some troops felt about what they had done or the significance of their return. In a scene in my documentary *Grounds for Resistance*, army veteran Joshua poignantly described his feelings about being treated as a war hero:

> I didn't feel that I was part of anything to be proud of. And them being proud of me just made me feel fucking terrible. The more they told me how happy they were to see me, the more they told me how proud they were of me, the more I just felt . . . shitty and wanted them to go away, the more I wanted to drink.

Being labeled heroes and thanked for one's service could help make some feel appreciated and that what they had endured was worthwhile. However, it could have the opposite effect of making some feel shut down and unable to express how they felt when feelings were dissonant with what families and communities expected. Some knew or at least thought that letting their family members know how they actually felt would disappoint them or even result in rejection.

In the few days after their return, it was common for there to be informal events at people's homes, bars, Veterans of Foreign Wars (VFW) establishments, or other meeting spaces where close friends and family could spend time together, usually someplace where there could be some privacy. Nate explained that sometimes at these events there were Bible readings; children read poems; and people told stories while laughing, eating, and often drinking, while also remembering anyone who did not come back alive. These close-knit events were helpful in the short run and for some were enough, but many returning troops did not engage in the kinds of social, psychological, or ritual processes necessary to gradually remove themselves from the reality and identity of a warrior into the roles that were expected of them in civilian life, as marine Pete explained:

> When I was in, you got a three-day set of classes to prepare you [for the transition], far from enough, and no money, just your last paycheck. I had more counseling on preventing sexual harassment and suicide prevention than what they give you to prepare to be a civilian. In my opinion, it was far from enough.

He elaborated:

> There's boot camp to indoctrinate you how to be a marine; there's not one on how to return to being a civilian. I was given thirty-two weeks to be trained before I was placed in my actual unit; I received three days to prepare me for deploying back to a civilian life—the ratios should be a closer number. Preparing for life after the military is almost as difficult as learning to BE in the military.

Nate referred to returning home as the "back home deployment." He felt fortunate that he went to a community college in his first year back where he found a mentor who was a "vet himself" of the Vietnam War. Nate reflected: "I don't know how I would have made out" without this man "guiding me through the initial transition." Nate was fortunate to happen upon someone well positioned and available to help him with the transition; others were less lucky.

With the lack of adequate processes for ritually reincorporating troops into their new civilian realities, troops were also faced with the multitude of tasks associated with establishing new lives or reestablishing themselves into existing lives. Those now out of the military had to find jobs, negotiate their relationships with friends and family members, figure out their identities, and deal with their own emotional struggles. Many described the transition period as being especially fraught with the intensity of memories of war, whether or not they had been formally diagnosed with mental health conditions.

As already detailed in previous chapters, combat veterans of these two wars suffered from staggeringly high rates of psychological as well as physical afflictions. In addition to stressors caused by trauma, many struggled with issues around the morality and ethics of some of what they had seen and done, as Joshua, interviewed on December 17, 2009, for my documentary project *Grounds for Resistance,* remembered:

> And still, just thinking about those incidents with those people that we fucked up, that comes back to me. That shame. That depression. And that's not something that's combat related. I experienced a roadside bomb. I was shot at a few times. It was just the stupid shit that we did. Like a man coming up to me, begging me to help his family. He's in tears, begging me, saying someone's hurting his family. And, I'm like "Oh shit, I have to help this guy." And I'm told to send him away. He's saying, "No, you have to help me." And I just say, "No, I can't help you. Get the hell out of here." And, I send him away. I'm becoming somebody that I don't want to be. Everything that I ever believed in, I just throw away and watch this man totally give up and walk away. And I see this guy's face. I'll never forget that man's face. The desperation in his eyes, and how I did nothing to help him. I completely failed as a human being.

Plagued by their physiological and physical struggles, outcomes of various dimensions of their military and war experience, many combat veterans were in need of professional medical and psychological attention.

The VA and other veterans' organizations provided resources for medical care, including mental health, and for finding educational and professional opportunities. Yet many of those I interviewed explained that these resources were inadequate and that they struggled profoundly when they returned, especially after they were discharged from the military and suddenly found themselves disconnected from the community that had been so important throughout their deployment and time in the military. Concerned about the lack of adequate resources for those returning from these two wars, the U.S. Congress required the Departments of Defense and Veterans Affairs to commission a study on troops' physical and mental health and other readjustment needs. The study was conducted by the Institute of Medicine of the National Academy (Veterans and Their Families 2013). The brief report associated with this study begins by stating: "Upon return, the vast majority report that their experiences were rewarding, and they readjust to life off the battlefield with few difficulties. Others, however, return with varied complex health conditions and find that readjusting to life at home, reconnecting with family, finding work, or returning to school is an ongoing struggle." The report clarifies that though a "majority" reported adjusting well, 44 percent reported difficulties, and for as many as half of these, the resources provided by the DoD and VA were inadequate to address their needs. The report also states that evidence from past wars indicates that "veterans' needs peak several decades after their war service, highlighting the necessity of managing current problems and planning for future needs." Among the problems emphasized are TBI, PTSD, depression, substance abuse, military sexual trauma, suicides, rise in domestic violence, and high unemployment rates. The report concludes by stating:

> Although the DoD and the VA actively seek to understand the scope of the readjustment challenges, implement appropriate policies, and provide programs and services, at many times their response is dwarfed by the magnitude of the problems.
> The urgency of alleviating these health, economic, and social issues is heightened by the number of people affected, the rapid drawdown of military personnel from Iraq and Afghanistan, and the long-term effects for service members, veterans, their families, and the nation.[3]

Efforts have been made in the last few years within the military to acknowledge the inadequacies of treatment and to provide increasing resources for returning troops. Yet the shortcomings of the VA remain a devastating reality. Allegations about systemic problems with the VA, including deaths at some centers possibly being due to patients not receiving treatment in a timely manner and the falsification of records to conceal this information to protect the reputation of VA hospitals and clinics, have been widespread.

The devastating number of veteran suicides (Friedman 2014) and the staggering statistics of veterans suffering from PTSD, military sexual trauma, and other forms of combat stress have forced the military to be more proactive in acknowledging the problems, helping troops identify and accept that what they are feeling is acceptable, and providing resources. Still, a large number of troops are suffering and will continue to suffer for a long time. As Nate explained, "I think all the branches are trying to step up, but now with everyone transitioning forces from desert to jungle and amphibious conflict (with downsized budgets and forces), it will probably be tough to really address the coming home transition."

As an example, Keith, mentioned in the last chapter, started suffering from PTSD while he was still in the military. A sergeant who himself had been diagnosed with PTSD helped Keith identify his problem and encouraged him to get help. But then the sergeant committed suicide four days before his retirement, which sent Keith into a major depression as he wondered, "Is this the rest of my life?" While he was still in the military and back from deployment, Keith described trying group and one-on-one therapy. He explained that the therapy was not very effective because most of the doctors that he saw would only come to base for three-month periods. He found himself not wanting to tell one therapist everything that was going on, only to have that person leave and then have to start over with the next one who came to base. He explained that he eventually began seeing a psychologist who specialized in PTSD and had been working in the area for twenty-five years. He finally began to open up and feel like he was getting the help he needed. But then (rumor had it) the therapist started having nightmares and suffering from PTSD herself, so she left her position, leaving Keith without her care. When I interviewed him, Keith was bitter about the quality of care he had received, "if you want to call it treatment." He elaborated that sometimes when he was in an emotional crisis, he would call the VA for an appointment and not be able to get one sooner than three weeks in the future. Keith's story echoes many others that I have heard over the course of doing this research.

Many interviewees also commented that the military did not do much to help troops transition to civilian life in terms of helping them find homes and ways of making a living. An article in USA Today provided figures from a VA memo released in January 2014, reporting that "nearly 50,000 Iraq and Afghanistan veterans were either homeless or in a federal program aimed at keeping them off the streets during 2013, almost triple the number in 2011" (Zoroya 2014). Due to the combination of lack of community, difficulty finding employment, and mental and physical health issues, many veterans that I know have found themselves homeless for varying periods of time.

While in the military troops were highly trained, and regardless of their positions, they served an important role in the larger system. Yet for most the skills and training they received in the military did not transfer into marketable qualifications in civilian life. Those I interviewed explained that after years of using their specialty training, they suddenly found themselves without work and often with skills and a resume that were not marketable. Medic Danny was responsible for his unit's health needs and had regularly done such extensive treatments as amputations and emergency surgeries. Back in Oregon his qualifications meant nothing, and he had to start all over. Those involved primarily in combat were trained to use complicated machinery and weaponry, and some were in leadership positions within their units. Once out of the service, these skills translated into qualifications for low-level positions as security guards or bouncers, or other jobs that many considered to be both unfulfilling and underappreciated. Nate explained that "the resources available for transitioning are often centered around turning military experience into a sales career (small business owner, salesman, finance), often using the military network to sell something that is military-related. For example, former Special Forces guys get recruited to sell and demonstrate the latest weapon systems. So you can imagine how frustrating/ limiting that can be for a grunt." Many described the transformation from having people count on them for their physical and emotional well-being, literally life and death in some situations, to feeling completely useless.

The social reintegration was also difficult. For many, their friends had gone on with their lives in their absence. Upon their return, though combat veterans often looked forward to reintegrating with their previous community of friends, they found themselves socially isolated. Angie described her transition out of the navy as being "catastrophic to her social life" and "devastating." She returned to her home in California only to find that "everyone was gone." She felt that she had nobody: "Everything and everyone was completely disrupted. And the way I grew up, my friends were kind of my family. I didn't have a lot of family, so my friends were it as far as my support system. And it's taken me years; still, it will never be the way it was." She explained that she felt further isolated because she did not feel that her friends wanted to hear anything about her experiences during their separation: "And they don't understand anything. They don't even ask. They don't give a shit. They really don't." This fissure in their social realm is particularly understandable for the large number of people I interviewed who entered the military right out of high school, a time of transition for all. Their friends back home had moved into their grownup lives distinct from their teen reality; yet the network of their youth was the only one to which the veterans had to return.

Substance abuse has been rampant among combat veterans as many turned to alcohol and other drugs, dulling their minds to keep from thinking or feeling too much. Having been restricted to a limited sexual pool, some engaged in lots of promiscuous sex, thinking little about the repercussions. Many who were married or in relationships struggled with the expectations of their loved ones, who were relieved to finally have their partners home again, only to find that they had each changed or that the combat veteran was not present or in the emotional state that the other person had hoped for.

As for many combat veterans, the transition out of the military and into civilian life was especially difficult for Pete. As he put it, "everything that you hear about happening to people happened to me." Pete elaborated that "he lost his family," went through periods of "homelessness," and received no help from VA for a long time. This was so even though he had "heard from a lot of my fellow marines that they now put more emphasis on transition." Pete did feel that the training he received as a marine "to get through any situation" had helped him with overcoming the issues he faced, though the commonality of the issues faced by Pete and others suggests that the military training to overcome adversity is not adequate for meeting all the challenges faced by troops as they attempt to transition into "normal" life.

HOME, MUSIC, REMEMBERING, COPING

Psychologists understand that individuals' memories about their own lives, or autobiographical memories, contribute to processes of self-structuration and, very importantly, can function to preserve a feeling of coherence over time, contribute to social bonds with others through sharing information about one's self, and enable people to use past experiences to understand their inner self in relation to others (Bijsterveld and van Dijck 2009). Memory making is a fluid, dynamic process that changes with reflection and over time. Through our memories, we "search for meaning" and make an active attempt to "make sense of our experience" (Crawford et al. 1992, 9). As already established, the relationship between musical listening and daily activities at war contributed to troops' memory making, and certain genres, artists, or musical selections became intertwined with salient events, thoughts, or emotional states from their time in combat (Petr et al 2007; Turino 2008; van Dijck 2006). These memories of what they saw, did, or experienced could be painful or disjunctive with how they previously understood their inner selves in relationship to their conceptualizations of self and in relation to others. The evocation of memories of war through music could thus contribute to a person's feeling of coherence over time, but it could also create fissures that were alienating and isolating, which could contribute to mental health issues.

Most people I interviewed recognized this mnemonic potential of music, and some reported consciously listening to particular music because of the memories it evoked. They sometimes chose to listen to certain music because it reminded them of their friends, places, and fun times. After returning from his last deployment, Mike continued to keep a cardboard shoebox with a selection of the CDs that he had listened to the most while in Iraq, a physical memorial to his musical listening at war.

Veterans also reported encountering music, without having chosen to do so, that triggered memories, disrupting their train of thought or what they were doing and transporting them to a different reality, physically, temporally, and emotionally distant from where they found themselves.

Some music evoked good memories, sometimes of positive experiences during deployments; at other times the memories of deployment reinforced their appreciation that they were no longer there. Angie still listened to the band Devo. She had many happy memories of singing along with the album with friends when she was in the navy, and these musical memories still made her feel cheerful. When Andy listened to "So-Cal music, what I call like Yellowcard bands," which he listened to a lot during his deployment because "there was this guy who was from California, and he had that on his playlist all the time," it reminded him of "hearing it when we'd play cards. It brings back the good time that we had." As they would listen to the music and play cards, they would tease the Californian, "'You know you're not working at Hollister or Abercrombie [trendy U.S. clothing chains] right now, turn that off!' We'd be acting out, you know, making fun of him."

Gabe reported that since his return, when he hears country music it makes him happy because it "reminds me of patriotism, it reminds me of patriotism very much." When Gabe was in Iraq, he listened to country music because it evoked feelings of patriotism and connected him to the United States. Since his return, when he listens to country music the same music now evokes memories of Iraq and reminds him of what it means to be an American, especially symbolic for him as a naturalized citizen.

Danny remembered:

Mike's box of CDs, a physical memorial of his musical listening at war. Courtesy of Mike.

I listened to James Taylor that my fiancée, and now my wife . . . . We both listened to certain songs on there, which really kind of spoke about how we felt, I guess. And I can listen to it now and remember and picture myself lying in my bed over there, just wondering when I was going to come home and see her again. Wondering if she's listening to the same music.

Danny listened to James Taylor after returning, not so much to remember being in Iraq, but to remind himself how much he wanted to be home and with his wife during his deployment, and thus it helped him appreciate his life away from war.

When I asked Josh about music that reminded him of Iraq, he mentioned Steve Earle. Josh did not feel patriotic when he was in Iraq and did not choose to listen to country music for its evocations of patriotism, yet it was part of his soundscape during his deployment. Now that he was back in the United States, music by Steve Earle, which ironically is explicitly antiwar, reminded him of being in Iraq. Country music indexed his war experience, and he associated the country music he heard in Iraq with the pervasive patriotism emphasized in the military. When he encountered country music after his deployment, rather than the music making him feel patriotic, it reminded him of war, and because of his political perspective, it amplified his anger about U.S. imperialism.

The evocations of indexical connections through music could trigger negative feelings or even evoke trauma. Eric, who suffered from PTSD, explained that since his return he had found himself changing "the song a lot if I think it's reminding me of there [Iraq]. A song will come on, and I'll be reminded of something that happened, and I get sweaty, an anxious feeling, and I'll have to change the song." Eric's visceral reactions to certain music are typical of PTSD, and I asked him if this happened when he heard a song that he had listened to during something significant that happened in Iraq. He answered:

Just something about the song. It might not even be the same specific song, but it might just be something that reminds me. I mean, for me music plays a huge part in my life. If it's even the era or whatever, if it's the type of music that I listened to or music that came out while I was there or anything that I can attribute to being in Iraq or something that happened, that is stressful; I change the station.

Eric's response highlights the risks inherent in musical listening, because listeners cannot always control what is in their soundscapes, nor can they always predict the affective impact that a given musical selection will have on them. As noted previously, in their study of the effectiveness of musical therapy, Mitchell and MacDonald (2006) found that the ability of individuals to exercise control over their musical listening was more important than the sonic dimensions of particular pieces in determining whether music would have the desired effect of helping an individual relax. Eric's example highlights that for those dealing with trauma or difficult emotions and memories, this control over listening is important, but control over what one's sound track contains does not always correlate with control over the associations that a person will make or the affective response that a particular selection will invoke.

Benji, who also suffered from PTSD, similarly explained that the song "Bodies" evoked a negative psychological response for him: "If I go in a room and I hear that song, yeah, I might start getting that imagery and it's like, you know, it could put me in an uncomfortable position." Here, the aggressiveness of the sonic qualities of the song and its lyrics evoking images of dead bodies hitting the floor were both indexical and iconic: he heard this song a lot during war, thus it was indexical, so the song worked as a sign on multiple levels, intensifying its affective impact on him.

In chapter 4 I shared a quote from Andy, who was listening to the song "Angel" by Sarah McLachlan when his base was attacked, and "a lot of my friends died that day." After his return, the song continued to evoke memories for him. Sometimes he consciously chose to listen to the song in order to evoke the memories and associated emotions. At other times, when he encountered the song not by his own choice, "it throws me off completely." In chapter 4 I also included a quote by Keith, who found that listening to the Cranberries' song "Zombie" in combat shifted his perspective to the suffering that he was causing. As a reminder, he was listening to that song as he drove through a village and saw a baby dying, an image that continued to torment him and led to deep feelings of depression and guilt over the well-being of his own son, who was around the same age as the one he saw die. He explained that when he has heard the song since his return, it "just makes me cry and upset." He explained that now that he was home, listening to it was different and more emotional than when he was in Iraq, because these memories and visions are "all . . . in my head now." He continued, "We have a saying when you go to sleep, you're home. When I go to sleep, I go back to war." He explained that every time he hears the song or hears a baby scream, he has to "relive that child dying."

Inasmuch as musical memories could evoke difficult memories and for some PTSD, it could also have a role in coping with difficult memories and trauma, as established in the previous chapter. Listening could be so involving that it distracted people from thinking. Benji described using music since his return from Iraq to drown out his feelings:

> If I feel like I might be having an anxiety attack, you know, then I'm just turning the volume up the whole way, or sometimes like when you're in a really bad mental state, or you're walking down the street and you're kind of like, staggering you know and it's like, the music gets turned all the way up and you just kind of want to have no end on that volume. You just want to kind of turn it all the way up, so that's all you are, that's all you hear, like there's nothing else going on in your head except that feeling, that thought of whatever, nothing in Iraq is there.

Benji's use of music in this example was a coping strategy to suppress his thoughts and emotions. Others continued to use music listening in the ways described in the preceding chapters for mood management.

Because of close associations between musical listening and memory, music played a part in autobiographical memory making, and thus music could help to create continuity in a person's sense of self, in addition to contributing to an understanding of the world around oneself and relationships with others. Because at least some of the experiences of war were so far removed from "normal life," it could be difficult for former troops to integrate their war experiences into their perception of themselves as coherent individuals. This could be especially important when someone had experienced trauma. When individuals listened to the same music before and after a traumatic incident, it could help them create an associative link between who they were before and after—the same person—contributing to a sense of coherence, which could enable them to incorporate the event into their life stories, often a critical step in healing.

By contrast, many combat veterans described consciously choosing to listen to different music after their deployments in an attempt to create a separation between who they were at war and who they wanted to be after. This shift in musical listening could be attributed to the joy of increased access to new music and social scenes, or to boredom with the repetitiveness of what they had been listening to.

A SUPERHERO IN MUSICIAN FORM:
THE SOLDIER HARD PHENOMENON

As alluded to at the end of chapter 5, Keith suffered from extreme PTSD and a lack of adequate treatment. He shared that his depression plummeted and that late one night he was feeling "very low," was in a "deep hole," and had been drinking a lot. He was prepared to give up. In front of his computer, with a gun in his hand and his finger on the trigger, he decided to peruse YouTube. "For some reason" he stumbled on the song "Support Us" by Soldier Hard. Keith listened to the song, and "it brought me down to the level" of knowing that "I'm not alone. I'm not alone going through this. If he can find a way to this, I can too." He put down the gun and listened to the song over and over, crying for hours. I asked him why he chose to search YouTube rather than calling a suicide hotline, and he said that it never occurred to him to call a hotline, that he didn't even know they existed. To this day, Keith is thankful to Soldier Hard for saving his life, and he is not alone.

In an e-mail exchange in December 2012, Tyler explained that he too first listened to Soldier Hard when he was contemplating suicide: "I was really thinking of killing myself and a friend sent me a text saying look up his video 'Road to Recovery.' I was sitting there with a gun and searched it. [In the video] I saw someone [Jeff Barillaro] going through the same stuff I am and I started to cry." This video combines music, song text, and visuals to tell a powerful story about a veteran successfully struggling with PTSD. The video starts with an audio track by Soldier Hard and probably other musician veterans mimicking the official communications that happen as a unit prepares for an operation, the mission here being the performance of this song. Soldier Hard appears in a black POW-MIA (prisoner of war-missing in action) T-shirt on a stage, surrounded by military personnel in full official military attire, complete with firearms. As they stand at attention, salute, and aim their guns, he raps. The phrase "I'm on the road to recovery" is repeated over and over and interspersed with lyrics about what he has been through and where he is at. The visual images tell the story most powerfully. Images of his wife emerge throughout. Toward the beginning, the lyrics express that he wants to be the way he used to be, and the viewer sees an image of him and his wife, smiling and enjoying one another's company. It then turns to the harsher realities of images of his face, tense with anxiety and agony. We see him taking the narcotic pain reliever Percocet, reaching for a gun, waking up from nightmares, and fighting with his wife. The lyrics verbally emphasize the "road to recovery" interspersed with images of him with what looks like a support group and in one-on-one sessions with a therapist. As the song winds down, things appear to be getting better. Wearing the words "Unapologetically American" on a black T-shirt, he appears with his wife, who is once again smiling. Soldier Hard hugs her, and he hugs children, maybe his own. The song ends at a barbecue where he is cheerfully grilling for a large crowd of people. As he smiles and hugs his cheerful wife, he looks over and sees what looks like a young veteran, sitting by himself, sullenly staring at the ground. Soldier Hard walks over to him and reaches out, and the two embrace as the images fade away and the line "I'm on the road to recovery" repeats over and over. As the song fades, the following quote emerges in white lettering on a black screen:

We have come too far to turn back, we owe ourselves to live again. Yet, we owe it to our fallen comrades. Let us live life for them . . . in their honor.

In this and many other videos, Soldier Hard poignantly presents himself as the protagonist, the veteran struggling with and surviving from mental health issues. Soldier Hard knows that he is not alone, and he is able to effectively tell his own story knowing that it is shared by so many others. His message is hopeful. He was the one taking Percocet, the one reaching for the gun, yet things are getting better, and he is there to help other veterans, such as the one pictured at the end of the video, because Soldier Hard understands, he was also there and in many ways still is. The story of his journey demonstrates that things are getting better. He now has the emotional capacity to love and be loved, to cook for his friends, and to support others. He provides evidence to Keith, Tyler, and so many others in the midst of their struggles that they too can survive, and tells them that they have the responsibility to do so because "we owe it to our fallen comrades."

A glance at Soldier Hard's Facebook site demonstrates the impact he is having on other veterans. On December 11, 2012, he had 4,999 Facebook friends. Soldier Hard is one of many musicians who are part of Redcon-1 Music Group, a collective of musicians, all of whom have served in the military, who produce music related to their military experiences.[4] Themes that dominate their original lyrics are PTSD, memories of war, struggles with returning home, and above all, supporting other troops and veterans.

Soldier Hard and other military musicians are aware of the high rate of suicide and other mental health issues and the impact that they are having. On the Web site for Redcon-1 they declare "Suicide? Please No!" and request:

Soldier Hard performing and in the studio while simultaneously managing
his Facebook site. Courtesy of Jeff Barillaro (Soldier Hard).

Brother's & Sister's in arms: If you have thoughts of suicide, please contact us
first! A Redcon-1 staff will be with you IMMEDIATELY![5]

They also provide a national suicide hotline number. Their role as combat veteran musicians thus extends far beyond producing music and interacting with
fans about it.

I contacted Soldier Hard to ask him if I could interview him and whether he
would put me in touch with any of his fans who might be willing to talk to me.
He posted on his Facebook site that there was a professor interested in talking
to his fans and received replies from many people, including Keith, Tyler, Pete,
Amy, and others who were enthusiastic about sharing with me just how important
Soldier Hard has been to them. Family members as well as veterans were among
those who responded. Soldier Hard's music has played an important role in helping family members understand what their veteran relatives are going through
and how they can help them. It also helps them realize that they are not alone
in the challenges they face in their relationships.

Soldier Hard's music is very direct and explicit in its treatment of the experience of what it was like to be at war and to struggle with the aftermath. His goal
is to be productive, not to complain but to help people survive. As he puts it, he
uses his music to express his own emotions, but also those of other people. After

hearing Keith's story, for example, Soldier Hard incorporated the story into his song "See Clearly Now." The two men met after a Soldier Hard show and spent time together after the performance. As he was leaving to catch his flight home, Soldier Hard handed Keith a CD with this song on it, which Keith later realized was about him. It meant a lot to Keith that Soldier Hard cared enough to convey his story to a wider audience.

Soldier Hard explained in an e-mail to me that he is not much of a "speaker" and "can't sit and tell my feelings to another person, I can NOT do that. Never have, and never will, but when I make a song about what I feel, it's as if I'm telling many others' story, not just my own." He explains that he often puts himself aside and "speaks for others who refuse to speak about how they are feeling or thinking. They NEED a voice." He explained that he feels that God has given him

a gift to turn something negative into a positive through music, and so I have to speak for those who CAN'T . . . so when I make music [about what] most NEVER talk about, I tell myself, "This is NOT the time to be selfish or prideful, you owe it to thousands of your military brothers and sisters to speak up for them, speak loud so that others will hear all their cries, speak loud, let the world hear who they are . . ." and I tell myself this over and over until I come to the conclusion that THIS IS WHAT I'M MEANT TO DO! so I just do it and hopefully I can HELP other people to cope, or to even understand who we are. Kinda like a super hero in a musician form, well that's what I believe, and NO one can tell me different.

Amy and her army veteran husband Sean agree:

Personally we feel we can talk to him about ANYTHING and EVERYTHING! Soldier Hard, aka Jeff, is an amazing individual. He deserves mad props for all he's done! We will support him and the Redcon-1 Music Group always. Never back down! He is inspirational, he has done what my husband does. He gets us. He is simply amazing, a true hero, whether he claims the title or not. He is saving troops daily through music.

The thousands of people who follow him on his Web site, the hundreds who are active participants on his Facebook site, and the fans who attend his performances and listen to his recordings are evidence that many feel he is indeed playing this role for them.

Soldier Hard has such an impact because he is a veteran expressing the struggles he is experiencing and increasingly the difficulties of other veterans that he has come to know, either during his time in the military or through his music making. When I asked Tyler whether the music would impact him the same if Soldier Hard were not a veteran, he explained that it would be "really different" because "only another veteran should sing about war because we lived it." Pete similarly explained that it's important that Jeff is a fellow veteran and really understands what it was like to be at war and how it felt afterward. As Pete put it, it helps him to know that the "person he is listening to has been through firefights, ambushes, and has been where he has." He elaborated that the music gives him strength because Jeff is "alive, he's making music. If he can do it, I can do it." Given my discussion with Shannon (mentioned in chapter 4) about his choice to listen to music about war by civilian artists, I asked Pete whether the music about war by civilians is similarly helpful. He answered that it was not as effective because "they either have a 'political feel'" or they romanticize soldiers.

Before finding Soldier Hard, Pete listened to "a lot of rock and country" and "never listened to any mainstream rap about chicks and guns." He was attracted to Soldier Hard's music because of the lyrics, and he thinks of it as "spoken word with a fast beat" more than as rap. As Keith and Tyler did, Pete first listened to Soldier Hard when he was having an especially rough time. A "buddy," another veteran who was aware of how he was feeling, sent him a link to a song by Soldier Hard because he thought it would be helpful. Pete found the song to be "spot on" and "felt immediately that there was someone else out there who knows exactly what I'm going through." He felt that the words matched "what he was feeling" so well that he "could have been the one saying the words." After hearing this song, he started stockpiling all the military music that he could find, and at the time of the interview, he reported that he rarely listened to anything else.

Pete went into great detail about how he consciously used Soldier Hard's music both to express himself and to manage his feelings. At the time of the interview, Pete ran a small business from a room in his house that he shared with his wife, children, and mother-in-law. Everyone in the house knew that Pete suffered from PTSD, though Pete rarely talked about his war experiences or his emotions with members of his family, and "they don't ask." Yet he had learned to communicate to them about both his experiences and his emotional struggles through his musical listening. Pete explained that throughout the day, he played "military music," usually in the room where he conducted his business. Having his own space allowed him to spend time alone where he could control the soundscape and thus to some extent his mood. He selected songs based on his emotional state and needs at any given time. When he was feeling a high level of anxiety, he listened to a song called "Last 48" by the rap band 40 Glocc. He described it as "a song about wrapping up loose ends the last few days before you step off and may not make it back. It's about accepting what you're about to do and just being ready to go." The song was about "knowing that things are going to change and that this was how life was and that it may be the last time that the soldier experienced life like this or at all." He described the song as "very mellow," and explained that it helped him calm down. When he felt anxious and that he had no control over his situation, songs could help him put his circumstances into perspective, remind him "that there are guys right now getting laid to rest, others being picked up for funerals." The songs helped him realize that there "is something that I can do," which enables him to "get out of this funk for an hour or so," so that he "can get back to my life."

In addition to Soldier Hard, Pete listened to other music by artists who are also combat veterans, including Sgt. Leo Dunson or 4th25. Again, he picked the music depending on his mind-set and emotional needs. Pete described this music as much more of the "hard core military mind-set" than was Soldier Hard's. Pete defined this mind-set as the attitude that "we can do as we please. We can take down a whole city, a 'don't fuck with me' type of thing." Sometimes when he felt that things were not fair or that someone had done something unjust to him, he listened to Sgt. Dunson to remember that at one point "I was this baddest guy. I had this power and did all that stuff, and I am still that guy." At times, however, he found that listening to this music did not end up helping him emotionally, because it got him "worked up" and "complicate[d] things more" because it made him "want to blow things up."

In these examples, Pete described selectively choosing music for his emotional needs, but he also said that he always had music playing in the background. Sometimes he was making very conscious choices about what to listen to; otherwise, "military music" accompanied him as he went through his life. These songs kept him connected to his war experience and could evoke memories. He explained that sometimes he would stop what he was doing and listen, sometimes playing the song over and over in order give him time to think about it. A song about a firefight, for example, "will make me stop to think about how insane it is and that I could have said the same thing as the one who wrote the song." Eventually he would stop repeating the song and would return to whatever he had been doing before.

Pete explained that people who have not been to war would understand these songs differently. For example, Soldier Hard has a song in which is the line "he used to scream hella loud in a firefight or on the battlefield." He explained that a civilian might think that the song was about how loud a firefight was with all "the guns and airplanes overhead." However, that's not what the song was about for him. It made him remember time. A firefight often could be as brief as two minutes, which to the inexperienced might not seem like a long time. But, he clarified, "it isn't quick. So much is going on and so much has to be taken into account and done. It goes by extremely slowly. The ambiguity of the songs allows any listener to take the little snippets" and "expand them into their own memories and thinking." Though he didn't think that civilians would interpret the songs the way he did, he nevertheless thought these songs "give a civilian a glimpse of the experience."

Pete was also drawn to writing by veterans about their experiences. I asked him whether he felt that there was a difference between hearing the kinds of messages that Soldier Hard was imparting through music or reading. He explained that he felt that music was more available and accessible than were poetry or memoirs. He felt that most people did not want to hear others talk about the "worst day of their life." Yet when this same information was "packaged in a song, it gets the word out in a more socially acceptable way." People could learn about the war experience in a "more easily digestible way."

Pete took advantage of what he considered the more digestible packaging about the war experience to communicate his own experiences to his family members. Because his wife and mother-in-law had also heard the songs by veterans he listened to, he felt that they often understood how he was coping based on his song selection. He could also communicate to them through the sound level. As an example, he said that on a day when he was struggling with PTSD, he could go into his room and "turn up the music a couple of notches." Doing so helped him both manage his own feelings and communicate to them that he "needs some space," and so they "leave him alone."

Similarly, Keith explained that he listened to Soldier Hard "every single day." At the time of our interview, he had been married for one year and with his wife for three years. As with most combat veterans who are in relationships, their partners have to learn to cope with their combat stress and find ways of giving them space and supporting them. Keith explained that he "can be a pain in the ass at home." He suffered from "bad anxiety, and one little thing, a word in the wrong tone can set me off," and he would "go off." He said that his wife understood and that when he responded in this way, she knew to give him space, "that he needs an hour or so by himself." She often would suggest that he listen to a Soldier Hard CD in order to calm down. Soldier Hard's music had become a tool for both of them to manage the intensity of his emotions.

Furthermore, Pete and others used music by veterans as a way to try to communicate something about what war was like to their loved ones. Pete explained that though he shared little about his experiences with his wife, he regularly played veteran music in her presence, for example, when they were driving together. Because some of the songs described war, such as the firefight example, by playing this music in their shared soundscape, Pete felt that he was sharing something about the experience with and fostering some understanding from his wife.

Soldier Hard's music also provided an avenue through which Pete and a few close friends who were in his unit with him could communicate with and provide support for one another. He explained that they all struggled on the anniversaries of traumatic events. No one other than the people in his unit knew the significance of these particular dates, yet each of them struggled on these days. He explained that they rarely talked about what had happened or acknowledged the significance of these dates directly. Instead, on each of these dates, they sent each other links to relevant songs that let the others know that they, too, were remembering the events of that date, and the lyrics were intended to provide some comfort.

SOCIAL MEDIA, MUSIC, AND VETERAN NETWORKS

In addition to the music itself, Soldier Hard and other musicians associated with the military provided a communication hub for social networking where listeners could interact to form virtual networks and forge communities. They did this by making connections with one another, discussing song lyrics, sharing how they were feeling, and being supportive. Connected through these musicians, troops constructed and engaged in community. Many veterans had difficulty sleeping, and they found that they could post at any time of day and night and receive a response. On Soldier Hard's Facebook page, Jeff was a constant contributor, posting about his own struggles, responding to other people's posts, and always updating information about his upcoming shows, recordings, and materials for sale.

The fellowship provided through this and other social networking sites replicated in some ways the profound sense of community that many troops experienced during their deployments when they lived so closely with others in their units. The loneliness of suddenly feeling cast off into a very different environment, where they felt isolated and no longer needed, without people in their immediate vicinity who understood their needs and were committed to being available for them, was partially mitigated by the virtual community created around music by fellow veterans. The social distance and anonymity afforded by the sites, such as Facebook, made it possible for veterans to express things to others that they might not without the cloak of anonymity.

Soldier Hard's Redcon-1 Facebook site provides an excellent example because it was so active. He posted multiple times daily, and his posts were always followed by numerous responses. In addition to giving updates about what he and others were up to musically, he shared information and photos about his family life, his successes and joys, and his struggles with physical and emotional issues. Soldier Hard, much admired by his fans for the courage and tenacity and survival of his musical messiahdom, presented himself as a struggling human who was also in need of affirmation. The responses to his and others' posts on the site were almost always supportive and full of praise. On February 19, 2013, Soldier Hard posted this:

> Holy crap, again on and off, I get some major headaches, and NOT like a normal headache or a migraine either, it's wors[e]! I feel excruciating pain in the back of my HEAD, which causes pain there and in between my eyeballs, makes me want to dig whatever is there causing the pain out! I bang my head with my fist thinking it will take the pain away! No luck! Then my upper LEFT side of my body starts shaking really fast and I can't control it! I went to the VA and told 'em about it, they just told me, its just a normal "headache" but no, I know me! This ain't normal at all!!! Anyone out there got this problem?

Following are a few of the sixty-two responses that flooded the page within one hour of his post:

> I had pressure headaches that stemmed from the back of my head going towards the front. My hands would shake all the time and they still do today.

> Listen brotha. I had a history of chronic headaches and that is not even a migraine. . . . I know the VA is free but I've heard cases of brain tumors and

aneurysms that can cause those symptoms. The brain is highly important brother. I recommend seeing a doctor asap to do proper scans and other tests. Just to be on the safe side. . . .

Probably a dumb question, but have you eaten??

This used to happen to me when I was in Iraq mainly from stress. How much pressure you been under, bro?

Soldier Hard responded to some of the questions and comments, answering that he had indeed eaten. After several posts mentioned the possibility of neurological problems, cancer, and chemical sensitivity, and a joke about his being on crack, he posted:

on the phone with the VA now to see if I can get in, I'm hurry up and waiting now! and I never did crack in my life!

The conversation continued, and a number of people, obviously with their own frustrating experiences with the VA, made comments about the VA and that he shouldn't let the "VA give you the brushoff." Ten hours later, he posted:

Headache's gone!!! I'm Up! Time to hit the lab!!!! Late Night Session!!! Gonna finish up a track I was working on earlier!

This comment precipitated messages of encouragement, and everyone followed his shift from talking about his physical issues back to music by posting questions about whether he was recording a new album.

This conversational thread was one of thousands of examples of similar interactions on this and other social network sites. Soldier Hard, the musician *and* veteran, shared his experiences and humanity through his music, but also by being a real person who was very human in his own pain and struggles and who was always accessible. It was his music and the potency of his lyrics and videos that put him at the center of this community. Not just any veteran with heart could bring together all these people and be the focus of so much supportive and jocular interaction. That he was a musician whose music spoke to so many was what brought them together and made them want to be active participants in the community. The daily interactions fostered through this site not only promoted his music but brought together veterans and their familial members into a supportive network. Amy explained:

> Redcon-1 Family was there for me throughout [her husband's] deployment. . . . When I needed someone to talk to, they were always there. None of them hesitated one bit to contact me to make sure we were okay, that Sean's condition was okay. They are amazing individuals. We love all of them, and sometimes I do not think they realize how much they really do mean to us!!! which is A LOT.

Other musicians who were veterans used the site to promote their music and let people know about other military musicians, thus expanding the musical network and audiences for military artists.

Pete explained that he felt that Soldier Hard was not only helping other veterans, but also helping himself through ongoing efforts to assist other vets through his music. He explained that in war, even when things were really tough, "you know that what you're doing is helping others." This "makes it easier to deal with what is going on." Similarly, he felt that helping others "makes it easier for Soldier Hard to deal with what he's going through." Jeff's response after reading a draft of this chapter reinforced how much his efforts help him as much as others:

> It's funny because I just got done reading the chapter. . . .I love it. I got emotional a lot throughout it, only because it's nice to hear how I help others. That's healing. . . . I have this new mindset [that] I've really embraced this past six months. I can heal myself if I keep staying busy servicing others. The more people I help, the more broken pieces of me will [be put] back together . . . so I can be whole again.

Inspired by Soldier Hard and others, Pete similarly started to dedicate a lot of his time to helping other vets, not through music, but through a variety of activities, including most recently collecting oral histories.

Pete cautioned that though he very much appreciated and benefited from social network sites, the anonymity could be negative. He explained that he worked at home and spent all day on his computer. A major source of his support came through music and his interactions with other veterans virtually, which meant that he "spen[t] all day in front of a computer by myself." Though he might be connected to other people online, he also felt that he often "suffers in silence." After reading this paragraph in an earlier draft, Pete elaborated:

I feel like I used it [social media] tactically as a tool to put a barrier between me and people. It's easier to look up someone before meeting them vs. an on-the-spot in a meet and greet. As part of having the anxiety we [combat veterans] try to avoid triggers, but by using social media you can almost go too far. Now that I'm working out of the house and forced to interact with people person-to-person, I'm doing a bit better. Before I had become almost awkward from not interacting with people outside of my family in person and conducting so much of my day-to-day on the computer working.

This chapter on coming home is difficult to bring to a close because there are so many stories, so many perspectives, and so many experiences, and none of these stories is over. As with any life experience, especially those so memorable and associated with trauma, troops continue to live their lives, remembering and forgetting, in an ongoing process of forging their identities and interpreting and reinterpreting all that they have done in the framework that makes sense to them at any given moment. As the distance from their time at war expands, the political landscape changes, and their personal lives evolve, what stories they tell about war, their musical listening, their memories, their relationships, and their politics will solidify, merge, change, or be forgotten. The memories and the explanations of significance in this chapter and others are themselves shifting. If I reinterviewed these people, many would probably have something different to say; even some of those I know well have different perspectives and stories at the time of this writing than they did during the interview.

What is clear despite all this fluidity is that music has been an invaluable resource for many troops when they return, to celebrate, grieve, remember, connect, and forget. Inasmuch as music has been a source of stress and trauma and an avenue for expressing difficult, sometimes destructive emotions, it has also been an integral mechanism for coping and healing; musical listening has helped war veterans in ways that have sometimes been more meaningful and long-lasting than the services provided by the institutions intended to serve them.

EIGHT

Music and Political Transformation

As I was doing this research and listening to some of my interviewees' descriptions of their negative feelings about the military and war and, for some, narratives about their transformations from service man or woman to antiwar activist, I became very interested in the process through which an individual goes from being someone who voluntarily joins the U.S. military into someone who adamantly opposes the military and its wars. This interest led me to make the documentary *Grounds for Resistance*. Here I explore the role that music played in these conversions, focusing on the stories of political transformation and musical listening shared with me by a few of the people I interviewed.

SHIFTING POLITICS WHILE STUCK AT WAR

A part of the daily experience of many troops was the ongoing reflection or deflection of coming to terms with what they were doing. Everyone knows that war is physically, emotionally, ethically, and politically difficult. Troops engaged in war are in the difficult position of having little control over what they are tasked to do and often have limited outlets to discuss their thoughts about the wars in general or their feelings about specific things they have seen or done. Furthermore, some people who fought in these wars found themselves in paradoxical situations in which they came to fervently disagree with the wars, but they had little choice but to continue fighting them. As Noah poignantly put it,

"I was not afraid of what was going to happen to me. I was terrified of what my country was going to ask me to do." Because war requires cooperation among many, if one person did not do a job, it could jeopardize the unit and put others at risk, something that many were not willing to do. Many of those I interviewed explained that these internal conflicts between what they were doing and their thoughts about it were too much to bear, so they had strategies, some of which included music, to try to keep themselves from reflecting on what they were doing. For others, music gave them a space to think or even introduced them to different political perspectives.

Publicly, when in uniform U.S. troops represent the government and become symbols and enactors of its policies. Carol Burke puts it well when she notes that the combination of uniform and required distinct hairstyle is "so thoroughly perfected and indelibly impressed as the military carriage that it speaks clearly to all who view it" (2004, 79). Regardless of what individual soldiers, marines, sailors, or airmen might have thought about themselves or the government, they nevertheless served as symbols and a communicative mechanism for the government. They were free to discuss their politics in private, though whether or not they found others similarly motivated to talk about issues or how much doing so was accepted in more public spaces depended greatly on the makeup of a particular unit or the perspectives of commanding officers. Some people I interviewed reported having one or two friends within their unit with whom they felt safe discussing politics; others expressed far more freedom or had relationships with their officers that allowed for some dissent. Others felt that there was no one in their units with whom they could discuss any dissenting view, which contributed to their feelings of isolation.

Of the people I interviewed, many described themselves as having been largely apolitical at the time of joining. Mark, for example, described himself as "not political at all. I was too self-absorbed when I was younger. I sort of thought of myself as a liberalish type of person, but I didn't give a shit really about any of that stuff." As previously mentioned, many, including Mark, were young people just out of high school who joined not because of a strong sense of duty, but rather because it was an option, sometimes they felt the only option, for their professional and economic development. Others described joining because of a desire to serve their country, and of those, some specifically chose to serve after the 9/11 attacks because they wanted to contribute by avenging the wrong and protecting their country by reducing the threat of terrorism. By contrast, a few remembered that even when they joined the military, they already were critical of the U.S. government's decision to engage in these wars; for example, Seth explained that he "had a real kind of academic opposition to the war." He surprised everyone in his family because he had always been vocal about his opposition to government policies. However, as a husband and the father of a young child, when he lost his job at a gun store he felt that he had few other options. The military recruiters promised to fund not only his education, but also his wife's, so despite his politics, he decided to join because it seemed like the best decision for his family.

Many people felt committed to contributing to their society, and some saw the military as a way to do that. They understood that the military was involved in lots of different types of activities across the world, most of which were not characterized as war. Moreover, the jobs offered by the military included a wide range of different types of occupations, many of which did not involve direct combat, including mechanic, cook, medic, computer technician, pilot, pharmacists, and so on. For those who joined because they wanted to serve their country, this motivation did not always imply strong support for war as the answer to resolving conflict. Gabe, for example, explained that "I identify myself as an educated American; when I was there, I really wanted to bring peace to Iraq. I thought I was one of those Americans that wanted good for the country, that wanted good for Iraq."

Regardless of a person's political perspective upon joining, for many the reality of serving one's country in real wars prompted political engagement and critical thinking about the missions to which they were contributing. For some, participating in the military fostered their political growth in the direction of increased patriotism and respect for the political and economic objectives of their government. Others experienced war as inherently contradictory. Some people listened to music to help them interpret their conflicted feelings about what they were doing. Gabe, who believed in war only as a vehicle toward a more peaceful world, discovered that his goals sometimes differed from some of what he found himself doing in Iraq:

My political point of view is that a peaceful world would be a better world. At the same time, I am in the army. I'm a medic. So, in my point of view, we were doing God's work in Iraq. We were bringing, we were trying to bring peace to Iraq, that's how I saw it. So, the reason why I listened to The Beatles, it was not so much because they were antiwar, it was more because they were peaceful.

He understood the irony of being a soldier participating in a war who was also deeply committed to peace. He was attracted to music by The Beatles because he felt that their lyrics promoted peace rather than explicitly opposing war.

All those I interviewed, regardless of their political views, were very reflexive and articulate about how they thought and felt about their war experiences. Being critical of the government, these particular wars, or how they were treated by their command did not necessarily imply a political stance. Plenty of troops who considered themselves to be patriots who supported their government were nevertheless critical about certain aspects of the war effort, and conversely, plenty of those who honorably served their country in these wars did not politically agree with some or all of what they were required to do.

Here I focus on those who did frame their feelings about war and the military in political terms, those troops who came to question their government's policies and in some cases became very critical of these wars, and especially of the sacrifices they and others were asked to make for wars they came to believe were not necessary. Some critiqued their own roles and came to the feeling, as Josh cogently put it, that, "we weren't really liberating occupied countries anymore. We were occupying countries now." Quite a number of those I interviewed explained the sense of disillusionment and alienation that came with this realization.

This disillusionment extended from the details of the mundane through much more profound experiences. Benji remembered listening to the song "Calling in Sick" by Buck-O-Nine, which was about someone pleased to finally have a job with sick leave benefits. He listened to this song over and over while he reflected about the irony that in his job, at least while he was at war, calling in sick was not an option. He would listen to it, frustrated, thinking, "I don't want to be here, what am I doing here?" For Mark, a particularly poignant traumatic event served as an epiphany for how he interpreted what he was doing. He explained that "when I was there, I started to realize pretty quickly that this is a complete farce, like everything about this war, everything that we'd been told is totally bullshit." He remembered a transformative incident when he was waiting for someone to finish showering in "these very rickety showers that were set up by the contractors, by KBR or Halliburton or whatever." Because of a problem in the electrical wiring, the man showering was electrocuted while Mark waited. This incident hit close to home for Mark, as he would have been the next one to shower and thus could easily have been the victim. He subsequently became very bitter about the private contractors who had been responsible for this shower, who were also U.S. citizens working for the war effort, but who he claimed were doing a "sliver of the same amount of work as me making thousands more without putting their lives at risk, really in the same way we [soldiers] do." That incident impacted his perspective profoundly, and he explained that:

> I really started to see what it was all about. We were all pawns for a big money-making scheme. Everything that we were told about it was a lie. We are there killing people in their own country. How can we feel good about this? How can I feel noble? There is nothing noble about this, at all. There is no great enemy. We were not fighting Nazis. We're fighting people who just want us to get out of there. And then they kill some of my friends, and then we take revenge. It's just, like, pointless. And all at the same time, there's these people there making vastly huge, way more money than us, and obviously, all the oil and everything, it became so clear to me. And I was like, I can't, there is not a part of me that can believe in this. I can't agree with this at all. . . . Anybody who thinks that way is just deluding themselves or doesn't want to deal with the fact that they were mercenary killers.

Unlike almost all other jobs that many of us have, troops did not have the option of quitting without suffering extreme consequences, which added additional pressure. Some members of the U.S. forces did desert while deployed, suffering a variety of consequences. Army Sergeant Bowe Bergdahl purportedly walked off a U.S. Army base in Afghanistan in June 2009 unarmed, possibly having left a note explaining that he was seeking a new life because he had become disillusioned with the war and was going forth to a new life. He was captured by the Taliban and was a prisoner of war for five years. On June 4, 2014, U.S. president Barack Obama announced that he had brokered a deal to release five Taliban prisoners from the U.S. Guantánamo Bay detention camp in exchange for Bergdahl's release. The arrangement was heavily criticized because of the danger associated with releasing the Guantánamo prisoners, top Taliban operatives who may very well participate in additional attacks against U.S. interests as a result of being released. An outcry also emerged immediately because Bergdahl was perceived by many to be a deserter and even a traitor and thus undeserving of having the U.S. government negotiate for his release (Goodman 2014). The details of what happened during his deployment and his motivation for leaving his unit have yet to be made public. In March 2015 he was officially charged with desertion (Lamothe 2015).

For those I interviewed who came to feel strongly against what they were doing, stopping or leaving the war zone was not an option unless they were willing to face capture as did Bergdahl; they still found themselves at war and most felt duty bound to carry out their jobs.[1] Many, regardless of their own political perspectives, felt that as service men and women they were obligated to do what was commanded of them and not to question it. This did not mean that they did not have their own opinions, but rather that they accepted the expectations that had been placed on them and understood the hierarchy in which they operated and feared the consequences of doing otherwise. This idea was repeatedly reinforced in military discourse. In response to the desertion of Camilo Mejía for political reasons, Tad Warfel, the commanding officer of his National Guard unit, was reported to have said: "His duty is not to question myself or anybody higher than me. . . . His duty is to carry out the orders that I give him or his platoon leader gives him. We're not paid in the military to form personal opinions or to doubt what our leaders say" (McDermitt 2004). Many told me that they were completely unaware during the time that they were in the military and deployed that there was any antiwar movement, much less that a veterans' antiwar movement existed, or that troops ever refused service for political reasons. If they did consider the option of refusing to serve or deserting, most did so very much alone, fearfully, and without support. Navy veteran Matt, who participated in *Grounds for Resistance,* explained:

> I was out of active duty for almost three full years before I met another vet who openly admitted to be being opposed to the war. I can really clearly remember the first time I met the guy. I almost felt my whole world shift. "What? There's another person out there that had a similar experience?"

This feeling of isolation with one's thoughts and feelings of dissent added to troops' confusion, lack of opportunities to fully explore and accept their perspectives, and lack of awareness of options other than fulfilling their obligation to the military. Most reported knowing nothing about the existence of war resisters, GI resistance, or the process for filing for conscientious objector status, which could have enabled some to legally discontinue their service. Benji remembered thinking that "GI resistance was something that happened in Vietnam." Filing for conscientious objector status was a long, drawn-out process that was not always successful; the status was not always granted. Furthermore, filing for this status was not an option for troops already at war. Even when back in the United States, some troops have gone AWOL (absent without official leave) in order to have the time to prepare their conscientious objector applications in time to avoid deployment, which has landed some in prison for desertion, for example,

Travis Bishop, who tells his story in *Grounds for Resistance*. Other options while at war, such as simply refusing to do one's job, could lead to punishment and ultimately dishonorable discharge, which would have lifelong implications for veterans' access to benefits, certain types of jobs, and general respect within their families and communities.

As with other dimensions of their lives, the ability to put on headphones and escape into a private sound bubble provided a space within which troops could think. Sometimes the politics of their musical choices were not very significant, in that they listened to music that they knew allowed them the headspace to reflect, but the music itself was not political. All genres of music had this capacity, though different individuals were drawn to different styles depending on their tastes, their musical listening, their identities, who was around them, their politics, and so on. Others listened to music whose lyrics evoked specific political perspectives, ethical issues, or attitudes about war, such as the patriotic country music previously discussed. Though these patriotic lyrics could affirm or reinforce a person's sense of belonging and contribution to the government's mission, for others the same music could evoke criticism or cynicism, because the listener disagreed with the perspective expressed in the song lyrics; as DeNora cautions, how music is interpreted by individuals is "constituted reflexively, in and through the practice of articulating or connecting music with other things" (2000, 33).

Other music contained sentiments that were generally antiwar, anti-U.S. government, anti-imperialist, or pro-peace, and some bands or songs were explicitly critical of these particular wars. This music provided an alternate perspective from that which dominated troops' environments.

Joseph

Joseph remembered that by his second deployment to Iraq:

I was totally, I was absolutely against the war, but I was also a 50-Cal gunner on convoys. I had to play this weird dual role. I had to be against the war and mad and angry at [President] Bush, and at the same time, I had to channel this anger into something constructive, which was to keep myself alive, which was ultimately destructive. It was ultimately destructive across the board because there [in Iraq], I hurt or affected negatively far more people's lives than would have been affected if I had simply died.

Joseph, who was very frustrated and politically minded by his second deployment, tried to manage this disjuncture by escaping into a sonic sound bubble of aggressive antiwar music as an outlet for his anger. He listened to this music while working out, which gave him a physical as well as psychological outlet:

> I would listen to really angry music when I'd work out because I wanted to get that anger out. Because I was angry at Bush, I was angry for being there, I was angry about being away from my wife, I was angry at the fucking army, I was angry at the American people. . . . When I wasn't working out, I would listen to a lot of music that was antiwar, like there was a *Rock Against Bush* CD that came out from Fat Records, which is owned by Fat Mike from No Effects. I would listen to [the band] Against Me!, which has a lot of antiwar lyrics. I would listen to [the band] Anti-Flag, which is antiwar too, I listened to all this really antiwar music.

Joseph listened to punk bands while exercising as a mechanism for expressing, sinking into, and managing his anger, "get out my aggression" as he put it. Joseph's reflection on what was happening when he listened to this aggressive music while working out emphasized the ambivalence and the disjuncture between his desire to be a good soldier and his anger against the war:

> I felt that this music was helping to fuel this very strong physiological response that I get from working out. . . . I would try to put everything that I was feeling into my workouts. . . . It's really hard to describe because it's the same emotions, but they are linked to two very different, they're two emotions that fed into the way I felt physically. . . . I have no words for it. It's linked to two very different attitudes. One was that I'm in Iraq. I'm a soldier and I'm supposed to be here to protect my friends on my convoys. And then at the same time, I was working out because I was really angry with [President] Bush and really angry with the American people for letting this happen to me and angry about being at war.

Joseph struggled putting into words such an emotional and visceral experience. What is clear from his explanation is that music helped drive his physical workout, and the two together provided an avenue for expressing and releasing the increasing ambivalence, confusion, and anger that were building in him. By contrast, in "calm moments on base," he sometimes listened to antiwar music reflectively in order to explore and reinforce what he thought about the war.

Though he explained that he listened to antiwar music during calmer times, he emphasized that "it wasn't this big peaceful antiwar music like John Lennon. It was really aggressive antiwar music, such as the band Propagandhi," a Canadian punk band.

Danny

Danny was especially articulate about how he used music to cope with conflicts arising from his sense of obligation and politics as his thinking developed over the course of his deployment. In addition to the regular stressors of war and of being a medic, as previously described, Danny emphasized his frustration with his leadership and the lack of opportunities to participate in decision making as being especially challenging:

> And being in a military environment and the rank structure, you can't tell your superiors what you really think of them. You know, whether or not they're doing their job correctly, or whether you just don't like them. You can't get into a fight with them. Because they would always threaten that you would be brought up on charges and you would be going to jail and you would get this, that, and the other thing. So the anger would just, it would build up. But for me it would always end up [with me] not feeling anymore. You go to, I like to say, you just feel numb because you can't be angry, because you can't be happy, you can't be sad. You just don't feel because there's absolutely nothing you can do, and in a sense it's kind of like prison because you know, you're waiting for that time when you can go home, but in the meantime you're just trying to survive.

He remembered one incident that especially outraged him, after which he felt especially imprisoned:

> They give you these night vision goggles, which are heavy as hell, and they weigh your head down. They don't have enough of the high-speed ones for everybody, so you end up with [this] broke-ass Vietnam era equipment. I couldn't get it working right, and here's this guy just bleeding out. And you know, he's one of my first casualties, so I'm just nervous. I'm like, "What do I do?" I took my Kevlar off. I just took my hat off, put it on the ground, picked up, I had a headlamp that I bought here [Eugene, Oregon] at REI, and put that thing on and went to work, and you know, I stopped the bleeding. I got his

heart rate stable. I filled him with fluid. I felt like I saved that guy's life, you know. . . . And so I'm feeling a little better because this guy's stable, and I'm working on some of the other casualties. And most of the guys, because of where the bullets went in, had a lot of lower leg injuries, and they weren't too bad, no amps, amputations or stuff like, like a broken fibula or something like that. And so through this situation I would just do an anatomical splint: put both legs together and grab them up. So I'm in the process of doing that, and our battalion commander comes over and starts yelling at me for not having my hat on, and I'm thinking, "You can't be serious?" I'm here saving these people's lives and he has the guts to say, "Well this area's not secure." And I'm like, "I'm the fucking medic. That's your job." And I ended up getting pulled into his office and threatened that if he ever caught me in that situation again, I would wear my entire uniform every single day, I would sleep in it."

After these descriptions of feeling trapped by unreasonable expectations and not being respected by his command, I asked him how he dealt with not being in a good mental situation while having to be the support person for others. He answered:

That's part of being a medic, you have to throw all of that out. You don't get to do that. You don't get to cry. You don't get to be angry. You can be angry behind closed doors and scared, but, I mean the last thing you want is for the guys that trust you . . . I mean, it's just like the leadership. If they saw the platoon sergeant crying or confused or whatever, then they would lose faith in them and so that was my standpoint on that.

He explained that one of the ways that he coped was to close himself in his own room and listen to music. Asked if he could recount a memorable experience of doing this, he told the following story:

I remember feeling numb over there, feeling like I couldn't do anything, feeling trapped. I'd go in my room, close the door. I had some candles lit, and I listened to a Dave Matthews song, it's called "I Let You Down." And just that line had several different meanings. Feeling like I was letting my family down if I went home, but that I was letting myself down if I didn't do something, stand up and be a man, and get out of there. I mean, being a soldier in a sense, I just felt like I was a lemming. I was walking along with everybody else, you know.

There's a lot of references to cattle calls and stuff like that, when you're there, because that's all you do is you follow the person in front of you. And for me, I could [lie] there and listen to that and zone out and it really was comforting. I guess in some regards, because I could just sit there and wonder what I was going to do, whether it was worth it, wondering whether I should tell them, "I don't want to do this anymore."

The multiple pressures on Danny, as on many others, to be a good soldier, follower, caregiver, and ethical human—all while controlling his emotions, whether sadness, frustration, disillusionment, anger, or disappointment—coalesced, producing a combat veteran who continued to struggle with these emotional and intellectual conflicts long after his last deployment. Danny exemplified the difficulties in assessing veterans' mental health when such things as PTSD and TBI diagnosis are restricted to specific symptoms associated with trauma. All troops in these wars experienced some type of trauma, and all must contend with the aftermath. Some were able to process and heal relatively quickly, while for others, the experiences continued to impact them far into the future, sometimes for their whole lifetimes. That the trauma and dark memories overlapped with mazes of often contradictory emotions associated with gender identity, morality, ethics, and politics makes it difficult not only for service providers to comprehend, diagnose, and treat the mental issues faced by many veterans, but for the veterans themselves to understand what they are feeling, justify it to themselves, and pursue mechanisms of healing.

Benji

When I interviewed Benji on April 29, 2009, he was twenty-two years old and had been out of the Marines for two years after serving for four. By that time he was an antiwar activist with Iraq Veterans Against the War and Veterans for Peace. He identified himself as a collective anarchist and described the veteran antiwar movement as "all over the political spectrum," including, "radical leftists," and then "you've got these people who are on the far right who are very pro-mission, pro-military, maybe perhaps still alienated from society or from within the military itself, but they're just opposed to the Iraq war."[2] Music played a role in enabling Benji to reflect upon and learn about political perspectives in addition to providing an outlet for expressing political views.

Benji explained that over the course of his deployment he found himself listening to more and more artists whose lyrics contained commentary on the Iraq war or more general antiwar sentiments. He did not think that it was a conscious decision for him to listen to this music. Rather, in the period since his two deployments he had spent a great deal of time piecing together the history of the development of his political consciousness. Benji was only seventeen years old when he joined the U.S. Marine Corps. He explained that some of his favorite bands at the time, including Catch-22, Riddlin' Kids, and Midtown, were comprised of young musicians whose lyrics resonated with his adolescent concerns with "girls and partying." As the musicians matured, they started coming out with songs with social messages, some specifically about the wars, which resonated with his own developing maturity and his conflicting feelings about what he was doing in Iraq. As an example, he mentioned the album *Permanent Revolution* by Catch-22.

As with many others I interviewed, it was only after Benji was home and far away from war that he could really reflect on and explore more fully the political implications of what he had done and make decisions about his political future. As he put it, echoing Danny, while in Iraq, "you don't think about what's going on because it's the same thing, like you're just numb to it. You don't process it until later."

Benji found himself increasingly depressed and struggling with mental health issues after returning from his second deployment. He explained that by the end of his second deployment, most members of his unit were no longer "pro-mission." Already feeling disillusioned, he also struggled with living in the barracks and feeling that his superiors were treating him and others in his unit like children, which was especially troublesome given the intensity of what they had been expected to do in Iraq:

> No way am I going to spend twelve hours every Thursday scrubbing stupid refrigerator coils with toothpicks and rubbing alcohol. I'm not going to get up to get into formation every day at six in the morning and stand there for half an hour and then walk around for forty-five minutes picking up cigarette butts. I wanted to get out of that really slaving and demeaning atmosphere. I was just sick of it. I had been to Iraq twice by now, I'd been in the Marine Corps a long time, and I was sick of being treated like a piece of shit.

During this time, a close-knit, small group in the unit spent a great deal of time together, drank lots of alcohol, and talked about how they were feeling about the war and the military.

As with other changes in his life, Benji traced this transition musically. He explained that the iPod that he had while at war had broken, which marked "the end of a legacy." He remembered going to the store Best Buy:

> Basically what I did was I got back from Iraq, [I went to Best Buy], I got a big cart, and I just went through and I picked out every single CD that I wanted. . . . and then I got my sound system for my car. I drove around and I listened to music at blaring levels.

In addition to listening to recorded music, he and his friends also traveled around the country to see bands perform, many of which he described as political, including Pepper, Fishbone, Hoodoo Boneskulls, Dispatch, and State Radio.

He explained that at this time he started getting in good physical shape and eating better than he ever had, but that he also started to have significant mental health issues. He had always struggled with depression, but it reached a new severity, and he found that he had trouble sleeping and suffered from increasing anxiety. He started to realize that he was not "normal." He described being out with civilians and telling a joke that would have been funny to his fellow marines, but instead was a conversation stopper due to its perceived inappropriateness. At the time he was working as an urban combat instructor for the Marines, and he remembered that he "would get very irate and angry and would throw stuff and kick stuff" and was "scaring people," all behaviors that were inconsistent with his typical "mellow" self. He later learned that these were the "first signs of post-traumatic stress," although at the time he had "no idea because the military really discourages you from thinking that you have post-traumatic stress."

It was around this time that he heard the song "Camilo," by State Radio, a song about Camilo Mejía, the first war resister of the Iraq War. Mejía deployed to Iraq in 2003 and served five months in active combat followed by two months in Jordan. In late 2003 he "deserted" from the army during a leave in the United States when he decided on political and ethical grounds that he could not return to Iraq to continue his deployment. He was arrested and imprisoned for desertion and ultimately received a bad conduct discharge, which bars him from any benefits he would otherwise have earned for his eight years of service. Since his release from prison he has become an activist in the veteran antiwar movement and an inspiration to those in the military seeking alternatives to continuing their service.[3] Following are the lyrics to the State Radio song about him:

"CAMILO"

Woke him up with a barrel to his head
His eyes shut tight bracing for the blow
Resigning his life to the metal held
In another man's hand

Twenty days in a concrete fallout
What life have I to take your own
Oh my country won't you call out
Doorbells are ringing with boxes of bones
And from another land's war torn corners
To a prison cell in my own
Punish me for not taking your orders
But don't lock me up for not leavin' my home

Your words just a bloody fallacy
A house of cards you painted white
You tried to recreate Normandy
But you made up the reason to fight
And now red oil is spillin' down on the street
And your eyes too big for the belly is weak
Will you not refuse this currency
Or is blood money just money to you

Is blood money just money to you

Twenty days in a concrete fallout
What life have to take your own
Oh my country won't you call out
Doorbells are ringing with boxes of bones
From another land's war torn corners
To a prison cell in my own
Punish me for not taking your orders
But don't lock me up for not leavin' my home

Camilo
Camilo
Leavin' my home
Camilo

Benji and his friends were really inspired by this song, because this was the first time they had heard about the existence of war resisters. Benji explained that they would listen to this song "over and over and over again. Listening to these same songs and starting to talk about, 'Wouldn't it be great to war resist?' We really started to idolize this concept of a war resister, someone who had the strength to stand up." Previously they had had no idea that there was a veteran antiwar movement. They began talking about the possibility of resisting, and they anticipated that if they were called to deploy, they would refuse, regardless of the consequences.

Benji was honorably discharged in 2007 at the conclusion of his four-year contract. Once out of the military and twenty-one years old, Benji stayed in California and moved into a house with housemates, where he had his own room for the first time in his adult life. This privacy increased his opportunity for musical exploration. Depressed and struggling, he continued to use music as he always had. He listened to more and more political music, which both enabled him to reflect on his experience and political perspectives and triggered emotions:

> I was reflecting a lot and I was thinking about specific memories, some very brutal memories, and remembering a lot of things . . . . I spent all my time, you know, keeping up with it. Horrible things are happening all the time, and I counseled GIs. Like now I'll listen to a lot of Streetlight Manifesto, which is the new band on the ska scene . . . . They are completely innovative, completely creative, very original lyrics. And the lyrics like "this one's for the boys who fought all the wars who'll never fight for themselves," lyrics like "the last two soldiers on the battlefield, survivors of the storm, they invent one another while their mothers beg the lord, if you're missing him, I, if you're listening I'm missing him, so somehow bring him home, how did it come to this?" And then the end of the song is two soldiers are on the battlefield and they're pointing, pointing the rifles at each other, and as they pull the triggers you know, they say "How does it, how did it come to this?"

He explained that this and other music helped him "validate" his "political thoughts." He also rediscovered Goldfinger. As a teenager he had associated the band's lyrics with the conflicts of childhood. Now he interpreted them to be about international conflict, demonstrating the creative ways that music listeners engage with music and continually reinterpret pieces based on their current needs or perspectives.

As others I interviewed told me they had done, at this time he also frequently chose to listen to certain music depending on the mood that he was trying to evoke. When he was feeling really "downtrodden," he would listen to the album *The Wander Souls of Flame* by the band O.A.R., or sometimes he would listen to music because it would trigger his anger:

Sometimes I'm heavily buzzed, and I want that trigger and I just want to be angry. That's how I channel it. I think music's always been helpful for me because it helps me to deal with my triggers and conflicts and thoughts. I channel without it ever being harmful to anything external. Like I'm angry, and I want to be angry. I can listen to angry music, and I'm not going to destroy property. Or if I'm sad and I want to be sad, you know. . . . I dealt with depression a lot as a kid, and I just kind of got exasperated in the Marine Corps. So I spent a lot of time feeling out my triggers and knowing my triggers. There is certain music that I can reach for to avoid that, to not even get to that point.

He explained that while he started to listen to a greater amount of explicitly political music about war and democracy, it took him a while to "connect the dots" and realize that he was actually changing his own thinking. Benji eventually became involved in veteran antiwar activism, and he said that it was at this time that his "PTSD really 'kicked off.'"

About a year after his discharge, Benji received reactivation orders, which he decided to refuse. He went to Portland, Oregon, for the Winter Soldier, organized by Iraq Veterans Against the War in March 2008 (Courage to Resist 2008). Inspired by a similar event by the same name that had taken place in 1971 during the Vietnam War, Winter Soldier featured firsthand testimony from combat veterans of the Afghanistan and Iraq wars, "giving an accurate account of what is really happening day in and day out, on the ground."[4] Through his participation in Winter Soldier, Benji publicly declared his intention to be a war resister and refuse his reactivation orders.

Though the song "Camilo" had been an important anthem for him, up until Winter Soldier Benji assumed that the song was based on a fictionalized protagonist. He was astonished to meet Camilo Mejía at the event and remembered thinking, "What? You're real?" Meeting Camilo and others helped bolster his courage to publicly express his experiences and refuse to continue to participate in the war effort.

As Danny described about the Dave Matthews song "I Let You Down," the song

"Camilo" and other songs, though inspirational for Benji, also evoked troubling emotions and feelings of inadequacy:

> When I listen to "Camilo" or the "The General" [by the band Dispatch], both those songs bring back images of Iraq, but they also bring up personal, negative feelings too, like personal inadequacy. I feel like I'm doing stuff now, and I'm atoning for some of the things I did, you know. We always felt like we didn't have the personal courage, that [refusing to participate in the war] was what courage really was. And we'd spend three years on our courage commitment. Every day, that's what we heard, courage, courage, courage, courage, right? And now instead of associating courage with something like charging the hill, we're associating courage with standing up and saying "no" and being free and true to ourselves.

These songs about veteran resistance inspired him politically, but they also made him feel bad, adding to his guilt that he did not have the courage to resist earlier, though his explanation hints at how confused he was while still at war: "Part of me feels bad for not having the courage to stand up then when I knew it was wrong, because I knew it was wrong, but I didn't really know it was wrong, you know?"

When Benji moved from California to Oregon in the year before the interview, he sought change far away from the Marines and enrolled in a community college in an attempt to figure out who he was and what his next steps would be. Part of his plan was to seek new music to help shape this change, just as music had played a role in his previous transitions. By the time I met Benji, he was taking classes at a community college in Corvallis, Oregon, and was an activist with Iraq Veterans Against the War and Veterans for Peace. He joined a peace group in the area and visited high schools on counter-recruiting projects: antiwar activists vie for the opportunity to visit high schools and provide an alternate message to those provided by the military recruiters who visit schools in order to sell the military experience. As did many of the young veteran activists I met, he continued to feel lost and struggled with PTSD, and he considered his activism a way to somehow atone for what he had done.

NINE

As Time Goes By

The context for this book about musical listening and war is big conflicts, the multination "global war on terror," and the more situated yet still enormous wars in Afghanistan and Iraq. As explained in the introduction, Sweeney (2001) argues for the study of music and conflict because it takes us from the business of politicians to the realm of those in the trenches. In the foreword to *My Music: Explorations of Music in Daily Life,* George Lipitz writes that examining the ways that individuals engage with music in everyday life reveals the "complicated and contradictory ways that people use music to make meaning for themselves" (1993, x). This study about troops' musical listening, their informal everyday expressivity, sheds light on the complex experiences and perspectives of those individuals whose boots were "on the ground," yielding insight into how individuals experienced and felt about these wars and how they used music in "complicated and contradictory" ways to make meaning for themselves during the wars and after.

New technological developments that increased the ubiquity of musical listening and individuals' capability to acquire and exchange music expanded the ways that music could contribute to contemporary large-scale conflicts. Through individual and collective listening, music in these wars has been used to disseminate competing ideologies at the same time that it has been used more explicitly as a tool of war by U.S. troops when certain selections become unifying pro-war or patriotic anthems and when individuals in the military listen to privately selected tracks to motivate and personally legitimize their participation in battle. Within these wars are other types of conflicts, not between states or global enemies, but associated with occupational and political hierarchies, power differentials, social status, ethnicity, gender, politics, musical taste, and so on. As this study demonstrates, music played a part in these layers and layers of conflict, sometimes as a mechanism for conflict resolution when music was used in community building, cross-cultural sharing, mutual support, and shared grieving, at the same that it also contributed to conflict, for example in its role in solidifying divides between hierarchies and various social groupings and when it was used as a weapon of war.

What becomes clear from this exploration of everyday musical listening at war is that all those intimately involved were thinking and feeling agents who were deeply impacted by their contribution to these overlapping webs of conflict (whether deemed positive or negative), their memories of what they saw and did, their moral reflections, and their subsequent psychological wounds. Not always having access to the necessary resources for healing and reestablishing themselves within the civilian world; through music combat veterans remember and sometimes forget, process, and hopefully heal, and ideally create new realities for themselves postconflict.

In the years that I was doing research for this project, from 2005 through the completion of a draft of the book in 2014, the wars droned on, attracting varying attention from the U.S. public, with spikes at moments of heightened engagement, for example when there were "surges" in the number of troops deployed, events that resulted in large numbers of casualties, stories of victories, and the occasional burst of media coverage around issues of PTSD and military sexual trauma, and after reports of an egregious act committed by a combat veteran. In 2015, though U.S. engagement in Iraq and Afghanistan and the region more broadly continues, public attention has dimmed. Fewer U.S. troops are deployed, and there are fewer news stories about U.S. casualties. Many civilians who are not directly impacted by the wars because their family members and loved ones did not participate can go on with their lives, largely oblivious of the impact of these wars on the people who fought them.

I am always struck by the number of male veterans sitting on U.S. street corners, emotionally and physically unwell, begging for any little bit that will enable them to make it through another day. It used to be that these men were older than me, often grey-haired men, many of whom never recovered from their service in the Vietnam War. Having spent so much time with young veterans of the contemporary wars, I now look at these men differently, seeing through their bedraggled faces into whom they must have been when they deployed: strapping young men, the same as those I have interviewed. Hearing about the experiences and struggles of those who have fought in Iraq and Afghanistan, I envision some of those I interviewed being these bedraggled street corner sitters of the future, and increasingly I am seeing more younger men and women sitting on corners, begging, with signs that claim veteran status.

My description of the struggles faced by combat veterans is not intended to portray troops as broken victims of war. On April 23, 2014, retired marine general Jim Mattis, an outspoken and controversial figure, talked about PTSD to a large crowd of veterans at San Francisco's Salute to Iraq and Afghanistan Veterans. Military advisor and combat veteran William Treseder (2014) reported on what Mattis had to say about PTSD, adding his own thoughts. According to Treseder, Mattis told the crowd: "You've been told that you're broken, that you're damaged goods and should be labeled victims of two unjust and poorly executed wars. The truth, instead, is that we are the only folks with the skills, determination, and values to ensure American dominance in this chaotic world." Treseder went on to echo Mattis and criticize the victimization of veterans and suggested that instead of characterizing trauma as something that breaks people, it was more productive to emphasize ways in which trauma can contribute to personal growth:

Why do we think that the story of our personal development ends when we go to war? The myth of Post-Traumatic Stress Disorder tells us that we are now broken and cannot be repaired. We are a threat to ourselves and others. We need medication to be stable. We will be constantly challenged by the civilian world as we stumble along, out of phase with the safe and boring environment back home.

What if instead we could look forward to rapid growth as we heal from our wounds stronger than ever before? What if we could rebuild ourselves, and all we needed was the loving support of those around us and a little bit of time? Progress, evolution, healing, restoration—these are watchwords of Post-Traumatic Growth.

I agree with Mattis and Treseder. The portrayal and treatment of combat veterans as broken victims is not productive. However, their presentation of the problem is overly simplified because it ignores the fact that within the military, alongside and perhaps stronger than the discourse about brokenness, is the omnipresence of the stereotypical and hypermasculine portrayal of troops as heroes and warriors. This image underscores that real warriors are not too phased by trauma and should be able to *rapidly* "heal from our wounds" and "rebuild ourselves." This perspective undermines the complexity of how individuals experience war and the very real need that people have for appropriate resources to process and heal.

From my interviews, press coverage, and other information readily available, we know that many veterans do feel that they are "broken" or at least struggling; unfortunately, all too many have chosen to end their lives to save themselves and others from the pain that suffocates them. I explained to my students in a class I was teaching at the time of writing about the problem of perceiving war veterans as "broken." It was the day after Memorial Day in 2014. A student, the only veteran in the class, listened to me quietly and then spoke up to explain that he was troubled by what I had just said because of how saddened he is each Memorial Day, noticing how many more of his friends are no longer with us, alluding to the frequency of veteran suicides.

Indeed, the goal should be for all troops to heal from trauma or at least to grow from it. However, we must acknowledge the challenges that troops face. We cannot ignore the reality that killing another human, regardless of how much one may feel that it is justified, is always associated with very real moral and ethical dilemmas or that observing, experiencing, or inflicting pain, fear, and suffering are difficult for all. If the U.S. military, U.S. government, and U.S. communities do not provide appropriate resources to enable troops to heal physically and mentally and to transition socially and occupationally into being productive civilians, unfortunately some veterans, and I argue too many, will not "in a little time" progress, evolve, heal, and restore, the "watchwords of Post-Traumatic Growth" (Treseder 2014).

I wrote this book because of my interest as a folklorist and ethnomusicologist in expressive culture and how it operates in everyday life, and I was especially interested in reflecting on the important role that music can play in war where troops have access to so little to enable them to cope with multiple demands. Yet ultimately, the project has been as much about personal experience narratives, very intimate and personal stories of life, war, and war's aftermath. Talking about music was an effective means to engage with war veterans and provide an opportunity for them to talk about the war without putting pressure on them, to create an interactional space in which combat veterans could share only that which they were willing to talk about.

I am very appreciative and honored by the trust that many put in me, sharing so much about their experiences, thoughts, and struggles. It is my hope that in reading this book, audiences will not only be interested in the discussion about musical listening, but will be interested in the people whose stories emerge throughout and recognize the importance of separating the politics of the wars from the very real human beings who gave so much in serving their country, regardless of whether it was what the reader believes the U.S. government should have been doing. These are people whose stories deserve to be heard and whose needs have to be met so that we do not have another generation of young people whose war experiences and how they were treated afterward devastate them to the extent of producing large numbers of people who never quite figure out how to exist after war and thus either end their lives, as so many have already done, or struggle at the margins, never quite fitting in.

Music has long been part of war experience in all different historical and cultural settings. Collective musicking has been used to create identity, forge bonds of solidarity, energize troops, provide respite, and express support or criticism, and as a weapon against the enemy. Private engagement with music—singing, listening, or playing an instrument—has long provided soldiers the opportunity to withdraw, express, reflect, feel, and sometimes act. Recent technological developments have precipitated a significant shift in the ways that people access and engage with music. This transformation has had a big impact on U.S. troops, who were already used to integrating music into war activities and can now do so in new and nuanced ways.

Scholars like Bull and DeNora rightfully emphasize how headphones and individualized listening devices enable people to withdraw into a private world, allowing the possibility of effecting control over one's soundscape to create a private bubble within which to move through the social world. This capacity is especially crucial to troops who have few private physical or psychical spaces within which to operate and so creatively manipulate their sonic environments to meet their social and psychological needs. These private soundscapes allow for personal reflection and private identity construction in addition to mood management.

The individualism of listening with new technologies should not be over-emphasized. Clearly, as much as these technologies allow one to isolate oneself while surrounded, they also in many ways expand social interaction, allowing people to connect across time and space, for example when troops share music with loved ones across the world or when veterans create online communities to participate in musicking and to support one another. The ability to share music allows people to forge identities or alternately to transcend identity boundaries and experiment with different soundscapes, thereby coming closer to those with whom they might otherwise find little reason to share.

Because music is so pervasive and intricately linked to so much of the day-to-day experience of war, it has an important role in mediating experience and becomes tied to identity construction and memory making in complicated ways that have implications for veterans' long-term processing and healing from combat. Some memories associated with music are cherished forever, as they invoke warm feelings of friendship and accomplishments. Others are tied to pain, fear, suffering, and questioning.

Memories of sadness and trauma fade, but they never go away. After awhile, though the amount of time varies from person to person, and depending on the nature of the trauma and what one is doing to process it, the memories recede into the background, becoming not so prominent on a day-by-day basis, allowing individuals to proceed with the present without the past always intruding at the forefront of their mental state, thinking, and interpretations.

Some find ways of trying hard to keep even painful memories alive because they want them in the forefront of their minds, afraid that if they start to forget, so too will everyone else, letting the reality of war become an illusion, something too easily abstracted, made hypothetical. Josh strives to maintain a lively memory of his war experiences, and he explained that he does not avoid music that reminds him of Iraq because he does not want to lose the anger he feels, he does not want to become complacent and stop thinking about the people, soldiers and Iraqis who are "right now" experiencing the things that make him so angry:

I don't really mind listening to music that reminds me of Iraq; it doesn't really bother me, I think it's good. If I forget Iraq too much, I think I would be less angry and just fall back into the space of every other American and forget that there's stuff going on. It's like weird to think, but like right now there's someone in Iraq being shot at, you know what I mean, or there's some guy on patrol, on a vehicle with his gun pointed at some Iraqi, that's happening right now, as we speak, guaranteed somewhere overseas; you know, it's easy to forget about that. I don't think I want to forget about that and just kind of like, you know since I'm not in Iraq anymore, just forget how everyone else is over there.

Josh's memories and the anger they evoke drove the political activism that was the focus of his life at the time of the interview.

Others work just as hard to put the memories aside, enfolding them into deep recesses in their psyches, from which they hope those thoughts will never emerge. It is sometimes these people who suffer the most, because they are not necessarily prepared to address these memories when they do emerge; when the irritability, sadness, anger, and aggression explode, they do not have the tools available to manage their emotions.

The receding of memories allows many veterans to carry on with their lives and return to a sense of normalcy with less anxiety, visions, startles, and nightmares. Yet once in awhile something, such as a phrase from a memorable song, triggers a memory, positive or negative, and they will each deal with it differently, depending on the individual and the memory. Sometimes, as Pete already explained, they will stand by and allow themselves a moment to reflect and feel, process the feeling, and think about who they are now in relationship to who they were before they went to war. When feelings and emotions start to emerge, some find ways of giving themselves time to think and feel. Nate explains that he sometimes takes his truck and drives deep into the mountains while listening to Bruce Springsteen's album *The Rising*. Each song is about 9/11 from a different person's perspective. Nate listens to each of the songs and "just cries, I ball my eyes out." Sometimes he feels he needs to be "a little honest with my feelings, allow myself to cry." He listens closely to each song and thinks about the story Springsteen is telling. In the past the songs would evoke personal memories, the details of stories of people he knew and some whom he lost. Now he listens differently. Instead of focusing on his own memories, he listens to the stories told by Springsteen, often visualizing all the details of the narratives in his mind. Though he no longer thinks about his own memories, he explained that while listening to the album, "obviously, I'm *feeling* things from other stories, from other things that have happened to me and people I knew." It's easier to allow himself to feel in response to Springsteen's stories about those unknown to him than to open up the wounds from his own losses. The music playing while he is in his truck, which he considers in some ways to be "an extension of my body," provides him with a contained space in which he feels safe to feel, especially out all alone on country roads in the mountains of Oregon.

APPENDIX

People Interviewed

I have chosen to use only first names or pseudonyms to respect people's privacy, unless they are public figures.

Titles, jobs, and dates of service or deployment history are presented as given by interviewees, so this information is not provided consistently.

Ages are those at the time of the interviews.

Ethnic identification is inherently problematic. I refer to people of European descent (white) as Euro-American to be consistent with how I refer to those with heritage from other regions of the world. Otherwise, I respected people's self-identification as much as possible. Throughout the text I mostly use the term "white," following popular conventions.

Name: Amy
Age: 29
Ethnicity: Euro-American
Sex: Female
Branch: Spouse of U.S. Army combat veteran of OIF and OEF
Date of interview: 12/5/2012
Medium of interview: E-mail

Name: Andrew
Age: 28
Ethnicity: Euro-American
Sex: Male
Branch: U.S. Marine Corps
Deployment history: Iraq

Date of interview: 6/9/2009
Medium of interview: In person

Name: Andy
Age: Late 20s
Ethnicity: Euro-American
Sex: Male
Branch: U.S. Army
Title(s): Surgical technologist, combat medic (E5)
Deployment history: Iraq
Date of interview: 2/12/2008
Medium of interview: In person

Name: Angie
Age: 30
Ethnicity: Euro-American/Native
  American/Mexican
Sex: Female
Branch: U.S. Navy
Title(s): E2–E5
Deployment history: March–June 2003,
  Gulf
Date of interview: 10/16/2012
Medium of interview: In person

Name: Benji
Age: 22
Ethnicity: Euro-American
Sex: Male
Branch: U.S. Marine Corps
Title(s): Mortarman, infantry
Deployment history: Iraq
Date of interview: 4/29/2009
Medium of interview: In person

Name: Bob
Age: 31
Ethnicity: Euro-American
Sex: Male
Branch: U.S. Army
Title(s): CW2, army aviator
Date of interview: 7/24/2006
Medium of interview: In person

Name: Chris
Age: Late 20s
Ethnicity: Euro-American
Sex: Male
Branch: U.S. Army
Date of interview: 6/13/2012
Medium of interview: E-mail

Name: Craig
Age: 30
Ethnicity: Euro-American
Sex: Male
Branch: U.S. Army
Title(s): Armored crewman
Date of interview: 8/12/2008
Medium of interview: Phone

Name: Danny
Age: Late 20s
Ethnicity: Euro-American
Sex: Male
Dates of service: 2001 through time of
  interview in 2007
Branch: U.S. Army National Guard
Title(s): Platoon medic
Deployment history: 2002, Iraq
Date of interview: 2/9/2007
Medium of interview: In person

Name: Dave
Age: 35
Ethnicity: African American
Sex: Male
Branch: U.S. Army
Title(s): Enlisted, E6
Date of interview: 7/19/2006
Medium of interview: In person

Name: Eric
Age: Late 20s
Ethnicity: Euro-American
Sex: Male
Branch: U.S. Army National Guard
Title(s): Emergency treatment
  noncommissioned officer
Date of interview: 2/26/2007
Medium of interview: In person

Name: Evan
Age: 31
Ethnicity: Euro-American
Sex: Male
Branch: U.S. Army
Title(s): Scout helicopter pilot, W2
Date of interview: 10/11/2006
Medium of interview: In person

Name: Gabe
Age: Early 30s
Ethnicity: Peruvian American/Latino
Sex: Male
Branch: U.S. Army National Guard
Title(s): Specialist E4/medic attached to
    infantry unit
Dates of service: 2001–?
Deployment history: 2005, one year in
    Iraq; 2007, Kuwait (supposed to be
    one year but returned early because of
    severe injuries)
Date of interview: 4/27/2009
Medium of interview: Phone

Name: Jeff Barillaro (aka Soldier Hard)
Age: 36
Ethnicity: Italian and Filipino
Sex: Male
Branch: U.S. Army
Title(s): 19 KILO Armor Crewman
Deployment history: 1997–1998,
    Operation Southern Watch Iraq/
    Kuwait; 2005–2006, OIF; 2009–2010,
    OEF
Date of interview: 12/4/2012
Medium of interview: E-mail

Name: J. D.
Age: 31
Ethnicity: Euro-American
Sex: Male
Branch: U.S. Army
Title(s): Helicopter pilot, rank W2
Dates of interview: 7/24/2006 (in person)
    and 8/21/2006 (phone)
Medium of interview: In person
    and phone

Name: Joseph
Age: 25
Ethnicity: Euro-American
Sex: Male
Branch: U.S. Army
Deployment history: Iraq
Date of interview: 7/9/2009
Medium of interview: In person

Name: Josh
Age: 27
Ethnicity: Euro-American
Sex: Male
Branch: U.S. Army
Dates of service: 2001–2006
Deployment history: 2004, Iraq
Date of interview: 8/24/2009
Medium of interview: In person

Name: Joshua
Age: 20s
Ethnicity: Euro-American
Sex: Male
Branch: U.S. Army
Date of interview: 12/17/2009
Medium of interview: In person

Name: Julie
Age: 24
Ethnicity: Euro-American
Sex: Female
Branch: U.S. Army
Title(s): Pilot
Dates of service: 2004–
Deployment history: Not yet deployed at
    time of interview
Date of interview: 7/24/2006
Medium of interview: In person

Name: Keith
Age: 30
Ethnicity: Euro-American
Sex: Male
Branch: U.S. Army
Deployment history: Iraq (5 months in
    2003–2004 and 7 months in 2005)
Date of interview: 12/5/2012
Medium of interview: Phone

Name: Mark
Age: 30
Ethnicity: Euro-American
Sex: Male
Branch: U.S. Army
Title(s): Cavalry scout
Dates of Service: 2003–2008
Deployment history: February 2004–
    March 2005 Iraq
Date of interview: 2/3/2012
Medium of interview: In person

Name: Matt
Age: 26
Ethnicity: Euro-American
Sex: Male
Branch: U.S. Navy

Title(s)/jobs: Construction battalion
Dates of service: 2001–? (definitely out
    by 2007)
Deployment history: Iraq
Date of interview: 6/11/2009
Medium of interview: In person

Name: Mike
Age: 27
Ethnicity: Euro-American
Sex: Male
Branch: U.S. Army National Guard
Title(s): SPC line medi/ambulance crew
    member/OR tech/treatment assistant
Dates of service: 2003–?
Deployment history: January 2005–2006
Date of interview: 1/16/2009
Medium of interview: In person

Name: Nate
Age: 35
Ethnicity: Caribbean American
Sex: Male
Branch: U.S. Marine Corps, then military
    contractor
Title(s): Rifleman, human and
    counterintelligence, contractor; E-5
    (sergeant)
Dates of service: July 1996–2005
Date of interview: 11/20/2012
Medium of interview: In person

Name: Noah
Age: 31
Ethnicity: Euro-American
Sex: Male
Branch: U.S. Army, active duty and
    National Guard
Title(s): 19 KILO armor crewman

Dates of service: 1996–2006 (eight years in active duty, remaining time in National Guard)
Deployment history: November 2004–November 2005
Date of interview: 7/25/2009
Medium of interview: In person

Name: Paul
Age: 30
Ethnicity: African American
Sex: Male
Branch: U.S. Marine Corps
Title(s): Motor transport operator
Dates of service: 2002–2006
Deployment history: Iraq, July 2004–February 2005 and September 2005–January 2006
Date of interview: 12/16/2014
Medium of interview: Phone

Name: Penny
Age: 30
Ethnicity: Euro-American
Sex: Female
Branch: U.S. Army
Title(s)/job(s): 68Q pharmacy tech 27
Dates of service: 2004–2008
Date of interview: 10/16/2012
Medium of interview: In person

Name: Pete
Age: 26
Ethnicity: Euro-American
Sex: Male
Branch: U.S. Marine Corps
Dates of service: 2004–2008

Deployment history: Iraq, September 2005–March 2006 and January 2007–August 2007
Date of interview: 12/6/2012
Medium of interview: Phone and follow-up e-mail

Name: Phil
Age: 30
Ethnicity: African American
Sex: Male
Branch: U.S. Marine Corps
Title(s)/job(s): Motor vehicle operator
Dates of service: 2002–2012
Deployment history: Iraq, February–September 2004 and February 2005–February 2006; Afghanistan, March–September 2012
Date of interview: 1/5/2015
Medium of interview: E-mail

Name: Seth
Age: 29
Ethnicity: Euro-American
Sex: Male
Branch: U.S. Army
Title(s): Infantry/stryker driver
Dates of service: 2002–2006
Deployment history: Iraq, October 2004–September 2005
Date of interview: 8/10/2009
Medium of interview: In person

Name: Shannon
Age: Late 20s
Ethnicity: Euro-American
Sex: Male
Branch: U.S. Air Force, 2001–2005

Title(s): Senior airman (SrA), aircraft electronics specialist, and crew chief
Deployment history: Iraq/Middle East, 2003 and 2005
Date of interview: 2/7/2007
Medium of interview: In person

Name: Simon
Age: 38
Ethnicity: Euro-American
Sex: Male
Branch: U.S. Navy
Title(s): medic, rank E3–E4
Dates of service: 1993–1998
Date of interview: 10/11/2012
Medium of interview: In person

Age: Tina
Ethnicity: Euro-American
Sex: Female
Branch: U.S. Army, active duty
Title(s): Specialist 96B intelligence analyst
Date of interview: 3/3/2008
Medium of interview: In person

Name: Tyler
Age: 28
Ethnicity: Euro-American
Sex: Male
Branch: U.S. Marine Corps
Dates of service: 2003–2006
Deployment history: Outside of Fallujah, Iraq, 2004–2005
Dates of interview: 12/5/2012 and 12/14/2012
Medium of interview: E-mail

Name: Tyson
Age: Early 30s
Ethnicity: Euro-American
Sex: Male
Branch: U.S. Army
Title(s): Warrant officer, helicopter pilot in the army in the cavalry
Dates of interview: 7/24/2006 (in person) and 8/26/2006 (phone)
Medium of interview: In person and phone

NOTES

Preface

1. See http://www.ivaw.org/ for information about Iraq Veterans Against the War and http://www.veteransforpeace.org/ to learn about Veterans for Peace.

2. For more information about Coffee Strong, see http://www.coffeestrong.org/ and see Gilman 2012.

3. Inspired by the Vietnam-era coffeehouse movement, young American veterans of the Iraq and Afghanistan wars opened Coffee Strong some 328 yards outside Joint-Base Lewis McChord in Washington State in 2008. This nonprofit café is a space where soldiers, veterans, and their families discuss politics and the impact of war, and it provides resources for combat stress, sexual trauma, navigating veteran benefits, and legal issues. The film focuses on the veterans who run Coffee Strong, exploring their decisions to enlist, deployment memories, relationships with one another, and how their efforts to make a more peaceful world help them cope with their experiences of war. See http://www.groundsforresistance.com for more information.

ONE Introduction

1. See Arthur (2001); Cleveland (1985, 2003); and Fish (1989).

2. For discussions about complexities associated with generic classification, see Frith (1998); Lena and Peterson (2008); Krims (2000); Walser (1993); Weinstein (2000 [1991]); and Fox 2005.

3. See Ritter and Daughtry (2007); Wolfe and Akenson (2005; Schmelz (2007); Naroditskaya (2010); and Sweeney (2001).

TWO Setting the Scene

1. For detailed analysis of the use of music in military recruiting, see Pieslak (2009, 16–45).

2. Catherine Lutz explains that after the Vietnam War, many Americans were disillusioned and cynical about the U.S. military, which necessitated that the military increase its enticements in its recruiting efforts: "Congress tripled the recruiting budget, doubled enlisted pay, offered bonuses to those who signed up for combat units, and opened nearly all military positions to women" (2001, 167).

3. See Gutmann and Lutz's *Breaking Ranks: Iraq Veterans Speak Out Against the War* (2010) for additional narratives of veterans' motivations for joining the military; many of them similarly were struggling in their youth at the time of joining.

4. Figures from U.S. Department of Defense, *2011 Demographics Profile of the Military Community* (Updated 2012), http://www.militaryonesource.mil/12038/MOS/Reports/2011 _Demographics_Report.pdf (accessed November 19, 2013).

5. All demographic information is from *2011 Demographics Profile of the Military Community*. See also Lutz (2008).

6. The majority of those interviewed served in one or both of these wars. A few who served in the military before these wars provided valuable insights into both continuities and transformations in musical listening with changes in technology. One interviewee was never deployed. She served as a pharmacist based in the United States during the wars and interacted regularly with combat veterans; thus her perspectives on gender and the military are relevant even if she herself never went to war.

7. Catherine Lutz elaborates on ways in which the "military budget's benefits are neither race, gender, or class neutral, with the white middle and upper classes and males being the system's disproportionate beneficiaries in intended and unintended ways" (2001, 175).

THREE Musicking at Work and Leisure

1. Sebastian Junger's documentary film *Restrepo* provides an illustrative example of an isolated army outpost in Afghanistan where possibilities for mobility and activities were especially limited.

2. In the hierarchy of the military, ranks of enlisted men range from E1 to E9. There are two categories of officers, warrant officers and commissioned officers, in all branches but the air force, which does not have warrant officers. The ranking of warrant officers starts at W1 and goes up to W5, and of officers from O1 to O10. Commissioned officers hold the highest ranking, best paid, and most powerful positions in the military.

3. General Order No. 1 outlines standards of conduct for American military personnel in "countries where Islamic law and Arabic customs prohibit or restrict certain activities

which are generally permissible in western societies" (Desert Shield General Order No. 1). Consumption of alcohol was prohibited, as was "intimate behavior" between men and women not married to each other. In 2008 the ban on sexual intimacy was lifted, though it continued to be heavily discouraged because it "can have an adverse impact on unit cohesion, morale, good order and discipline" (Brown 2008).

4. Troops were occasionally based in places where these restrictions were lifted. Air force veteran Shannon remembered that when they were in Qatar, "the prince allowed us to drink and a lot of people were a little bit more happy there."

FOUR Music as a Sound Track of War

1. Interviewed by *MTV News*, the late Dave Williams described the song as "basically our perspective from the stage on what the crowd is doing. It's a mosh pit anthem. You have a bad week at work, you're not getting along with your folks, you're not getting along with your girlfriend, boyfriend, whatever. Things build up. Instead of reacting in a bad way, come to a show, get in the pit and get it out. It's awesome to see the floor just breathe. It looks like a swirling mass of flesh. I love that. It's very primal. That was my perspective, and I thought it would be cool to write a song about that. It has turned into a beast that we cannot even begin to tame. Every time that we play that song live, it's chaos." "Drowning Pool: Off the Deep End," http://www.mtv .com/bands/d/drowning_pool/NewsFeature_080401/feature.jhtml (accessed April 16, 2015).

2. For detailed discussion of the timbrel dimensions of metal and the lyrical dimensions of "gangsta rap" that make them especially relevant to troops engaged in war, see Pieslak (2009, 147–67).

3. See Christensen (2009) for more detailed analysis of music in these videos.

4. "Taliban Bodies Hit the Floor," YouTube, http://www.youtube.com/watch?v =ig92IfbQJdE (accessed January 25, 2013).

5. Thank-you to Nate for bringing this video to my attention.

6. Both the military and cheerleader videos are presented together in the video clip "Miami Dolphins Cheerleaders: 'Call Me Maybe' vs U.S. Troops: 'Call Me Maybe,'" You-Tube, http://www.youtube.com/watch?v=4HzlkqoSG-k (accessed January 16, 2014).

7. See Sugarman (2010) for a discussion of how different musical genres as well as specific songs were used for political identification and mobilization by different groups in the Yugoslav wars of the 1990s.

8. In the interview, Keith told me that the song was about the war in Bosnia, whereas in fact it is about the conflict in northern Ireland. This discrepancy reinforces the idea that individuals listen to music and interpret it, and it can mediate their understanding of what is happening in their surroundings in highly idiosyncratic ways often quite different from the messages intended by the artists.

FIVE Music, Gender, and the Paradox of Masculinity

1. Figures from *2011 Demographics Profile of the Military Community*.

2. An argument for removing the ban on women serving in combat units is that with irregular warfare becoming increasingly common, there is less difference between those serving on the frontlines or as support personnel. Policy changes have also led to reorganization and restructuring within the military that blurs the lines between combat and noncombat units (Mackenzie 2012).

3. In January 2013 the Department of Defense rescinded the 1994 Direct Ground Combat Definition and Assignment Rule, which restricted women's roles within the military. This change requires all military branches to assess their gendered policies to determine what role women will have in sectors previously restricted to men ("DoD Lifts the Ban" 2013).

4. This essay was originally published in *Theorizing Masculinities* (Brod and Kaufman 1994).

5. *2011 Demographics Profile of the Military Community*. See also Lutz (2008).

6. See Dundes and Pagter (1991) for examples and analysis of aggressive sexual terminology used in reference to domination in war.

7. The sexual violence and harassment in the military across branches is extremely widespread and was receiving much attention at the time of writing (e.g., Hoyt et al. 2011; Katz et al. 2012; Kimmerling et al. 2010; Pershing 2003; Valente and Wight 2007).

8. "Military Sexual Trauma," fact sheet, U.S. Department of Veterans Affairs, http:// www.mentalhealth.va.gov/msthome.asp (accessed March 7, 2014).

9. Veterans' discussions about masculinity in the military suggest the need for a study of how men use joking to expand the parameters of acceptable masculinity, a topic outside the scope of the current study.

SIX "Music Doesn't Judge": Managing Feelings at War

1. See Västfjäll et al. (2012) for some models for studying the emotional impact of musical listening in everyday life.

2. This type of humor about killing and the ugliness of war is complex and cannot be taken at face value, as is the case with the dark humor common among many occupational groups that confront trauma and pain on a regular basis, such as doctors and emergency responders. See Gabbert and Salud (2009); George and Dundes (1978); Moore (1991); and Odean (1995).

3. PTSD: National Center for PTSD, "What Is PTSD?," U.S. Department of Veterans Affairs, http://www.ptsd.va.gov/public/PTSD-overview/basics/what-is-ptsd.asp (accessed April 18, 2014).

4. The estimates of the prevalence of PTSD among combat veterans from these two wars vary widely, though it is widely agreed that the impact of these "invisible wounds" is staggering and will have long-term consequences.

5. See Addis and Mahalik (2003) for an overview of the literature on differences between men and women of different ages and cultural backgrounds seeking mental health care.

6. The Redcon-1 Music Group Web site is at http://www.redcon1musicgroup.org.

SEVEN Coming Home

1. "101st Airborne Division (AASLT): Welcome Home Ceremony," Fort Campbell and the 101st Airborne Division, http://www.campbell.army.mil/campbell/directorates /DPTMS/Pages/flights.aspx (accessed May 1, 2014).

2. The Welcome Home Project is an interesting example of a community in Oregon, aware of the need for rituals of integration for troops, that came together to organize an opportunity for a small group of veterans to write about their experiences, share them with the community, and be ritually accepted by the community after performing their stories. See The Welcome Home Project, http://www.thewelcomehomeproject. org (accessed on May 1, 2014) for information about the project and the documentary "The Welcome."

3. These quotes are from Institute of Medicine of the National Academies, "Returning Home from Afghanistan: Assessment of Readjustment Needs of Veterans, Service Members, and Their Families," *Report Brief* (March 2013), http://www.iom.edu/~/media /Files/Report%20Files/2013/Returning-Home-Iraq-Afghanistan/Returning-Home-Iraq-Afghanistan-RB.pdf, accessed on 5/9/2014. The full publication is available in print (Veterans and Their Families Committee 2013).

4. "Redcon" is military slang, a shortened form of "Readiness Condition," which refers to having everything prepared for an operation.

5. Accessed at http://www.redcon1musicgroup.org (accessed February 20, 2013).

EIGHT Music and Political Transformation

1. Several of those I interviewed described that there was dissent across a unit, which allowed for subtle strategies for avoiding participation in activities that they felt would lead to unnecessary suffering. Many others described feeling that they had no other options. Many had never heard of war resisters and did not even consider that refusing to do something they were ordered to do was possible.

2. See Gutmann and Lutz (2010) for additional perspectives from veterans of the Iraq war speaking out against the war.

3. See Ensign (n.d.); Robert Shetterly's Americans Who Tell the Truth.

4. See "Winter Soldier" on the Iraq Veterans Against the War Web site, http://www
.ivaw.org/wintersoldier (accessed May 15, 2015). *This Is Where We Take Our Stand,* a film
by David Zeiger, documents the event, provides context and interviews with participants,
and explores its impact.

REFERENCES

Addis, M. E., and J. R. Mahalik. 2003. "Men, Masculinity, and the Contexts of Help Seeking." *American Psychologist* 58 (1): 5–14.

Andén-Papadopoulos, Kari. 2008. "US Soldiers Imaging the Iraq War on YouTube." *Popular Communication* 7 (1): 17–27.

Anderson, Ben. 2004. "Recorded Music and Practices of Remembering." *Social and Cultural Geography* 5 (1): 3–20.

Arnett, Jeffrey Jensen. 1991. "Adolescents and Heavy Metal Music: From the Mouths of Metalheads." *Youth and Society* 23 (1): 76–98.

———. 1996. *Metal Heads: Heavy Metal Music and Adolescent Alienation.* Boulder, CO: Westview Press.

Arthur, Max. 2001. *When This Bloody War Is Over: Soldiers' Songs of the First World War.* London: Piatkus Books.

Baade, Chrstina. 2012a. "Between the Lines: 'Lili Marlene,' Sexuality, and the Desert War." In *Music, Politics, and Violence,* ed. Susan Fast and Kip Pegley, 83–103. Middletown, CT: Wesleyan University Press.

———. 2012b. *Victory through Harmony: The BBC and Popular Music in World War II.* Oxford: Oxford University Press.

Bachman, Jerald G., David R. Segal, Peter Freedman-Doan, and Patrick M. O'Malley. 2000. "Who Chooses Military Service? Correlates of Propensity and Enlistment in the U.S. Armed Forces." *Military Psychology* 12 (1): 1–30.

Bauman, Richard. 1972. "Differential Identity and the Social Base of Folklore." In *Toward New Perspectives in Folklore,* ed. Américo Paredes and Richard Bauman, 31–41. Austin: University of Texas Press.

Belkin, Aaron, and Geoffrey Bateman, eds. 2003. *Don't Ask, Don't Tell: Debating the Gay Ban in the Military.* London and Boulder: Lynne Rienner Publishers.

Berger, Harris. M. 1999. *Metal, Rock, and Jazz: Perceptions and the Phenomenology of Musical Experience.* Hanover, NH: Wesleyan University Press.

Berger, Harris M., and Giovanna P. Del Negro. 2004. *Identity and Everyday Life: Essays in the Study of Folklore, Music, and Popular Culture.* Middletown, CT: Wesleyan University Press.

Bernard, H. Russell, and Grey W. Ryan. 1998. "Text Analysis: Qualitative and Quantitative Methods." In *Handbook of Methods in Cultural Anthropology*, ed. H. Russell Bernard, 595–646. Walnut Creek, CA: AltaMira Press.

Bijsterveld, Karin, and José van Dijck. 2009. Introduction to *Sound Souvenirs: Audio Technologies, Memory and Cultural Practices*, ed. Karin Bijsterveld and José van Dijck, 11–20. Amsterdam: Amsterdam University Press.

Bourdieu, Pierre. 1984. *Distinction: A Social Critique of the Judgement of Taste.* Cambridge, MA: Harvard University Press.

Branum, James. 2014. "'There Were No Good Options': Bergdahl Should Get Honorable Discharge, Says Lawyer for Deserters," http://newsle.com/person/jamesbranum /5178526 (accessed June 4, 2014).

Braudy, Leo. 2003. *From Chivalry to Terrorism.* Random House Book.

Brighton, Shane. 2004. "The Embodiment of War: Reflections on the Tour of Duty." *Journal of Cultural Research* 8 (1): 51–54.

Brod, Harry, and Michael Kaufman, eds. 1994. *Theorizing Masculinities.* Research on Men and Masculinities Series. Thousand Oaks, CA: Sage Publications.

Bronner, Simon J. 2007. *Crossing the Line: Violence, Play, and Drama in Naval Equator Traditions.* Chicago: University of Chicago Press.

Brown, Drew. 2008. "Ban on Sex for Soldiers in Afghanistan Lifted . . . Sort Of." *Stars and Stripes*, March 15.

Bryant, Jerry H. 2003. *"Born in a Mighty Bad Land": The Violent Man in African American Folklore and Fiction.* Bloomington: Indiana University Press.

Bull, Michael. 2000. *Sounding Out the City: Personal Stereos and the Management of Everyday Life.* New York: Oxford University Press.

———. 2007. *Sound Moves: iPod Culture and Urban Experience.* London and New York: Routledge.

———. 2009. "The Auditory Nostalgia of iPod Culture." In *Sound Souvenirs: Audio Technologies, Memory and Cultural Practices*, ed. Karin Bijsterveld and José van Dijck, 83–92. Amsterdam: Amsterdam University Press.

Burke, Carol. 2004. *Camp All-American, Hanoi Jane, and the High-And-Tight: Gender, Folklore, and Changing Military Culture.* Boston: Beacon Press.

Burns, Richard Allen. 2003. "'This Is My Rifle, This Is My Gun . . .': Gunlore in the Military." *New Directions in Folklore* 7. https://scholarworks.iu.edu/dspace/handle/2022/6906 (accessed May 3, 2015).

Cavicchi, Daniel. 2011. *Listening and Longing: Music Lovers in the Age of Barnum.* Middletown, CT: Wesleyan University Press.

Christensen, Christian. 2009. "'Hey Man Nice Shot': Setting the Iraq War to Music on

YouTube." In *The YouTube Reader*, ed. P. Snickars and P. Vonderau, 204–17. Stockholm: National Library of Sweden.

Cleveland, Les. 1985. "Soldier's Songs: The Folklore of the Powerless." *New York Folklore* 11: 79–97.

———. 2003 [1988]. "Songs of the Vietnam War: An Occupational Folk Tradition." *New Directions in Folklore* 7. https://scholarworks.iu.edu/dspace/handle/2022/6908 (accessed May 3, 2015).

Coles, Tony. 2007. "Negotiating the Field of Masculinity: The Production and Reproduction of Multiple Dominant Masculinities." *Men and Masculinities* 12 (1): 30–44.

Connell, John, and Chris Gibson. 2003. *Sound Tracks: Popular Music, Identity, and Place*. London and New York: Routledge.

Connell, R. W. 1987. *Gender and Power: Society, the Person, and Sexual Politics*. Sydney: Allen and Unwin.

———. 1993. "The Big Picture: Masculinities in Recent World History." *Theory and Society* 22: 597–623.

Cook, Nicholas. 1998. *Music: A Very Short Introduction*. Oxford: Oxford University Press.

Courage to Resist. 2008. "Marine Benjamin Lewis Pledges Recall Refusal." http://courage toresist.org/2008/10/marine-benjamin-lewis-pledges-recall-refusal/ (accessed April 16, 2015).

Crafts, Susan D., Daniel Cavicchi, Charles Keil, and the Music in Daily Life Project. 1993. *My Music: Explorations of Music in Daily Life*. Hanover, NH: Wesleyan University Press.

Crawford, June, Susan Kippax, Jenny Onyx, Una Gault, and Pam Benton. 1992. *Emotion and Gender: Constructing Meaning from Memory*. London: SAGE Publications.

Cusick, Suzanne. 2006. "Music as Torture/Music as Weapon." *Revista Transcultural de Música/Transcultural Music Review* 10. http://www.sibetrans.com/trans/articulo/152/music-as-torture-music-as-weaponhttp (accessed April 16, 2015).

———. 2008. "'You Are in a Place That Is Out of the World . . .': Music in the Detention Camps of the 'Global War on Terror.'" *Journal of the Society for American Music* 2 (1): 1–26.

Daughtry, J. Martin. 2012. "Belliphonic Sounds and Indoctrinated Ears: The Dynamics of Military Listening in Wartime Iraq." In *Pop When the World Falls Apart: Music in the Shadow of Doubt*, ed. Eric Weisbard, 111–44. Durham, NC: Duke University Press.

DeGregory, Lane. 2004. "Iraq 'n' Roll." *St. Petersburg Times*, November 21, 2004. http://sptimes.com/2004/11/21/Floridian/Iraq__n__roll.shtml.

Demaria, Christina, and Colin Wright. 2006. "What Is a Post-Conflict Culture?" In *Post-Conflict Cultures: Rituals of Representation*, ed. Christina Demaria and Colin Wright, 5–12. London: Zoilus Press.

Dempsey, Jason K. 2010. *Our Army: Soldiers, Politics, and American Civil-Military Relations*. Princeton, NJ, and Oxford: Princeton University Press.

DeNora, Tia. 2000. *Music in Everyday Life.* Cambridge, UK: Cambridge University Press.

Desert Shield General Order Number 1. "Bulletin for New Members: Join the 3rd Armored Division Association Board of Governors." Available at http://www.3ad.com/ (accessed February 28, 2013).

Dibben, Nicola. 2002. "Gender Identity and Music." In *Musical Identities,* ed. Raymond A. R. Macdonald, David J. Hargreaves, and Dorothy Miell, 118–33. Oxford: Oxford University Press.

"DoD Lifts the Ban on Women in Combat." 2013. *Army* 63 (3): 9–14.

Douglas, Susan. 2004. *Listening In: Radio and the American Imagination.* New York: Times Books.

Dundes, Alan. 1980. *Interpreting Folklore.* Bloomington: Indiana University Press.

Dundes, Alan, and Carl Pagter. 1991. "The Mobile SCUD Missile Launcher and Other Persian Gulf Warlore: An American Folk Image of Saddam Hussein's Iraq." *Western Folklore* 50 (3): 303–22.

Enloe, Cynthia. 1983. *Does Khaki Become You? The Militarization of Women's Lives.* Boston: South End Press.

——— 2000. *Maneuvers: The International Politics of Militarizing Women's Lives.* Berkeley: University of California Press.

Ensign, Tod. N.d. "Camilo Mejia Is Free: Conviction to Be Appealed." Citizen Soldier. Retrieved from http://www.citizen-soldier.org on May 28, 2014. (Web site no longer active.)

Faris, John H. 1981. "The All-Volunteer Force—Recruitment from Military Families." *Armed Forces and Society* 7 (4): 545–59.

Fast, Susan, and Kip Pegley. 2012. Introduction to *Music, Politics, and Violence,* ed. Susan Fast and Kip Pegley, 1–33. Middletown, CT: Wesleyan University Press.

Fish, Lydia. 1989. "General Edward G. Lansdale and the Folksongs of Americans in the Vietnam War." *Journal of American Folklore* 102 (406): 390–411.

———. 2003. "Informal Communication Systems in the Vietnam War: A Case Study in Folklore, Technology and Popular Culture." *New Directions in Folklore* 7. https://scholarworks.iu.edu/dspace/bitstream/handle/2022/6907/NDiF_issue_7_article_4.pdf?sequence=1&isAllowed=y (accessed May 18, 2015)

Flueckiger, Joyce Burkhalter. 1991. "Genre and Community in the Folklore System of Chattisgarh." In *Gender, Genre, and Power in South Asian Expressive Traditions,* ed. Arjun Appadurai, Frank J. Korom, and Margaret Mills, 181–200. Philadelphia: University of Pennsylvania Press.

Fox, Aaron A. 2005. "'Alternative' to What? O Brother, September 11, and the Politics of Country Music." In *Country Music Goes to War,* ed. Charles K. Wolfe and James E. Akenson, 164–91. Lexington: University Press of Kentucky.

Francke, Linda Bird. 1997. *Ground Zero: The Gender Wars in the Military.* New York: Simon and Schuster.

Friedman, Matthew J. 2014. "Suicide Risk Among Soldiers: Early Findings from Army Study to Assess Risk and Resilience in Service members (Army STARRS)." *JAMA Psychiatry* 71 (5): 487–489.

Frith, Simon. 1998. *Performing Rites: On the Value of Popular Music.* Cambridge, MA: Harvard University Press.

Gabbert, Lisa, and Anton Salud, MD. 2009. "On Slanderous Words and Bodies Out-of-Control: Hospital Humor and the Medical Carnivalesque." In *The Body in Medical Culture,* ed. Elizabeth Klaver, 209–27. Albany: State University of New York Press.

Garofalo, Reebee. 2007. "Pop Goes to War, 2001–2004: U.S. Popular Music After 9/11." In *Music in the Post-9/11 World,* ed. Jonathan Ritter and J. Martin Daughtry, 3–26. New York: Routledge.

George, Victoria, and Alan Dundes. 1978. "The Gomer: A Figure of American Hospital Folk Speech." *Journal of American Folklore* 91 (359): 568–81.

Gilman, Lisa. 2010. "An American Soldier's Ipod: Layers of Identity and Situated Listening in Iraq." *Music and Politics* 4 (2). http://www.music.ucsb.edu/projects/musicandpolitics/archive/2010-2/gilman.html (accessed May 3, 2015).

———. 2011. *Grounds for Resistance: Stories of War, Sacrifice, and Good Coffee.* Distributed by Films Media Group.

———. 2012. "Oppositional Positioning: The Military Identification of Young Anti-War Veterans." In *Warrior Ways: Explorations in Modern Military Folklore,* ed. Tad Tuleja and Eric Eliason. Logan: Utah State University Press.

——— 2013. "Troupes Hors-Sol: Music, Espace, Mémoire dans la Guerre en Irak (Grounding the Troops: Music, Place, and Memory in the Iraq War)." *Volume! The Journal of Popular Music Studies* 10 (1): 171–88.

Gittoes, George. 2004. *Soundtrack to War: The Movie.* Melee Entertainment.

Goodman, Amy. 2014. "Father of Freed U.S. Soldier: 'Nobody Can Relate to Guantánamo Prisoners More Than Our Family.'" *Democracy Now.* Transcript of radio report. http://www.democracynow.org/2014/6/3/father_of_freed_us_soldier_nobody (accessed April 16, 2015).

Gutmann, Matthew, and Catherine Lutz. 2010. *Breaking Ranks: Iraq Veterans Speak Out Against the War.* Berkeley: University of California Press.

Gutmann, Stephanie. 2000. *The Kinder, Gentler Military: Can America's Gender Neutral Fighting Force Still Win Wars.* New York: Scribner.

Hargreaves, David J., Dorothy Miell, and Raymond A. R. Macdonald. 2002. "What Are Musical Identities, and Why Are They Important?" In *Musical Identities,* ed. Raymond A. R. Macdonald, David J. Hargreaves, and Dorothy Miell, 1–20. Oxford: Oxford University Press.

Heuer, Martin. 2003. "Personal Reflections on the Songs of Army Aviators in the Vietnam War." *New Directions in Folklore* 7. https://scholarworks.iu.edu/dspace/bitstream

/handle/2022/6909/NDiF_issue_7_article_6.pdf?sequence=1&isAllowed=y (accessed May 18, 2015).

Hoyt, Tim, Jennifer Klosterman Rielage, and Lauren F. Williams. 2011. "Military Sexual Trauma in Men: A Review of Reported Rates." *Journal of Trauma & Dissociation* 12 (3): 244–60.

Huron, David. 2006. *Sweet Anticipation: Music and the Psychology of Expectation.* Cambridge, MA: MIT Press.

Iraq Veterans Against the War and Aaron Glantz. 2008. *Winter Soldier: Iraq and Afghanistan Eyewitness Accounts of the Occupations.* Chicago: Haymarket Books.

Jakupcak, M., R. K. Blais, J. Grossbard, H. Garcia, and J. Okiishi. 2014. "'Toughness' in Association with Mental Health Symptoms among Iraq and Afghanistan War Veterans Seeking Veterans Affairs Health Care." *Psychology of Men & Masculinity* 15(1): 100–104.

Jansen, Bas. 2009. "Tape Cassettes and Former Selves: How Mix Tapes Mediate Memories." In *Sound Souvenirs: Audio Technologies, Memory and Cultural Practices,* ed. Karin Bijsterveld and José van Dijck, 43–53. Amsterdam: Amsterdam University Press.

Johnson, Bruce, and Martin Cloonan. 2009. *The Dark Side of the Tune: Popular Music and Violence.* Burlington, VT: Ashgate Publishing Company.

Johnson, J. D., L. A. Jackson, and L. Gatto. 1995. "Violent Attitudes and Deferred Academic Aspirations: Deleterious Effects of Exposure to Rap Music." *Basic and Applied Social Psychology* 16: 27–41.

Junger, Sebastian. 2010. *War.* New York: Hachette Book Group.

Juslin, Patrik N., and John A. Sloboda, eds. 2001. *Music and Emotion: Theory and Research.* Oxford: Oxford University Press.

———. 2010a. *Handbook of Music and Emotion: Theory, Research, Applications.* Oxford: Oxford University Press.

———. 2010b. "Introduction: Aims, Organization, and Terminology." In *Handbook of Music and Emotion: Theory, Research, Applications,* ed. Patrik N. Juslin and John A. Sloboda. Oxford: Oxford University Press. Kindle edition (no page numbers).

Kassabian, Anahid. 2001. "Ubisub: Ubiquitous Listening and Networked Subjectivity." *Echo: A Music-Centered Journal* 3 (2). http://xenopraxis.net/readings/kassabian_ubiquitous.pdf (May 18, 2015).

Katz, Lori S., Geta Cojucar, Sayeh Beheshti, Erin Nakamura, and Michelle Murray. 2012. "Military Sexual Trauma During Deployment to Iraq And Afghanistan: Prevalence, Readjustment, and Gender Differences." *Violence and Victims* 27 (4): 487–99.

Kaufman, Michael. 2006. "Men, Feminism, and Men's Contradictory Experiences of Power." In *Men and Masculinities: Critical Concepts in Sociology,* ed. Stephen M. Whitehead, 1:183–202. New York: Routledge. (Originally published in Brod and Kaufman 1994, 142–165.)

Keil, Charles. 1993. Introduction to *My Music: Explorations of Music in Daily Life,* ed.

Susan D. Crafts, Daniel Cavicchi, Charles Keil, and the Music in Daily Life Project, 1–3. Hanover, NH: Wesleyan University Press.

Kimmerling, Rachel, Amy E. Street, Joanne Pavao, Mark W. Smith, Ruth C. Cronkite, Tyson H. Homes, and Susan M. Frayne. 2010. "Military-Related Sexual Trauma Among Veterans Health Administration Patients Returning From Afghanistan and Iraq." *American Journal of Public Health* 100 (8): 1409–12.

Krims, Adam. 2000. *Rap Music and the Politics of Identity.* Cambridge, UK: Cambridge University Press.

Lamothe, Dan. 2015. "Bowe Bergdahl, Once-Missing U.S. Soldier, Charged with Desertion." *Washington Post*, March 25, 2015. http://www.washingtonpost.com/news/ checkpoint/wp/2015/03/25/bowe-bergdahl-once-missing-u-s-soldier-charged-with-desertion (accessed May 3, 2015).

Laser, Julie, Anne Stephens, and Paul M. Stephens. 2011. "Working with Military Families Through Deployment and Beyond." *Clinical Social Work Journal* 39: 28–38.

Lena, Jennifer C., and Richard A. Peterson. 2008. "Classification as Culture: Types and Trajectories of Music Genres." *American Sociological Review* 73 (5): 697–718.

Lipsitz, George. 1993. Foreword to *My Music: Explorations of Music in Daily Life,* ed. Susan D. Crafts, Daniel Cavicchi, Charles Keil, and the Music in Daily Life Project, ix-xix. Hanover, NH: Wesleyan University Press.

———. 1994. "We Know What Time It Is." In *Microphone Fiends: Youth Music, Youth Culture,* ed. Andrew Ross and Tricia Rose, 17–28. New York: Routledge.

Litman, R. E., and N. L. Farberow. 1994. "Pop-Rock Music as Precipitating Cause in Youth Suicide." *Journal of Forensic Sciences* 39: 494–99.

Lutz, Amy. 2008. "Who Joins the Military? A Look at Race, Class, and Immigration Status." *Journal of Political and Military Sociology* 36 (2): 167–88.

Lutz, Catherine. 2001. *Homefront: A Military City and the American Twentieth Century.* Boston: Beacon Press.

Mackenzie, Megan H. 2012. "Let Women Fight." *Foreign Affairs* 91 (6): 32–42.

MacLean, Alair, and Nicholas L. Parsons. 2010. "Unequal Risk: Combat Occupations and the Volunteer Military." *Sociological Perspectives* 53 (3): 347–72.

Malone, Bill C. 2002. *Don't Get Above Your Raisin': Country Music and the Southern Working Class.* Urbana: University of Illinois Press.

McDermitt, Tricia. 2004. "AWOL from Iraq." *60 Minutes*, March 29. http://www.cbsnews. com/news/awol-from-iraq/ (accessed May 16, 2014).

McKelvey, Tara, ed. 2007. *One of the Guys: Women as Aggressors and Torturers.* Emeryville, CA: Seal Press.

Mechling, Jay. 2005. "The Folklore of Mother-Raised Boys and Men." In *Manly Traditions: The Folk Roots of American Masculinities,* ed. Simon J. Bronner. Bloomington: Indiana University Press.

———. 2012. "Soldier Snaps." In *Warrior Ways: Explorations in Modern Military Folklore,* ed. Eric A. Eliason and Tad Tuleja, 222–47. Logan: Utah State University Press.

Messner, Michael A. 1997. *Politics of Masculinities.* Lanham, MD: Altamira Press.

Miranda, Dave, and Michel Claes. 2004. "Rap Music Genres and Deviant Behaviors in French-Canadian Adolescents." *Journal of Youth and Adolescence* 3 (2): 113–22.

Mitchell, Laura A., and Raymond A. R. MacDonald. 2006. "An Experimental Investigation of the Effects of Preferred and Relaxing Music on Pain Perception." *Journal of Music Therapy* 63: 295–316.

Moore, Jamie. 1991. "Poetry, Puns, and Pediatrics: The Verbal Artistry of Dr. James L. Hughes." *North Carolina Folklore Journal* 38 (1): 45–71.

Morris, Madeline. 1996. "By Force of Arms: Rape, War, and Military Culture." *Duke Law Journal* 45 (4): 652–81.

Mosher, Donald L., and Mark Sirkin. 1984. "Measuring a Macho Personality Constellation." *Journal of Research in Personality* 18: 150–63.

Naroditskaya, Inna. 2010. "Musical Enactment of Conflict and Compromise in Azerbaijan." In *Music and Conflict,* ed. John Morgan O'Connell and Salwa El-Shwan Castelo-Branco, 46–66. Urbana: University of Illinois Press.

North, Adrian C., and David J. Hargreaves. 2012. "Pop Music Subcultures and Wellbeing." In *Music, Health, and Wellbeing,* ed. Raymond A. R. MacDonald, Gunter Kreutz, and Laura Mitchell, 502–12. Oxford: Oxford University Press.

Obajtek-Kirkwood, Anne-Marie, and Ernest A. Hakanen, eds. 2007. *Signs of War: From Patriotism to Dissent.* New York: Palgrave MacMillan.

O'Connell, John Morgan. 2010. "Introduction: An Ethnomusicological Approach to Music and Conflict." In *Music and Conflict,* ed. John Morgan O'Connell and Salwa El-Shwan Castelo-Branco, 1–14. Urbana: University of Illinois Press.

Odean, Kathleen. 1995. "Anal Folklore in the Medical World." In *Folklore Interpreted: Essays in Honor of Alan Dundes,* ed. Regina Bendix and Rosemary Lévy Zumwalt, 137–52. New York and London: Garland Publishing.

Pegley, Kip, and Susan Fast. 2007. "'America: A Tribute to Heroes': Music, Mourning, and the Unified American Community." In *Music in the Post-9/11 World,* ed. Jonathan Ritter and J. Martin Daughtry, 27–42. New York: Routledge.

Pershing, Jana. L. 2003. "Why Women Don't Report Sexual Harassment: A Case Study of an Elite Military Institution." *Gender Issues* 21(4): 3–30.

Petr, Janata, Stefan T. Tomic, and Sonja K. Rakowski. 2007. "Characterisation of Music-Evoked Autobiographical Memories." *Memory* 15 (8): 845–60.

Petrie, Phil W. 2000 [1987] "Real Men Don't Cry . . . and Other 'Uncool' Myths." In *Reconstructing Gender: A Multicultural Anthology,* 2nd ed., ed. Estelle Disch. Boston: University of Massachusetts Press. (Originally published in *Essence* [November 1982]).

Pieslak, J. R. 2007. "Sound Targets: Music and the War in Iraq." *Journal of Musicological Research* 26: 123–49.

——. 2009. *Sound Targets: American Soldiers and Music in the Iraq War*. Bloomington: Indiana University Press.

Pin-Fat, Véronique, and Maria Stern. 2005. "The Scripting of Private Jessica Lynch: Bio-politics, Gender, and the 'Feminization' of the U.S. Military." *Alternatives* 30: 25–53.

Rauscher, F. H., G. L. Shaw, and K. N. Ky. 1995. "Listening to Mozart Enhances Spatial-Temporal Reasoning: Towards a Neurophysiological Basis." *Neuroscience Letters* 185: 44–47.

Ritter, Jonathan, and J. Martin Daughtry, eds. 2007. *Music in the Post-9/11 World*. New York: Routledge.

Robert Shetterly's Americans Who Tell the Truth. n.d. "Camilo Mejia: Biography." http://www.americanswhotellthetruth.org/portraits/camilo-mejia (accessed May 28, 2014).

Robinson, Victoria, and Jenny Hockey. 2011. *Masculinities in Transition*. New York: Palgrave.

Rose, Tricia. 1994. *Black Noise: Rap Music and Black Culture in Contemporary America*. Hanover, NH: Wesleyan University Press.

——. 2008. *The Hip Hop Wars: What We Talk About When We Talk About Hip Hop—Why It Matters*. New York: Basic Books.

Rosen, Leora N., Kathryn H. Knudson, and Peggy Fancha. 2003. "Cohesion and the Culture of Hypermasculinity in the U.S. Army." *Armed Forces and Society* 29 (3): 325–51.

Rudder, Randy. 2005. "In Whose Name? Country Artists Speak Out on Gulf War II." In *Country Music Goes to War*, ed. Charles K. Wolfe and James E. Akenson, 208-26. Lexington: University Press of Kentucky.

Sacks, Oliver. 2007. *Musicophilia: Tales of Music and the Brain*. Rev. and exp. ed. New York: Vintage Books.

Sampert, S., and N. Treiberg. 2007. "Red, White and Blue: American Foreign Policy in Country Music." Paper presented to the Canadian Political Science Association, Saskatoon, Saskatchewan.

Saucier, Karen A. 1986. "Healers and Heartbreakers: Images of Women and Men in Country Music." *Journal of Popular Culture* 20 (3): 147–66.

Sax, D. 2006. "Combat Rock." *Rolling Stone* 1002: 42.

Schmelz, Peter J. 2007. "'Have You Forgotten?': Darryl Worly and the Musical Politics of Operation Iraqi Freedom." In *Music in the Post 9/11 World*, ed. Jonathan Ritter and J. Martin Daughtry, 123–54. New York: Routledge.

Seeger, Anthony. 2010. "The Suyá and the White Man: Forty-five Years of Musical Diplomacy in Brazil." In *Music and Conflict*, ed. John Morgan O'Connell and Salwa El-Shwan Castelo-Branco, 109–25. Urbana: University of Illinois Press.

Silva, Jennifer M. 2008. "A New Generation of Women? How Female ROTC Cadets Negotiate the Tension between Masculine Military Culture and Traditional Femininity." *Social Forces* 87 (2): 937–60.

Sloboda, John. 2005. *Exploring the Musical Mind: Cognition, Emotion, Ability, Function.* Oxford: Oxford University Press.

Small, Christopher. 1987. *Music of the Common Tongue: Survival and Celebration in African American Music.* Hanover, NH: Wesleyan University Press.

Smith, Christina M., and Kelly M. McDonald. 2011. "The Mundane to the Memorial: Circulating and Deliberating the War in Iraq Through Vernacular Soldier-Produced Videos." *Critical Studies in Media Communication* 28 (4): 292–313.

Smith, Clive Stafford. 2008. "Welcome to 'the Disco.'" *The Guardian,* June 8.

Stahl, Roger. 2010. *Militainment, Inc.: War, Media, and Popular Culture.* New York: Routledge.

Sterne, Jonathan. 2012. *MP3: The Meaning of a Format.* Durham, NC, and London: Duke University Press.

Stokes, Martin. 1997 [1994]. "Introduction: Ethnicity, Identity, and Music." In *Ethnicity, Identity and Music: The Musical Construction of Place,* ed. Martin Stokes, 1–27. Oxford: Berg Publishers,.

Sugarman, Jane C. 2010. "Kosova Calls for Peace: Song, Myth, and War in an Age of Global Media." In *Music and Conflict,* ed. John Morgan O'Connell and Salwa El-Shwan Castelo-Branco, 17–45. Urbana: University of Illinois Press.

Sweeney, Regina M. 2001. *Singing Our Way to Victory: French Cultural Politics and Music During the Great War.* Middleton, CT: Wesleyan University Press.

Tanielian, Terri, and Lisa H. Jaycox. 2008. "Summary." In *Invisible Wounds of War: Psychological and Cognitive Injuries, Their Consequences, and Services to Assist Recovery,* ed. Tanielian, Terri and Lisa H. Jaycox, xiix–xxxiii. Santa Monica, CA: RAND Corporation.

Treseder, William. 2014. "General Mattis' Next Mission: Destroying the PTSD Victim Myth." Military 1. http://www.military1.com/army/article/461498-general-mattis-next-mission-destroying-the-ptsd-victim-myth (accessed May 16, 2014).

Tuleja, Tad. 2012. "'America's Best': Cultural Poaching on 'Ballad of the Green Berets.'" In *Warrior Ways: Explorations in Modern Military Folklore,* ed. Eric A. Eliason and Tad Tuleja, 248–70. Logan: Utah State University Press.

Tuohy, Sue. 1999. "The Social Life of Genre: The Dynamics of Folksong in China." *Asian Music* 30 (2): 41–86.

Turino, Thomas. 2008. *Music as Social Life: The Politics of Participation.* Chicago: University of Chicago Press.

Turner, Victor W. 1969. *The Ritual Process: Structure and Anti-Structure.* Chicago: Aldine Publishing.

Valente, Sharon, and Callie Wight. 2007. "Military Sexual Trauma: Violence and Sexual Abuse." *Military Medicine* 172 (3): 259–65.

Van Dijck, José. 2006. "Record and Hold: Popular Music between Personal and Collective Memory." *Critical Studies in Media Communication* 23 (5): 357–74.

Van Gennep, Arnold. 1960. *The Rites of Passage*. Chicago: University of Chicago Press.

Van Goethem, Annelies, and John Sloboda. 2011. "The Functions of Music for Affect Regulation." *Musicae Scientiae* 15 (2): 208–28.

"Vanishing Volunteers." 2006. *Congressional Quarterly's Magazine on Government, Commerce, and Policy* 64 (47): 3277–78. http://library.cqpress.com.libproxy.uoregon.edu/cqweekly/document.php?id=weeklyreport109-000002414406&type=hitlist&num=0& (accessed February 28, 2013).

Västfjäll, Daniel, Patrik N. Juslin, and Terry Hartig. 2012. "Music, Subjective Wellbeing, and Health: The Role of Everyday Emotions." In *Music, Health, and Wellbeing*, ed. Raymond A. R. MacDonald, Gunter Kreutz, and Laura Mitchell, 405–23. Oxford: Oxford University Press.

Veterans and Their Families Committee on the Initial Assessment of Readjustment Needs of Military Personnel. 2013. *Returning Home from Iraq and Afghanistan: Readjustment Needs of Veterans, Service Members, and Their Families*. Washington, DC: The National Academies Press.

Vincente, Victor A. 2012. "Pax Mevlana: Mevlevi Sufi Music and the Reconciliation of Islam and the West." In *Music, Politics, and Violence*, ed. Susan Fast and Kip Pegley, 150–70. Middletown, CT: Wesleyan University Press.

Walser, Robert. 1993. *Running with the Devil: Power, Gender, and Madness in Heavy Metal Music*. Hanover, NH: Wesleyan University Press.

Weber, Heike. 2009. "Taking Your Favorite Sound Along: Portable Audio Technologies for Mobile Music Listening." In *Sound Souvenirs: Audio Technologies, Memory and Cultural Practices*, ed. Karin Bijsterveld and José van Dijck, 69–81. Amsterdam: Amsterdam University Press.

Weems, Mickey. 2012. "Taser to the 'Nads: Brutal Embrace of Queerness in Military Practice." In *Warrior Ways: Exploration in Modern Military Folklore*, ed. Eric A. Eliason and Tad Tuleja, 139–60. Logan: Utah State University Press.

Weinstein, Deena. 2000 [1991]. *Heavy Metal: The Music and Its Culture*. Rev. ed. New York: Da Capo Press.

West, Candace, and Don H. Zimmerman. 1987. "Doing Gender." *Gender and Society* 1: 125–51.

White, Miles. 2011. *From Jim Crow to Jay-Z: Race, Rap, and the Performance of Masculinity*. Urbana: University of Illinois Press.

Williams, Kayla, with Michael E. Staub. 2005. *Love My Rifle More Than You: Young and Female in the U.S. Army*. New York: W.W. Norton.

Willman, C. 2005 *Rednecks and Bluenecks: The Politics of Country Music.* New York: The New Press.

Wolfe, Charles K., and James E. Akenson, eds. 2005. *Country Music Goes to War.* Lexington: University Press of Kentucky.

Young, Kristi. 2012. "Making Lemonade: Military Spouses' Worldview as a Coping Mechanism." In *Warrior Ways: Explorations in Modern Military Folklore,* ed. Eric A. Eliason and Tad Tuleja, 161–80. Logan: Utah State University Press.

Zoroya, Gregg. 2014. "Up to 48,000 Afghan, Iraq Vets at Risk for Homelessness." *USA Today,* January 17. http://www.usatoday.com/story/news/nation/2014/01/16/veterans-homeless-afghanistan-iraq-wars/4526343/ (accessed May 3, 2015).

INDEX

Page numbers in *italics* refer to illustrations.

biographical sketch, xi; on "Bodies," 54; combat experiences, 77, 171; enlistment, 25–26; on music as privacy, 4; music preferences of, 32; preparation for deployment, 36; PTSD experience, 154–55

Bergdahl, Bowe, 172–73

Bernard, H. Russell, 10

Bijsterveld, Karin, 14–15

Bishop, Travis, 173–74

"Bodies" (Drowning Pool song), 45, 53–57, 94, 118, 154, 201n1

boom boxes, 6, 43

boot camp, 24, 26, 47–48, 54

Bosnian War, 201n8

Bourdieu, Pierre, 85

Braudy, Leo, 92

Brickell, Edie, 48

Brighton, Shane, 67

Brooks, Garth, 76

Buck-O-Nine, 171

Buffett, Jimmy, 48

Bull, Michael: on music as emotion management, 113; on music as memory trigger, 15, 138; on music in everyday life, 10; on personal stereo listening, 2, 4, 6; on the private auditory bubble, 70–71, 73–75, 189

Burke, Carol, 169

Bush, George W., 174–75

"Busted Stuff" (Dave Matthews Band song), 69

"Bye Bye Blackbird" (Edie Brickell), 48

Caillat, Colby, 97

"Calling in Sick" (Buck-O-Nine song), 171

"Call Me Maybe" (Carly Rae Jepsen song), 58–59

"Camilo" (State Radio song), 180–81, 184

Cash, Johnny, 131

cassettes, 6

Catch-22, 179

Cavicchi, Daniel, 10

Chris, 45–46

Christensen, Christian, 56

classical music, 72, 114

Cloonan, Martin, 10–11

Coffee Strong, xi–xii, 199n2

Coldplay, 35

Coles, Tony, 83–84

combat: aggressive music as preparation for, 5, 27, 44–45, 60, 91–92, 117–19; collective identity in combat, 15–16, 26, 30; combat soundscape, 19, 59–60; danger in, 14, 22, 73–74, 116; emotions related to, 116–21; invasions, 12, 19, 44–45, 69–70, 118; music and conflict approaches, 10–12; peace objective associated with, 109; PTSD/ TBI "invisible wounds" and, 15, 123–24, 142, 147–48, 153–56, 164–65, 178; training compared with, 65; unit video depiction of, 55–59; witnessing violence and death, 127–28; women in combat, 80, 202nn2–3 (Chap. 5). *See also* war experience

"Come Monday" (Jimmy Buffett song), 48

compact discs (CDs): boom boxes, 43–44; as care packages, 35; as commemoration of deployment, 151–53, *152*; mixtape productions on, 49–50; portable CD players, 6; post-combat life and, 180; preparation for deployment, 36; sharing of, 94; warzone recording, 3; warzone use of, 6–8, 45, 135

concurrent experience (music and life): memory triggers and, 2; multiplicity of engagement and, 11–12; music as clarifying medium, 65–69; music as disjunctive normalcy, 73–74; semiotics of music and, 52; unit theme songs, 54–55; Vietnam-era music and, 66–69. *See also* war experience

Connell, John, 63

Connell, R. W., 83

Cook, Nicholas, 86

country music: base western nights, 50–51; as boot camp relief, 48; as homeplace memory trigger, 72–73; listening experiences with, 44; military masculinity and, 89–91; patriotism in, 27, 61–64, 151

"Courtesy of the Red, White, and Blue (The

psychological and physiological effects; social effects

ideoculture, 29

"If I Was KIA" (Redcon-1 Music Group song), 128

"I Let You Down" (Dave Matthews song), 177, 183–84

Indie Rock, 72

industrial techno music, 89

Internet: as base leisure resource, 48; home leave use of, 140; Internet fieldwork, xii; limited warzone access, 36, 37; soldiers' access to music trends, 7–8; unit commemorative videos, 56–59; veteran social media network, 157–59, 163–67

iPod. *See* personal stereo

Iraq and Afghanistan Wars: antiquated equipment in, 171–72, 176–77; Baghdad wartime experiences, 69; base leisure limitations, 47, 200–201nn3–4; Bowe Bergdahl capture and release, 172–73; combat danger in, 22, 73–74; combat soundscape, 19, 60; as context for this book, 186–87; emotional experience of troops, xii–xiii, 1–2, 128; heavy metal music popularity in, 59–60; Iraq invasion, 44–45, 118; mythologizing narratives for, 20–21; occupation of government palaces, 37; unit videos of, 55–59; use of private contractors, 171–72. *See also* 9/11 World Trade Center attack

Iraq Veterans Against the War (IVAW), xi, 178, 183

Iraq War (Operation Iraqi Freedom, OIF). *See* Iraq and Afghanistan Wars

Islam, 47, 200–201nn3–4

Jakupcak, Matthew, 125

Jaycox, Lisa H., 123–24

J. D., 40

Jepsen, Carly Rae, 58–59

Johnson, Bruce, 10–11

Joint Base Lewis-McCord, xi

Jones, Norah, 93, 128–29

Joseph: antiwar sentiment of, 174–76; on controlling anger, 122–23; on country music, 63; listening tastes, 73; on male bonding, 110–11; on military masculinity, 83, 106; music friendships of, 48; on the pervasiveness of wartime music, 4; on preparation for combat, 60–61, 118–19

Josh, 73–74, 153, 190

Joshua, 144, 146

Junger, Sebastian, 41, 46–47, 200n1 (Chap. 3)

Juslin, Patrik N., 13

Juvenile, 46

Kassabian, Ahahid, 5

Kaufman, Michael, 82

KBR Corporation, 171

Keil, Charles, 10, 29

Keith: on "American Soldier," 62; on military masculinity, 111–12; PTSD experience, 125–26, 148, 154, 156; as Soldier Hard fan, 157–60, 162–63; on war and music, 65–67; on warzone isolation, 41, 130; on warzone music collections, 34; on "Zombie," 201n8

Keith, Toby, 62, 64, 90–91, 130

Kevin, 30

"Last 48" (40 Glocc song), 161

Latin Americans. *See* Hispanic or Latino Americans

Lennon, John, 176

"Let Me Love You" (Mario song), 100–101

"Letters from Home" (John Michael Montgomery song), 63

Lewis, Benjamin. *See* Benji

Lil John, 55

Lil Scrappy, 30

Lil Wayne, 46

Linkin Park, 56

Lipitz, George, 185

Lisa, 96

listening: command regulation of, 5; dedicated and secondary listening, 3–4; hiding small devices, 6, 8–9; individual "ideoculture" of

Index **223**

effects, 73; heavy metal sensory intensity, 59–60; morale building, 12; postwar social reintegration, 12, 149, 161–63; psychological turmoil and, 13; relief of suffering, 5, 19, 113, 126–33; use by medics, 5, 134–36. *See also* identity; memory; social effects

PTSD/TBI "invisible wounds": depression and, 183; early symptoms of, 180; gender and, 125, 187–88; hypermasculinity and, 187–88; music effect on, 15, 126, 128, 130–31, 153–57, 160–62; post-combat transition and, 142, 147–48; research and policy on, 123–25, 178; treatment for, 125–26; veterans social media network and, 164–65

punk music, 48–49, 89, 122–23, 175–76

R&B music, 126

race. *See* African Americans

radio, 5

Radiohead, 35

rap music: African American preference for, 86–87; "amp up" effect of, 27; as boot camp relief, 48; Dirty South rap, 30; gangsta rap, 89; listener demographics, 29; military masculinity and, 86–89, 109; music friendships and, 48–49; warnings about emotional effects, 113–14; women listeners and, 97

recording, 3, 5, 6. *See also* compact discs; listening; LPs; performance; reel-to-reel recording

Redcon-1 Music Group, 128, 156–57, 159, 164–65

"Red War" (Probot song), 60–61

reel-to-reel recording, 5

Reggae music, 74

Reserve military, 30–31

Restrepo (Junger film), 41, 46–47, 200n1 (Chap. 3)

Reznor, Trent, 131

Riddlin' Kids, 179

"Road to Recovery" (Redcon-1 Music Group song), 128, 156–57

Robert, 48

Ryan, Grey W., 10

Sacks, Oliver, 14–15

Sadler, Barry, 61

salsa music, 31–32

Sax, D., 55–56

Schriever Air Force Base, ix

Scott, Garrett, 44

Sean, 128, 159

"See Clearly Now" (Soldier Hard song), 159

Seeger, Anthony, 3, 19

Seth, 120, 170

sexuality: feminine music genres and, 92–94; heteronormative sexuality in music, 99–100; homophobia, 82, 104–6; homosexuality and alternate sexual orientations, 28, 99, 103, 104–5; male "brotherly" bonding, 80, 109–10; military policy and practice, 27–28, 47, 99, 200n3; music and private identity, 104, 106–7; pornography use and prohibition, 47; post-combat sexuality, 150; sexual harassment, 101–3, 131; shared sleeping spaces and, 37, 39; soldier childhood sexual abuse, 111. *See also* gender

SGT Dunson, 143, 161

Shannon: on civilian artists, 74, 160; on controlling anger, 122; on feminine music genres, 94; on leisure limitations, 46–47; on music during missions, 7, 42, 44, 46, 74; on shared sleeping spaces, 37, 39–40; on Vietnam-era music, 66–69; on warzone isolation, 117; on warzone musical instruments, 3, 48–49; on warzone social stratification, 30, 32

sharing: collective musicking, 189; friends/family musical bonding, 8; headphone sharing, 4, 95; mixed-sex group listening, 95–97; mixtapes, 6; mp3 file format, 7; musical sharing in friendships, 32, 95, 98–99; rank stratification and, 40, 95–96. *See also* social effects

silence, 78–79

Silva, Jennifer, 81–82

Simon, 6, 32, 42–43, 47–48, 105

MUSIC / CULTURE

A series from Wesleyan University Press
Edited by Deborah Wong, Sherrie Tucker, and Jeremy Wallach
Originating editors: George Lipsitz, Susan McClary, and Robert Walser

Frances Aparicio
*Listening to Salsa: Gender, Latin Popular
Music, and Puerto Rican Cultures*

Paul Austerlitz
*Jazz Consciousness: Music, Race,
and Humanity*

Harris M. Berger
*Metal, Rock, and Jazz: Perception and the
Phenomenology of Musical Experience*

Harris M. Berger
*Stance: Ideas about Emotion, Style, and
Meaning for the Study of Expressive
Culture*

Harris M. Berger and
Giovanna P. Del Negro
*Identity and Everyday Life: Essays
in the Study of Folklore, Music,
and Popular Culture*

Franya J. Berkman
*Monument Eternal: The Music
of Alice Coltrane*

Dick Blau, Angeliki Vellou Keil
and Charles Keil
*Bright Balkan Morning: Romani Lives and
the Power of Music in Greek Macedonia*

Susan Boynton and Roe-Min Kok, editors
*Musical Childhoods
and the Cultures of Youth*

James Buhler, Caryl Flinn
and David Neumeyer, editors
Music and Cinema

Thomas Burkhalter, Kay Dickinson,
and Benjamin J. Harbert, editors
*The Arab Avant-Garde: Music,
Politics, Modernity*

Patrick Burkart
Music and Cyberliberties

Julia Byl
*Antiphonal Histories: Resonant Pasts in
the Toba Batak Musical Present*

Daniel Cavicchi
*Listening and Longing: Music Lovers
in the Age of Barnum*

Preston Love
A Thousand Honey Creeks Later:
My Life in Music from Basie to Motown—
and Beyond

René T.A. Lysloff and
Leslie C. Gay Jr., editors
Music and Technoculture

Allan Marett
Songs, Dreamings, and Ghosts:
The Wangga of North Australia

Ian Maxwell
Phat Beats, Dope Rhymes: Hip Hop Down
Under Comin' Upper

Kristin A. McGee
Some Liked It Hot: Jazz Women in
Film and Television, 1928–1959

Rebecca S. Miller
Carriacou String Band Serenade:
Performing Identity in the
Eastern Caribbean

Tony Mitchell, editor
Global Noise: Rap and Hip-Hop
Outside the USA

Keith Negus
Popular Music in Theory: An Introduction

Johnny Otis
Upside Your Head!: Rhythm and
Blues on Central Avenue

Kip Pegley
Coming to You Wherever You Are:
MuchMusic, MTV, and Youth Identities

Jonathan Pieslak
Radicalism and Music: An Introduction
to the Music Cultures of al-Qa'ida, Racist
Skinheads, Christian-Affiliated Radicals,
and Eco-Animal Rights Militants

Matthew Rahaim
Musicking Bodies: Gesture and Voice
in Hindustani Music

John Richardson
Singing Archaeology:
Philip Glass's Akhnaten

Tricia Rose
Black Noise: Rap Music and Black Culture
in Contemporary America

David Rothenberg and Marta Ulvaeus,
editors
The Book of Music and Nature:
An Anthology of Sounds, Words, Thoughts

Marta Elena Savigliano
Angora Matta: Fatal Acts
of North-South Translation

Joseph G. Schloss
Making Beats: The Art of
Sample-Based Hip-Hop

Barry Shank
Dissonant Identities: The Rock 'n' Roll
Scene in Austin, Texas

Jonathan Holt Shannon
Among the Jasmine Trees: Music and
Modernity in Contemporary Syria

Daniel B. Sharp
Between Nostalgia and Apocalypse:
Popular Music and the Staging of Brazil

Helena Simonett
Banda: Mexican Musical Life across Borders

Mark Slobin
Subcultural Sounds: Micromusics of the West

Mark Slobin, editor
Global Soundtracks: Worlds of Film Music

Christopher Small
Music of the Common Tongue: Survival and Celebration in African American Music

Christopher Small
Music, Society, Education

Christopher Small
Musicking: The Meanings of Performing and Listening

Regina M. Sweeney
Singing Our Way to Victory: French Cultural Politics and Music During the Great War

Colin Symes
Setting the Record Straight: A Material History of Classical Recording

Steven Taylor
False Prophet: Fieldnotes from the Punk Underground

Paul Théberge
Any Sound You Can Imagine: Making Music/Consuming Technology

Sarah Thornton
Club Cultures: Music, Media and Subcultural Capital

Michael E. Veal
Dub: Songscape and Shattered Songs in Jamaican Reggae

Robert Walser
Running with the Devil: Power, Gender, and Madness in Heavy Metal Music

Dennis Waring
Manufacturing the Muse: Estey Organs and Consumer Culture in Victorian America

Lise A. Waxer
The City of Musical Memory: Salsa, Record Grooves, and Popular Culture in Cali, Colombia

Mina Yang
Planet Beethoven: Classical Music at the Turn of the Millennium

ABOUT THE AUTHOR

Lisa Gilman is an associate professor in the Department of English and Folklore Program at the University of Oregon. She is the author of *The Dance of Politics: Performance, Gender, and Democratization in Malawi* and director of the film *Grounds for Resistance: Stories of War, Sacrifice, and Good Coffee.*